REPARATIONS
PRO&CON

REPARATIONS PRO&CON

Alfred L. Brophy

OXFORD
UNIVERSITY PRESS

2006

Copyright © 2006 by Oxford University Press, Inc.

Published by Oxford University Press, Inc.
198 Madison Avenue, New York, New York 10016

www.oup.com

Oxford is a registered trademark of Oxford University Press

Library of Congress Cataloging-in-Publication Data
Brophy, Alfred L.
Reparations : pro & con / Alfred L. Brophy.
   p. cm.
Includes bibliographical references and index.
ISBN-13 978-0-19-530408-4
ISBN 0-19-530408-X
1. African Americans—Reparations. 2. African Americans—Legal status, laws, etc.
3. Compensation (Law)—United States. 4. Reparations for historical injustices.
5. Restorative justice. I. Title.
KF4757.B66 2006
342.7308'7308996073—dc22   2005037620

9 8 7 6 5 4 3 2 1

Printed in the United States of America
on acid-free paper

For my friends, most especially Dedi

ACKNOWLEDGMENTS

I HAVE been the beneficiary of a wonderful set of friends and colleagues. At the University of Alabama, William S. Brewbaker III and Utz Lars McKnight have generously offered their time (and opposing views) to help make sure that I treat positions with at least some rough justice. In addition, Arthur G. LeFrancois, Daniel M. Filler, Bryan Fair, Suzette Malveaux, Carol N. Brown, Kenneth Rosen, and Norman Stein have spent much time questioning my arguments. My dean, Kenneth Randall, has provided funding and a supportive atmosphere. My other friends on the University of Alabama campus, Damon Freeman, Greg Dorr, Pat Bauch, Lisa Lindquist Dorr, Joshua Rothman, and George Williamson, have helped as well.

The larger world of reparationists has been supportive as well. Randall Kennedy, Eric Miller, Charles J. Ogletree, and Kenneth W. Mack have all spent time improving my ideas. Professors Ogletree and Miller—the leaders of the movement for reparations litigation—have given me the pleasure of working with them on the Tulsa riot lawsuit, along with Agniezska Fryzman, Scott Ellsworth, Kimberly Ellis, and Michele Roberts. My other friends from the reparations world, including Roy Brooks, Alfreda Robinson, Mark Gibney, Angela Kupenda, Rhonda McGee Andrews, Michele Goodwin, Anthony Farley, Maria Grahn Farley, Kevin Hopkins, Keith Hylton, David Lyons, Calvin Massey, Catherine Manegold, Albert Mosley, Kaimipono Wenger, Robert Westley, and Eric Yamamoto, have taught me much. Members of the Brown University Steering Committee on Slavery and Justice, particularly its chair, James Campbell, and Michael Vorenberg, James Patterson, Seth Rockman, and Neta Crawford, are doing much to advance the academic study of these issues, and I have incorporated many of their ideas here. I have also learned much from friends whose primary area of work is outside reparations, including John Dzienkowski, John C. P. Goldberg, Ronald Krotozynski, Mark Brandon, Ellen Pearson, Sarah Nelson Roth, Stephen Siegel, Aviam Soifer, and Valorie Vojdik.

Many students at Alabama, Boston College, and Vanderbilt have taught me about reparations, including Janel Apuna, Elizabeth Tyler Bates, Becca Brinkley, Chad Bryan, Rebecca Schwartz, and Amy Leigh Wilson. As usual, my friends have supported this project. I am especially indebted to Felix Escamilla, Eva Gasser, Bryn Dinges, Mary Sarah Bilder, Daniel Hulsebosch, Barbara Thompson, Sanford Katz, Mark Brodin, Sara Patterson, Deana Pollard, and Scott England.

I have also benefited from audiences at the University of Alabama, Boston College Law School, Brown University, DePaul University, the University of Florida, the University of Kentucky and the Lexington Network, the University of Nevada at Las Vegas, New York University, Pendel Hill, Smith College, Swarthmore College, Thomas Jefferson School of Law, Vanderbilt University Law School, and Wayne State University.

Once again, as with my previous book, *Reconstructing the Dreamland: The Tulsa Riot of 1921—Race, Reparations, Reconciliation*, my editor, Dedi Felman (this time with help from Stephen Holtje and six anonymous readers), has mightily improved the manuscript. She first suggested the idea of a primer on reparations and has guided this book. Everything good in here, from the structure to the arguments, comes from Dedi. The digressions are my contribution.

CONTENTS

Appendices. Documents Related to Reparations

INTRODUCTION

FACED WITH differences between blacks and whites in wealth, poverty rates, educational achievement, and health care, scholars and activists in post–Civil Rights America have increasingly turned to "reparations talk." Indeed, reparations talk has grown exponentially. People are talking about whether there is a need to redress the years of unpaid labor and slavery from 1620, when the first African slaves were brought to the Virginia colony, until 1865, when slavery ended, and the decades of "Jim Crow" segregation that followed.

There has also been action. There have been apologies for slavery from the Southern Baptist Convention, the Presbyterian General Assembly, the *Hartford Courant*, JPMorgan Chase, and Wachovia, and an apology from the U.S. Senate for failing to pass antilynching legislation in the 1920s. Lawsuits have been filed, including one in 2003 by Charles Ogletree and Johnnie Cochran for victims of the Tulsa race riot of 1921 (dismissed in 2004). Bills have been introduced in Congress every term since 1989. There has been a law passed by the state of California to require insurance companies to disclose policies written on slaves' lives. In Chicago, Detroit, and Los Angeles, ordinances require companies doing business with those cities to disclose their connections to slavery. There are frequent references to reparations in political debates from the state to the national level and on radio and television talk shows, as well as editorials in the nation's newspapers and, of course, fervent debate on college campuses, where faculty, administration, or students at schools like Brown, Sewanee, Vanderbilt, Yale, and the Universities of Alabama, Mississippi, North Carolina, South Carolina, and Virginia are investigating their connections to slavery and the institution's defenders.

The two sides, reparations advocates and their opponents, however, rarely talk to one another. They exist in two parallel worlds and talk about different issues. Reparations advocates focus mostly on the harm of slavery and Jim Crow (the period between the end of the Civil War and the modern Civil Rights era of the 1950s, which witnessed limited voting, educational, and employment opportunities). They often refer to how harms that began in those times continue to limit the opportunities of blacks today and how those eras have left blacks with only a fraction of the wealth of whites. They speak in terms of the debt owed by white America and of the continuing benefits of "white privilege."

Reparations skeptics acknowledge the tragedy and injustice, as they must, of slavery and Jim Crow. President George W. Bush, for example, in his trip to Africa in 2003 called slavery one of the greatest crimes of history.[1] (His speech is reprinted in appendix 6.) However, reparations skeptics focus on the economic and educational opportunities that blacks have in the United States, as well as their achievements. They point out that discrimination is illegal and has been for decades, that trillions of dollars have been spent on social welfare programs, and that many of the problems with black educational and economic achievement seem to stem from single-parent families, rather than from the legacy of now decades-old crimes. And even with the discrimination in the United States, they ask, would blacks prefer that their ancestors had remained in Africa?

This book is an attempt to take seriously the arguments on both sides of the debate. There is a huge volume of literature on reparations. Dozens of journalists, politicians, and social activists, along with professors of philosophy, literature, history, sociology, and law, have written across a range of reparations issues. Serious reparations talk has engaged (and enraged) the nation for the past fifteen years and at other points in American history, too. The bibliography calls attention to some of the literature and the key contours in the debate, but in a subject that is moving so quickly and that encompasses such breadth and quality of writing, it is impossible to capture all the contours. This book will survey the major arguments, but first and most important, I want to make readers think about this important subject and to raise issues for further research. While it is not possible to reach definitive conclusions about these issues, it is possible to identify the key arguments on either side and to suggest some of the ways that we can focus the debate and evaluate the utility of reparations. I hope this book will provide a vehicle for moving the discussion of reparations to a new level.

The first chapter sets the stage for the discussion of the black reparations movement. Chapter 1 defines reparations and surveys the forms they take, such as truth commissions, apologies, community-building programs, and payments to individuals. It then turns to a basic definition of reparations: legislative and court action designed to address historic injustices. Reparations are programs that seek both to repair past damage and to build something that will help bring about racial justice and equality. They are about both "corrective justice" (correcting past harm) and "distributive justice" (redistributing wealth in the present). The movement is also divided between those emphasizing backward-looking remedies, designed to compensate for decades of slavery and Jim Crow, and those who emphasize forward-looking action, which focuses on building something better for the future, independent of evidence of specific harm.

Chapter 2 turns to the history of reparations in the United States. It looks to the programs of reparations that have been discussed (and sometimes granted), with particular emphasis on what has happened since World War II. This second chapter traces one of the longest-running battles for reparations: the efforts for reparations for slaves and their descendants since the Civil War. A brief window opened at the end of the Civil War in 1865, when there was serious discussion about providing land to help newly freed slaves get an economic start. But those grand promises of assistance went unfulfilled during the period of Reconstruction. Instead, Southern legislatures established "black codes," which restricted movement of the newly freed slaves and subjected them to arrest if they were unemployed. The Jim Crow system of segregation grew up about the same time. That system mandated segregation in housing, employment, education, and public accommodations. Frequently, the strict lines of segregation were enforced through violence. At bottom, the Jim Crow system dramatically limited the opportunities for educational and economic advancement. The legacy of Jim Crow suggests some of the reasons that we are talking about reparations now. Although slavery ended more than 140 years ago, there was not a clean break from the era of slavery. Reparations talk is often about repairing Jim Crow as much as about repairing slavery.

Once we locate the movement for slavery and Jim Crow reparations in its historical context, we can then begin to examine the relationship of the black reparations in America movement to other reparations movements. When we begin to look at American history, we see that the U.S. Congress, as well as state legislatures, has been granting reparations throughout American history. Decades before the American Revolution, for instance, families of those wrongfully executed during the Salem witchcraft scare received payments from the Massachusetts legislature. Similarly, victims of mob violence in the nineteenth century frequently had the right to sue the local government for failure to protect them from violence. One of the most surprising reparations programs is that provided by Congress in 1862 for slaves freed in the District of Columbia. Slaveholders who were loyal to the Union received compensation when their slaves were freed.[2]

In the twentieth century, there have been Congressional truth commissions and, recently, many apologies. Moreover, legislatures have frequently taken action to expose and repair past damage—such as the 1946 federal legislation to compensate Native tribes for their land claims and Florida's 1994 act to provide compensation to victims of the 1923 Rosewood Massacre in Florida. One of the most significant acts of slave reparations so far has been California's legislation that requires insurance companies doing business in the state to disclose the names of the slaves whom they insured, along with the names of the slave owners who purchased the policies. That registry, which is available on the Internet, provides stark testimony to the connections between our nation's slave past and the present.[3] Lawsuits have also resulted in reparations, such as the $9 million settlement that victims of syphilis experiments in Alabama received in 1976.

The next section of the book turns to the current debate and to possibilities for the future. Here we see the opposing arguments, the clash between reparations proponents and skeptics. Chapter 3 asks, Why are we taking about reparations now? Did the compensation received by the Japanese Americans interned during World War II through the Civil Liberties Act of 1988 lead to the dramatic growth in reparations talk? Why has it so captured the imagination of blacks and so few others? Why do two-thirds of blacks believe that reparations should be paid, while only 5% of whites support them? One clear factor is the continuing concern among blacks about the lack of progress in the post–Civil Rights era United States. The optimism of the Civil Rights movement of the 1950s and 1960s following such monuments as *Brown v. Board of Education*, the Civil Rights Acts of 1957 and 1964, the Voting Rights Act of 1965, the Fair Housing Act of 1968, the social welfare programs of the Great Society of the mid-1960s, and the affirmative action programs of the late 1960s and 1970s has not been fulfilled, at least in the minds of many blacks. As Congress and the U.S. Supreme Court cut back on affirmative action programs in the 1980s, many academics and community activists looked around for another language to use in talking about inequality. They sought a language of entitlement, of a debt owed the black community. They began to talk of reparations.

The third chapter also provides a roadmap for understanding "what reparationists want"—how they view the movement as fitting into the post–Civil Rights agenda. One problem with understanding the movement is that it is going in several different directions at once. Some moderate members of the movement see it as a way of correcting a historical injustice, which will ultimately move us toward an integrated America. Others are not interested in the goal of integration in itself. They see reparations as a way of obtaining justice and fairness, which they believe is not possible through integration. Some are not interested in integration; the most extreme reparations proponents advocate a separate state for blacks. For them, the reparations movement is about separation.

The chapter also explores the other factors leading to current reparations talk. The decline of affirmative action theories underlying reparations, such as the black power movement, critical race theory, and multiculturalism, opened the door for replacement. As activists were looking around and realizing that the Civil Rights movement had not brought economic equality, they saw other groups receiving limited reparations: Japanese Americans interned during World War II received compensation in 1988 from the U.S. Congress; some victims of the Holocaust received compensation as well; and Native Americans periodically received reparations, such as the 1971 Alaska Native Claims Settlement Act, which transferred billions of dollars of land to tribes to settle claims to Alaskan land. We are having this debate in 2006, rather than in 1876, 1906, or 1956, because many strands of thought came together: the search for new ideas in the aftermath of the Civil Rights movement; the international movement for reparations and apologies, such as the South African Truth and Reconciliation Commission; and the movement for reparations to other groups in the United States, such as to Native Americans and to survivors of the Nazi Holocaust and Eastern European communism.

Recently, opponents of reparations, or "reparations skeptics," have begun to take reparations arguments seriously and to question the moral and legal basis for reparations. Chapter 4 takes up their arguments. The arguments can be put into several broad categories:

1. That there have already been adequate reparations paid through the Civil War and social welfare programs, like the Great Society
2. That taxpayers should not have to pay, because they are innocent; that is, they have no culpability for the actions of past legislators and private individuals, and they have no benefit from the legacy of slavery and Jim Crow
3. That compensation is impracticable or politically unworkable
4. That reparations are divisive and focus attention of the black community in the wrong places
5. That slavery is, on balance, a benefit to the descendants of the enslaved

Reparations talk, with its focus on America's history and its effects on the present, is really one part of a much larger debate over race and equality in contemporary America. The arguments, pro and con, are another front on what we call the "culture wars." Where people stand in the culture wars is determined in part by such questions as: Do we view America as a land of opportunity or oppression? Is it a place where blacks are disadvantaged by a legacy of slavery or by their own culture? Who should bear the responsibility for correcting those past injustices? Should we even try to correct them? That debate frames the arguments advanced against reparations.

Turning from this debate, we then look at "reparations in practice," or ways to achieve those goals. Chapter 5 discusses the possibilities of reparations through lawsuits—what lawsuits require in terms of proof, the hurdles faced in court, and the types of relief they might provide. In short, lawsuits are poorly designed to provide the relief sought by reparations because they demand plaintiffs who can show they have been harmed unjustly by a defendant within the relatively recent past (known as the statute of limitations). Until now, lawsuits have been remarkably ineffective. In 1996, in the case of *Cato v. United States*, the U.S. Court of Appeals (the court just below the U.S. Supreme Court) dismissed a suit brought by slave descendants against the federal government. It rested its decision on a series of rationales, including an inadequate demonstration that the United States had taken any action that hurt the plaintiffs and that the plaintiffs had taken too long to file their claims (they were barred by the statute of limitations). Other suits have also foundered because of the statute of limitations and the failure to connect plaintiffs to harm caused by defendants. Still, plaintiffs continue to come forward.

Chapter 5 also explores some ways that plaintiffs might meet the burdens of a lawsuit. There may be some limited lawsuits that will be successful, such as suits for return of specific property taken from slaves, against universities that received donations from slaveholders who made fortunes off slave labor, for the possessors of art made by slaves that survives to the present, and for access to graves of ancestors who were held in slavery. There may also be lawsuits for specific Jim Crow crimes, such as the riots that terrorized black communities in the aftermath of World War I, for the thousands of lynchings presided over by government officials, and for segregated libraries. In some slavery era cases, there is specific, identifiable property that can be traced to slaves; in some Jim Crow cases, a few individuals who are still alive may be able to demonstrate specific harm that they suffered. They may be able to overcome statute of limitation defenses by showing that they did not have access to the courts, one well-known basis for overriding the statute of limitations.

Yet, the number of successful lawsuits is likely to be small and to offer only tiny relief compared with the huge harms of slavery and Jim Crow crimes. For the great crimes for which reparations are sought, relief would have to come through legislative action. So we turn in chapter 6 to legislative proposals. We examine what a legislature might do in terms of apologies and legislative action and what they are permitted to do under the Constitution. Because any legislature faced with reparations claims faces very difficult questions about collective guilt and moral issues along the lines of who should pay for past crimes and who is entitled to relief, there will be difficult issues of who should pay and who should benefit. There are also related questions about how much should be paid and how much evidence of harm beneficiaries must show.

The seventh chapter then turns to a series of discrete guidelines for "realistic reparations." It explores a series of increasingly controversial proposals, beginning with the (relatively) uncontroversial, such as public truth commissions, apologies, and statutes that impose duties on private corporations to disclose their complicity in slavery and Jim Crow. Then it moves to the more controversial, such as statutes that provide retroactive liability for businesses' and governments' complicity in long-ago racial crimes, to payments for community-based programs of reparations, and to payments to specific individuals. The proposals move from areas where most people can agree to areas where many will disagree. This way, readers can see what the entire field of opportunities looks like. The models are designed to provide grounding for the abstract discussions earlier in the book, to offer a sense of what reparations might look like, and to push forward discussion of what—if anything—we want to do. And chapter 7 concludes with some questions about reparations, which may be helpful to keep in mind as you read this book. Those questions include how much have the legacies of slavery and Jim Crow contributed to the gap between African American and white wealth? How much did the federal and state governments participate in slavery and Jim Crow? How much have those governments—and American society in general—provided benefits to victims of slavery and Jim Crow?

This discussion of reparations is gathering force. Each side will need to have a greater understanding and appreciation of the merits of the others' arguments. The scholarship both supporting and opposing reparations will set the agenda for future legislative action. Once there is a dialogue, we can more clearly see what, if anything, ought to be done.

PART I

Understanding Reparations

Reparations Definitions, Goals, History, and Theory

1

Reparations Definitions

In 1989, U.S. Representative John Conyers of Michigan introduced a bill, H.R. 40, to study slavery and understand its effects, both benefits it has conferred on American society and harms it has caused subsequent generations. Since then, discussion of reparations has grown explosively. Debate about reparations is now heard on college campuses, on the editorial pages of newspapers, even in political campaigns.[1]

Reparations talk has advanced from the circles of Black Power, where the idea floated in the late 1960s and early 1970s, though the time was not then ripe. In the 1980s, law professors again took up discussion of reparations for slavery and other racial crimes and identified the problems with lawsuits. That scholarship built on such prominent precedents as the Civil Liberties Act of 1988, which provided compensation to Japanese Americans interned during World War II, and Florida's payment to victims of the 1923 Rosewood Massacre. It contemplated what reparations might look like and how they might lead to interracial justice.[2] It also sought to identify new places, like the Tulsa race riot of 1921, where there should be reparations.[3] Yet, much of that scholarship was critical of the existing system, critical of American law's seeming inability to provide a language for thinking about reparations.

As other nations begin to discuss how they can repair past damage and obtain closure, the concept of reparations has gained momentum throughout the world.[4] As Nontombi Tutu has said, "The honest discussion of reparations has come of age in the United States and the world. Maybe I should say that the world has come of age for the discussion of reparations."[5] Even as discussion has grown and as reparations lawsuits have been filed, courts have been remarkably unreceptive to claims. In 1995, the U.S. Court of Appeals dismissed a reparations lawsuit brought against the U.S. government by descendants of slaves.[6] In January 2004, another set of cases filed against companies that profited from slavery was dismissed.[7] In February 2003, a serious claim was filed for reparations for victims of the 1921 Tulsa race riot; it was dismissed in March 2004.[8] The future of the movement will be determined in large part by how successfully reparations proponents can make a compelling moral argument for reparations and promote political support for the concept.

But reparations advocates have a very, very long way to go. It is a gross understatement to say that many people are unconvinced by the idea of reparations. Reparations payments, even apologies, are incredibly controversial and unpopular. When the *Mobile Register* polled Alabama citizens in the summer of 2002, it found that the question of reparations was the most racially divisive issue it had ever studied. The differences between whites and blacks outstripped even the gap seen by the paper during the Civil Rights struggle over integration. During the Civil Rights era, many moderate whites supported integration. That is not the case with reparations for slavery. As table 1.1 shows, whites overwhelmingly oppose reparations payments, and a majority of blacks support them. The contrast is stark. Only 5% of white Alabamians support reparations for slavery from the federal government, but 67% of black Alabamians support them. And perhaps that 5% is an

TABLE 1.1

Percentage of Alabamians Favoring Apologies and Payments

	Blacks	Whites
Government should apologize for slavery	73	24
Corporations that benefited should apologize	76	31
Corporations that benefited from slavery should establish scholarship funds for descendants of slaves	87	34
Corporations that benefited from slavery should pay descendants of slaves	69	15
Federal government should pay reparations	67	5

Source: Sam Hodges, *Slavery Payments a Divisive Question*, Mobile Register, June 23, 2002.

overestimate, for the poll may have had problems. Some whites became so enraged at the mere suggestion of reparations that they could not complete the poll.[9]

Lest one think that Alabama is out of step with attitudes elsewhere in the United States, that racial gap is fairly constant. According to a study by Harvard University and University of Chicago researchers reported in the spring of 2003 and listed in table 1.2, only 4% of whites support reparations payments. The bare poll numbers—revealing as they are—do not begin to capture the anger that many expressed at the mere suggestion of reparations. The antireparations Web site "We won't pay" expresses the feelings of many, apparently:

> No matter what pressure is brought up [sic] us, no matter what laws are passed, no matter what verdicts are handed down, no matter what consequences there are to following our conscience, and no matter what it is that we have to do to fulfill our pledge, we give our pledge that we will give in no further. Paying reparations in the year 2003 for an act that ended in 1865 is wrong, and we will not participate; and that is all there is to it.[10]

The opposition to even apologies, which are free from financial obligation, suggests that something very important is at stake—how we view ourselves and our place in the world. Reparations and apologies, in

TABLE 1.2
Attitudes of Blacks and Whites toward Apologies
and Payments from the Federal Government

The Federal Government Should	Blacks	Whites
Apologize for internment of Japanese Americans during World War II	75%	43%
Pay compensation to those interned	59%	26%
Apologize for slavery	79%	30%
Pay compensation for slavery	67%	4%

See Harbour Fraser Hodder, *The Price of Slavery*, Harvard Magazine, May–June 2003, available at http://www.harvard-magazine.com/on-line/050319.html; Michael C. Dawson & Rovana Popoff, *Reparations: Justice and Greed in Black and White*, 1 DuBois Review 47, 62 (2004).

short, are about what is known as the culture wars, a conflict between liberals and conservatives over how they view cultural issues as diverse as abortion, religion's role in public life, affirmative action, and U.S. culpability for racism.[11] Reparations touch on those issues, for reparations relate to how we view U.S. history. Is the United States a place of opportunity or oppression?

Reparations also relate to how we view the legacy of slavery and what we should do about it now. Is there continuing culpability? Do we need to do something to repair past harms? Do ideas of personal culpability free current taxpayers from liability? Have slaves' descendants received adequate compensation in the form of U.S. citizenship or in the grand opportunities available in this country? These are issues we take up, though by no means answer, in subsequent chapters. Reparations and apologies are about issues of racial justice and redistribution of wealth. Thus, they touch central issues of the American soul, of guilt for past sins, and contemporary issues in race.

There is something more at stake with reparations, though; there is more opposition to reparations than to most issues in the culture wars. In many issues of the culture wars, such as abortion, gay marriage, and what should be taught in elementary and secondary school history classes, there is some basic parity. With reparations, judging by public opinion, there is no parity. Reparations are simply viewed with disdain by the vast majority of Americans. Why is this? Perhaps it is because of a conflict that appears so frequently when race enters political discussion, because of fear of issues of group identity and group liability. So frequently, group members see themselves as being asked to pay more than their fair share. Other group members think they are receiving less than they deserve. Those sentiments are heightened when one deals with racial group identity.

Some of the opposition to apologies comes from the sense that they will lead to extraordinary liability and that there will be more humiliation attached to apologies and reparations payments. So far, reparations skeptics have won the hearts and minds of American voters, and it appears as though that dominance will continue. Yet, the idea of reparations is powerful in the black community. Alan Keyes, running on the Republican ticket for a seat in the U.S. Senate from Illinois, proposed reparations, perhaps as a way of appealing to black voters.[12] And so, as reparations begins appearing even in Republican platforms, let us turn to the definition of reparations, to gain a sense of what the debate is about.

Defining Reparations

When proponents ask for reparations, what do they have in mind? When opponents speak against them, what do they think they are opposing? The meanings vary, but at base each reparations program has the goal of building something better for the future by correcting for past injustice. Often that correction of the past includes a redistribution of wealth in the present.

Reparations proponents envision grand programs that will achieve racial justice and perhaps racial harmony. They often talk in vague terms about these programs, running from apologies and truth commissions, to community-building programs, and in rare instances individual payments. There has been little systematic effort to define reparations, however. And yet we need some kind of definition to give us a common language for talking about what reparations are, who ought to provide them and who will receive them, and what we might expect them to accomplish.

Often, reparations programs look backward. That is, they focus on measuring past harm and correcting for it. Thus, truth commissions, apologies, and individual payments are frequently aimed at correcting for some well-defined, identifiable past harm. Other programs are forward-looking. Community-building programs, designed to promote the welfare of an entire community through such actions as funding for schools, frequently make little effort to measure past harm; recognizing that a harm occurred in the past, they are more concerned with trying to design a program to improve the lives of victims into the future.[13]

Reparations proponents' discussions of backward-looking and forward-looking programs are similar to what is called "corrective justice," which refers to acknowledging and repairing past harm, and to "distributive justice," which refers to distributing property in a fair manner.[14] In essence, corrective justice seeks to put people back in the position they would have been in, absent slavery or other racial crime. That involves answering a complex question: what position would a given person be in without slavery? Is the appropriate comparison the standard of living for people on the west coast of Africa or in the United States? These issues are addressed in much more detail in chapter 5, which discusses various ways to measure harm due to slavery. Distributive justice is not concerned with measuring past harm; it is concerned with achieving a fair and appropriate distribution of property right now. Hence, it examines not the harm slavery imposed but what is fair today and going forward into the future. Nonetheless, deciding on a fair distribution involves questions of past harm. Often, corrective justice and distributive justice lead to similar calculations of the amount owed.

Thus, reparations proponents' discussion of backward-looking and forward-looking programs is closely related to well-established legal concepts. Backward-looking relief seeks to assess the exact harm of the past and compensate for it. Proponents of forward-looking relief, in contrast, recognize that past harm is having some continuing effect on the present, but they make little effort to assess the exact value of those past harms. In place of an exact calculation of past harm, they seek some compensation that attempts to improve lives into the future. The Civil Liberties Act of 1988 is an example of that kind of forward-looking relief, for it provided a flat payment of $20,000 to every Japanese American person interned during World War II who was still alive in 1986. The flat payment was not linked in any way to evidence of past harm. Forward-looking relief seems to be the dominant form among reparations proponents, for it provides flexibility in choosing the type and size of remedy. Many also believe that it offers the best way of tailoring a program that is suited to the nature of the harm.

Backward-looking programs seek to tie relief to specific findings of past harm. As the Civil Liberties Act of 1988 demonstrates, backward-looking programs are rigid (and thus problematic) because they provide compensation regardless of need and limit compensation to those who can prove their connections to specific past harm. Every reparations program is likely to look both backward and forward in certain ways. They will be backward-looking because they are justified on the basis of past harm and forward-looking because they are designed to enable a better future. Flexible, forward-looking programs can provide compensation for past injuries and still allow payments based on need, so that the amount of compensation is not necessarily closely tied to harm. To take an example from contemporary political debate, backward-looking programs are like our current Social Security program. Benefits depend in large part upon the amount of money paid in the past. Programs that would add means testing to Social Security and, thus, tie benefits to need are more similar to forward-looking reparations programs.

We might think of reparations, then, as *programs that are justified on the basis of past harm and that are also designed to assess and correct that harm and/or improve the lives of victims into the future.* That is a broad definition, indeed, but it also recognizes the diverse programs that are part of addressing past injustices.[15]

Further Defining the Reparations Movement through Its Goals

The reparations movement has defined itself largely through aspirational goals rather than specific definitions of what it sees as reparations. A movement that is still in its early stages and that is still formulating its strategies can identify its goals more easily than it can make plans. In social movements, goals often come first, followed by specific plans. There are several key goals of the black reparations movement: identification of past injustice and bringing those injustices to the public's attention so that they can be addressed, compensation and redress of those injustices to bring about racial justice, and reconciliation.

Harvard Law School Professor Charles Ogletree, a leader of the Reparations Coordinating Committee, a group of lawyers and social scientists whose goal is to coordinate reparations lawsuits and political activism, has recently emphasized four features of reparations:

1. A focus on the past to account for the present
2. A focus on the present, to reveal the continuing existence of race-based discrimination
3. An accounting of the past harms or injuries that have not been compensated
4. A challenge to society to devise ways to respond as a whole to the uncompensated harms identified in the past[16]

Ogletree sees "acceptance, acknowledgment, and accounting" as central elements of reparations.[17] Phrased another way, reparations include truth commissions that document the history of racial crimes and the current liability for those crimes, apologies that acknowledge liability, and payments to settle those accounts. Professor Ogletree concludes with an appeal to the consciences of his readers with a grand theme of empowering the powerless: "I envision an America where we focus not on our own personal, selfish needs, but on the needs of the voiceless, faceless, powerless, and dispossessed members of the African-American community. We must continue the fight for justice and equality by imagining a world that cares for those who would be left behind. It is a dream that we must make . . . a reality for everyone."[18]

Tulane University Law School Professor Robert Westley, a leading reparations theorist, defines reparations through its goals:

> Reparations include compensations such as return of sovereignty or political authority, group entitlements, and money or property transfers, or some combination of these, due to the wrongdoing of the grantor. It is obvious, then, that the form reparations will take depends on, among other things, the particular demands of the victimized group and the nature of the wrong committed.[19]

Like many others, Westley urges a focus on community-building programs, not payments to individuals, but he suggests that the very poorest may deserve direct payments. The goals of reparations proponents are broad and varied; they include money, political autonomy, and power. Those goals are to be achieved through a variety of means, what one might call the modes of reparations.

Modes of Reparations

A final part of defining reparations comes with identifying the kinds of programs that are part of redress. That is, what kinds of programs are part of redressing past injustices? The types of reparations are varied. Many begin by talking about modest programs, such as truth commissions, which study the scope of the problem, then move to discussions of apologies. From there, they move to more concrete programs, such as civil rights laws, community-building programs, and payments to individuals. Much reparations scholarship assumes that reparations include truth commissions, apologies, community development programs, individual entitlement programs, and cash payments. Both proponents and skeptics have included such diverse efforts as the emancipation of slaves through the American Civil War, the Great Society's welfare payments, the many apologies given by Congress and other government officials for past injustice, truth commissions, affirmative action programs in education and employment,[20] community empowerment zones, and payments to Japanese Americans interned during World War II. Professor John McWhorter of the University of California–Berkeley, a prominent reparations skeptic, claimed the Great Society as reparations:

> [F]or almost forty years America has been granting blacks what
> any outside observer would rightly call reparations. . . . For
> surely one result of that new climate of the 1960s—of the offi-
> cial recognition that America owed its black citizens some sort
> of restitution—was a huge and historic expansion of
> welfare.[21]

Some define reparations narrowly, as including only payments. They see truth commissions and apologies as adjuncts to reparations plans, which lay the groundwork for payments of some sort. But if we define reparations as programs designed to repair past injury, reparations do not *necessarily* have to include payments. Some injuries may be best repaired by study of the past injustice and by apology. Indeed, a sincere apology may be more valuable and meaningful to some victims than money. Even if, as is often the case, an apology is insufficient to repair all past harm, it can be part of a meaningful program of repair and reconciliation. So this section includes apologies and truth commissions as part of its catalog of modes of reparations.[22]

Apologies and Truth Commissions

Some of the more moderate proponents of reparations see truth commissions and apologies as critical first steps toward a plan of monetary reparations; they also see them as integral parts of a plan of reconciliation. The most prominent proposal for a truth commission for slavery is Congressman John Conyers's Bill H.R. 40 (appendix 3). That bill is primarily about studying the history of slavery. Truth commissions are central to many sophisticated blueprints for reparations. Similarly, University of Hawaii Law School Professor Eric Yamamoto's book *Interracial Justice* focuses on reconciliation. Yamamoto sees reconciliation as a multistep project. First, there should be truth commissions and apology; then payments can solidify that contrition. Following that, there should be forgiveness. Yamamoto sees several phases of the process of interracial justice, running from recognition, to responsibility, to reconstruction, and, finally, to reparation.[23]

Others propose truth commissions to address discrete events in the Jim Crow past, such as the Tulsa, Oklahoma, race riot of 1921; the Rosewood, Florida, massacre of 1923; and the thousands of wrongful prosecutions and lynchings and dozens of riots that took place throughout the country in the period from Reconstruction through the Civil Rights era.[24] Professor Sherrilyn A. Ifill has suggested that local communities ought to establish truth commissions to investigate local complicity in such crimes as lynchings. She makes a compelling case for the centrality of lynchings to American society in the early part of the twentieth century. Given that centrality, it makes sense that we do something to investigate them. Lynching truth commissions may teach us about the range of racial crimes that were sponsored or permitted by the government. Moreover, lynchings provide concrete examples of how the Jim Crow system left blacks without legal protection and how, in fact, that system often used law to oppress them.

Certainly, truth commissions will uncover ugly chapters of American history. But once that has happened, will they do anything else?[25] What good does it do to bring up that ugly past? How will that help repair the past?

The new knowledge that the truth commissions will produce will, one suspects, have several consequences. First, it will give a new sense of power to those whose version of history is vindicated. The power of historical stories is strong—they give listeners a sense of place and importance—and stories about the community will lead to a renewed sense of power and pride. The value of new and accurate accounts of past racial crimes appears to be great.

One can gauge the power of truth commissions, as well as apologies, by how difficult it is to obtain them. Look at the struggle that has taken place over whether the U.S. government will apologize for slavery. President William J. Clinton discussed the horrors of slavery when he visited Africa in 1998. "European Americans received the fruits of the slave trade, and we were wrong in that." Later on the trip, he flirted with an apology for slavery when he visited Goree Island, the place of embarkation for many slaves being taken to the Americas.[26] His remarks represent condemnation and contrition, even though he never apologized.[27] Why, one asks, is it enormously difficult to obtain even an apology?

Given how difficult apologies for slavery are to obtain, the apology must have meaning to the people who are asked to give the apology, as well as those seeking it. What is that meaning? It gives signals about blame and responsibility for the consequences of that crime. On his 2003 trip to Africa, President George W. Bush's statements (appendix 6) regarding the crime of slavery suggest both the power of reparations arguments and the current limitations on them.[28] It is doubtful that President Bush would have made such an acknowledgment about the harms of slavery if there had not been extensive reparations talk in the months leading up to his statement, but his refusal to apologize for slavery also suggests the limitations.[29]

Second, truth commissions' findings and apologies will serve as a basis for subsequent arguments about equality and reparations. Reparations proponents will argue that, with this new understanding of the centrality of race, we should take racial categories into account more often.[30] Far from leading to a society in which race is not important, reparations and truth commissions will probably lead in the short run to an even more color-conscious society.

This question of what truth commissions do is at the center of debates throughout the world on reparations.[31] There is a certain value in truth; it tells us about how we view the world.[32] One important truth commission, which is usually overlooked in discussion of reparations, is the Congressional investigation of the Ku Klux Klan, which took place in the late 1860s and early 1870s. That investigation led to thousands of pages of testimony about the behavior of the Klan. Historians are still returning to those rich records; much of what we know about the violence of the Reconstruction period comes from them.[33] Moreover, the hearings led directly to the Anti–Ku Klux Klan Act of 1871, which gave us the critical civil rights statute known as § 1983.

Although some may be satisfied with truth commissions and apologies and think that kind of disclosure and repentance is sufficient, for many the truth commission and apology are merely opening steps to a larger program of reparations. They are a way of putting a claim before the public and a way of preparing people to understand the nature of the harm and why reparations are needed. One recent anonymous assessment of reparations from the April 2002 *Harvard Law Review*, entitled "Bridging the Color Line: The Power of African-American Reparations to Redirect America's Future,"[34] focuses on winning political acceptance of the idea of reparations. The author observes, that to be successful, the idea of "African-American reparations must succeed in the court of public opinion."[35] Transformative reparations will almost certainly come through the legislature, if at all. "Bridging the Color Line" proposes a gradual, political[36] process of accommodating the national conscience to reparations—initially through study of the effects of slavery and Jim Crow and then through exploration of remedies, which emphasizes issues of justice and economics rather than race. That author sees studies of the impact of slavery on the nation and on slaves and their descendants as critical to the case for reparations—and as only the first step in making the case.[37] The initial study of the effects of slavery and Jim Crow would both lay the groundwork for a national consensus on reparations and serve a cathartic purpose in offering emotional closure for victims.[38]

Schools such as Brown University and private companies such as JPMorgan Chase and Wachovia are also participating in the reparations discussion. They are investigating their past connections to slavery and, in the cases of JPMorgan Chase, Lehman Brothers, and Wachovia, have apologized for the connections of their predecessors for their involvement in slavery.[39] Moreover, other institutions are considering renaming buildings or parks that bear the names of people with connections to the era of slavery. In 2002, Vanderbilt University tried to rename a dormitory on its campus from "Confederate Memorial Hall" to "Memorial Hall." Following protracted litigation, the United Daughters of the Confederacy, which contributed $50,000 in 1933 to the building cost, won. The building is still named Confederate Memorial Hall.[40] The Tennessee Court of Appeals opinion presents, one might suggest, a form of reparations for the United Daughters of the Confederacy, for it enforces a right that arose long ago. That right is strangely analogous to reparations claims, which seek to provide compensation for decades-old injuries. Moreover, a concurring opinion in the case by Judge William B. Cain shows, further, the power of the memory of the Civil War. Cain agrees that Vanderbilt cannot rename the building. But he goes on to discuss the meaning and suggest that the memorial is to soldiers who fought honorably, rather than to the memory of slavery. Judge Cain does this by quoting the memoirs of Union General Joshua Lawrence Chamberlain. Chamberlain fought and was wounded at Gettysburg, and he accepted the surrender at Appomattox. About the time of the fiftieth anniversary of the Battle of Gettysburg, as people North and South were struggling with the memory of the Civil War and with reunion, Chamberlain published his memoirs, which honored the soldiers of both North and South. Judge Cain quotes the memoirs extensively, including:

> Before us in proud humiliation stood the embodiment of manhood: men whom neither toils and sufferings, nor the fact of death, nor disaster, nor hopelessness could bend from their resolve; standing before us now, thin, worn, and famished, but erect, and with eyes looking level into ours, waking memories that bound us together as no other bond; —was not such manhood to be welcomed back into a Union so tested and assured? Instructions had been given; and when the head of each division column comes opposite our group, our bugle sounds the signal and instantly our whole line from right to left, regiment by regiment in succession, gives the soldier's salutation, from the "order arms" to the old "carry"—the marching salute. Gordon at the head of the column, riding with heavy spirit and downcast face, catches the sound of shifting arms, looks up, and, taking the meaning, wheels superbly, making with himself and his horse one uplifted figure, with profound salutation as he drops the point of his sword to the boot toe; then facing to his own command, gives word for his successive brigades to pass us with the same position of the manual, —honor answering honor. On our part not a sound of trumpet more, nor roll of drum; not a cheer, nor word nor whisper of vain-glorying, nor motion of man standing again at the order, but an awed stillness rather, and breath-holding, as if it were the passing of the dead! . . .

Ah, is this Picketts Divison? — this little group left of those who on the lurid last day of Gettysburg breasted level cross-fire and thunderbolts of storm, to be strewn back drifting wrecks, where after that awful, futile, pitiful charge we buried them in graves a furlong wide, with names unknown! Met again in the terrible cyclone-sweep over the breast-works at Five Forks; met now, so thin, so pale, purged of the mortal, — as if knowing pain or joy no more. How could we help falling on our knees, all of us together, and praying God to pity and forgive us all![41]

The appearance of Chamberlain's thoughts again, nearly a hundred years later, in a judicial opinion is a reminder of how North and South reconciled after the war. They also remind us of the meaning of the monuments to the Confederacy to many. As the concurrence later observed, "It is to the memory of these men that Confederate Memorial Hall was built and, to that end and at great personal sacrifice in the midst of the Great Depression, that the United Daughters of the Confederacy raised and contributed . . . more than one-third of the total cost of the construction of the dormitory."[42] Such is the nature of the conflict over memory and honor that the issues continue to generate much emotion, lo these many years later.

Meanwhile, across the state of Tennessee in Memphis, there is debate over whether the city should rename the Nathan Bedford Forrest Park. (Forrest was a founder of the Ku Klux Klan.)[43] And another great Tennessee institution, Sewanee: The University of the South, is now emphasizing the Sewanee part of its name. Southern flags have also been taken down from the chapel, the University's mace (which has a Confederate flag on it) has been at least temporarily retired from service, and alumni fear that other moves are afoot.[44]

Civil Rights Legislation, Community Building, and Payments to Individuals

Truth commissions and apologies (and the occasional renaming) are but the opening steps to further discussion. They are limited ways of remaking our understanding of the meaning of the past. Reparations proponents say that to be meaningful, there must be some concrete reparative action beyond a truth commission or an apology.[45] That leaves open the question, once we get past studying, talking about, and apologizing for slavery and Jim Crow: of what reparations will look like. Richard Newman of the W. E. B. DuBois Institute at Harvard University suggested a domestic Marshall Plan as an analogy to the Marshall Plan that rebuilt Germany after World War II.[46] He could not state, because indeed it is extremely difficult, the likely cost of reparations. In talking about reparations, one is talking, as Newman stated, "about something colossal."[47]

Part of the problem with evaluating reparations is that not only are the costs colossal but also we do not even know what they would look like. One of the surprising elements is that even one of the most recent major books on this topic, Raymond A. Winbush's *Should America Pay?* has hundreds of pages of discussion on whether the U.S. government and corporations should pay reparations but very little discussion on *what* they would pay, if they were going to do so, or of the form the reparations would take.

The specifics of what legislative reparations could look like will be discussed in substantially more depth. For now, we should note that reparations plans may sometimes include civil rights legislation, such as the Civil Rights Act of 1964, which guaranteed the right to use public accommodations, such as restaurants and hotels, regardless of race. The Civil Rights Act of 1964 put the power of enforcement in the hands of those who had the most interest in enforcing those rights. It empowered the black community. We might also look to the Voting Rights Act of 1965. It empowered the federal government to ensure the right of blacks to register and vote. Yet, civil rights legislation is rarely talked about as a form of reparations.

The most commonly discussed kinds of reparations are community-building programs and legislation to provide compensation to individuals, such as direct payments and affirmative action preferences. We are still a long way from having comprehensive plans about what community-building reparations programs would look like. But reparations proponents commonly speak in grand terms about programs modeled on President Lyndon B. Johnson's Great Society initiatives, which provided funding for health care, education, and welfare, as well as money for building housing and roads for neglected rural and urban communities. Some proponents also talk about direct cash payments to individuals, particularly those who are extremely poor. But as yet, the talk of cash payments to individuals has come mostly from people who seek to ridicule the idea of reparations. Why would we pay Oprah Winfrey or Michael Jordan reparations? they ask. Alternatively, direct payments were proposed as a way of cutting off all further race-based remedies. Charles Krauthammer proposed a reparations payment of $40,000 to every black person as a way of finally settling claims.[48]

With that basic understanding of what reparations are, we can now explore in the next chapter the history of the movement from the era of Reconstruction to the present. Then we can explore in detail the precedents for black reparations and the ideas behind them.

2

Black (and Other) Reparations in History

THE MOVEMENT for reparations has a long and distinguished lineage, as well as a rich recent history. Reparations talk has exploded since Randall Robinson's *The Debt: What America Owes to Blacks* was published in 2000. Robinson's idea, radical though it may be, is not new. In fact, it is old. Even before the Civil War ended more than 200 years of forced, uncompensated labor in colonial British North America and then the United States, there had been discussion of ending slavery and the need to do something to restore to slaves what had been taken from them.[1] There were other calls, primarily by those advocating abolition, to compensate those whose labor had been taken without compensation.[2]

An especially elegant appeal appeared in 1829. David Walker's "Appeal to the Colored Citizens of the United States" asked for some form of acknowledgment of the harms of slavery and something to make amends for it. He said, "The Americans may say or do as they please, but they have to raise us from the condition of brutes to that of respectable men, and to make a national acknowledgement to us for the wrongs they have inflicted on us." Then, in words that still ring true, he acknowledged that asking for some form of redress was unexpected and would likely be met with ridicule. Yet, Walker thought reparations were necessary: "As unexpected, strange, and wild as these propositions may to some appear, it is no less a fact, that unless they are complied with, the Americans of the United States, though they may for a little while escape, God will yet weigh them in a balance, and if they are not superior to other men, as they have represented themselves to be, he will give them wretchedness to their very heart's content."[3]

The idea of reparations is much older than the abolitionist period that preceded that American Civil War of 1861 to 1865, however. One of the most discussed cases was that of Quock Walker, a slave in Worcester, Massachusetts, who in 1781 sued his owner, Nathaniel Jennison, for freedom. Quock Walker said that he had been promised freedom at age 25. A jury found that he was, indeed, free, and he subsequently won a judgment against Jennison for assault and battery. The judgment was not for past labor, but it was for injury inflicted when Walker should have been freed.[4]

In other cases before the Civil War, people who had been wrongfully held as slaves were able to recover for their labor. In the 1801 case *Negro Peter v. Steel*, the Pennsylvania Supreme Court faced a claim by a man who was captured from behind British lines by an American officer during the Revolutionary War and brought to Lancaster, Pennsylvania, where he was held as a slave. After a few months, a court discharged the man from slavery, and he sued for payments for the time he was enslaved.[5] The Kentucky Court of Appeals issued a similar opinion in 1809, when it enforced a promise made by a slave owner to the woman who sold him the slave that he would free the man, known as Will, after seven years' service. The owner refused to free Will, and when the woman sued, Will was freed, and she received nearly $700 for Will's service beyond the time he should have been freed. The money was paid to her "in trust" for Will.[6] Other cases occasionally allowed similar recoveries when it was shown that a slave should have been free. Thus, even some Southern courts recognized the debt owed people who were wrongfully held in slavery. Of course, for those held in slavery according to law, there was no relief. Nor was there much in the way of compensation after emancipation, though in some instances, we know that the freed people believed themselves entitled to compensation.

The largest discussion of reparations naturally came at the time of emancipation, as the Civil War drew to a close in 1865 and as the country entered the period of Reconstruction, which lasted from 1865 to 1877. Slavery ended as the result of a war in which more than 600,000 people lost their lives. During the Civil War and Reconstruction, the world was remade. It was also a period when some former slaves sought compensation, when promises were made regarding assistance to former slaves, and when, amid great upheaval, the promises were not fulfilled.

A letter from freed slave Jourdon Anderson to his former owner, Colonel P. H. Anderson, captures well the desire of slaves to seek compensation for their years of unpaid labor in the wake of the Civil War.

Sir: I got your letter and was glad to find you had not forgotten Jourdon, and that you wanted me to come back and live with you again, promising to do better for me than anybody else can. I have often felt uneasy about you. I thought the Yankees would have hung you long before this for harboring Rebs they found at your house. I suppose they never heard about your going to Col. Martin's to kill the Union soldier that was left by his company in their stable. Although you shot at me twice before I left you, I did not want to hear of your being hurt, and am glad you are still living. It would do me good to go back to the dear old home again and see Miss Mary and Miss Martha and Allen, Esther, Green, and Lee. Give my love to them all, and tell them I hope we will meet in the better world, if not in this. I would have come back to see you all when I was working in Nashville, but one of the neighbors told me Henry intended to shoot me if he ever got a chance.

I want to know particularly what the good chance is you propose to give me. I am doing tolerably well here; I get $25 a month, with victuals and clothing; have a comfortable home for Mandy (the folks here call her Mrs. Anderson), and the children, Milly, Jane and Grundy, go to school and are learning well; the teacher says Grundy has a head for a preacher. They go to Sunday-School, and Mandy and me attend church regularly. We are kindly treated; sometimes we overhear others saying, "Them colored people were slaves" down in Tennessee. The children feel hurt when they hear such remarks, but I tell them it was no disgrace in Tennessee to belong to Col. Anderson. Many darkies would have been proud, as I used to was, to call you master. Now, if you will write and say what wages you will give me, I will be better able to decide whether it would be to my advantage to move back again.

As to my freedom, which you say I can have, there is nothing to be gained on that score, as I got my free-papers in 1864 from the Provost-Marshal-General of the Department at Nashville.

*Mandy says she would be afraid to go back without some proof
that you are sincerely disposed to treat us justly and kindly—and
we have concluded to test your sincerity by asking you to send us
our wages for the time we served you. This will make us forget
and forgive old scores, and rely on your justice and friendship in
the future. I served you faithfully for thirty-two years and Mandy
twenty years. At $25 a month for me, and $2 a week for Mandy,
our earnings would amount to $11,680. Add to this the interest
for the time our wages has been kept back and deduct what you
paid for our clothing and three doctor's visits to me, and pulling
a tooth for Mandy, and the balance will show what we are in
justice entitled to. Please send the money by Adams Express, in
care of V. Winters, esq, Dayton, Ohio. If you fail to pay us for
faithful labors in the past we can have little faith in your promises in the future. We trust the good Maker has opened your eyes
to the wrongs which you and your fathers have done to me and
my fathers, in making us toil for you for generations without rec-
ompense. Here I draw my wages every Saturday night, but in
Tennessee there was never any pay day for the negroes any more
than for the horses and cows. Surely there will be a day of reckoning for those who defraud the laborer of his hire.*

*In answering this letter please state if there would be any
safety for my Milly and Jane, who are now grown up and both
good-looking girls. You know how it was with poor Matilda and
Catherine. I would rather stay here and starve and die if it comes
to that than have my girls brought to shame by the violence and
wickedness of their young masters. You will also please state if
there has been any schools opened for the colored children in
your neighborhood, the great desire of my life now is to give my
children an education, and have them form virtuous habits.*

*P.S.—Say howdy to George Carter, and thank him for taking
the pistol from you when you were shooting at me.*
From your old servant,

Jourdon Anderson[7]

Anderson's letter, which is so perfect that one thinks it must have been
invented by some latter-day reparations proponent (or by someone

seeking to stir up anti-Southern feelings in the wake of the Civil War), captures the desire of slaves to be compensated for past labor, as well as their recognition that they were owed something.

Moreover, although we rarely think about the topic in these terms, the government has frequently paid reparations to people injured by the government's wrongful acts. In 1720, several decades after the disastrous miscarriage of justice of the Salem witchcraft trials, the Massachusetts legislature voted to give a substantial sum of money to each victim's family. That was not done because there was a legal duty to do so, or because those legislators (or taxpayers) had themselves done something wrong. It was done because the legislature realized that the government had mistreated its citizens and it wanted to do something to repair that damage.

Such payments continued throughout the eighteenth and nineteenth centuries, right through the Civil War. In many instances, legislatures voted to pay compensation—what we might now call reparations—even when there was no government culpability for losses. In the aftermath of the War of 1812, for instance, the U.S. Congress made sure that slaveholders whose slaves the British freed during the war received compensation. Revolutionary War veterans received pensions throughout their lives, even though there was no obligation to pay them. They received those pensions because the country recognized that they had sacrificed for the common good. In the 1830s, as mob violence became more prominent, many legislatures voted to give victims a right to sue the municipalities where the violence occurred. Thus, the legislatures created a duty of local government to protect their citizens from violence.

Slavery Reparations Discussion in American History

Given those precedents, Jourdan Anderson's request for compensation was, perhaps, not as radical as it might otherwise seem. Moreover, in a world that treated the labor of slaves as a commodity, there were many cases that allowed slave owners to recover when their slaves were injured by others—including for lost wages. The institution of slavery was based on the idea that one person could own the labor of another and that that labor was valuable. One Missouri court even awarded compensation to a former slave who was wrongfully held in bondage.

He should have been freed but was not. Therefore, the person who had wrongfully imprisoned him owed him compensation.[8]

Even among the pro-slavery forces, there was a recognition that slavery had taken slaves' labor and had left them, perhaps, unready for democracy. And that was precisely a basis for opposing emancipation. Before the Civil War, one of the most powerful arguments against abolition of slavery was made by Thomas Roderick Dew, a professor of history at William and Mary College in Virginia (and later its president), who wrote a pamphlet opposing the abolition of slavery, which the Virginia legislature was considering in the early 1830s. Slavery, the legacy of the millennia, might "require *ages* to remove," he told the legislature.[9] Dew understood, as did many others, that the legacy of slavery would require generations to eradicate—and he used that argument effectively to *prevent* efforts to end slavery. Dew, moreover, proposed no efforts to begin the abolition of slavery. His largely forgotten lectures on history, which were posthumously published in the 1850s under the grand title A *Digest of the Laws, Customs, Manners, and Institutions of the Ancient and Modern Nations,* give even more detail on Dew's worldview: he saw slavery and respect for individual private property as central to the advance of Western civilization. We now understand that the resilient human spirit could not be crushed by slavery and that newly freed slaves were entirely capable of participating in democracy. However, the argument illustrates the understanding that everyone had, when they were being honest, that it would require time and enormous expenditures to allow freed slaves to participate equally in the economy.

But the idea of compensating the former slaves did not have a strong hold on the American mind. President Lincoln's Emancipation Proclamation in July 1862 made clear that slavery would end when Union armies reached the slaves, and so planning for a United States without slavery had to begin. Lincoln urged the newly freed slaves to refrain from violence, except in self-defense, and to "labor faithfully for reasonable wages." There was no talk in the Emancipation Proclamation about restoring property that had been taken from those slaves, to say nothing of their ancestors. There was talk of providing land to freed slaves as part of a plan of making them economically independent. As Massachusetts businessman Edward Atkinson, a supporter of Republican Reconstruction, wrote during the discussion of compensation to slaves, providing land would "ruin the freedmen" because they would believe they would not have to work for it.[10]

So while the war proceeded, slaves were freed, and their former masters lost some of their property through confiscation. Indeed, Arlington National Cemetery sits on land confiscated from Robert E. Lee's family. Yet, the loudest talk about reparations at the time was of compensation to Northern slaveholders whose slaves were freed. Congress made sure that slave owners in Washington, D.C., received compensation.[11] And so, when we speak of reparations for slavery, it is important to remember that some reparations have been paid—to slaveholders.

When the Union Army liberated slaves, it made the first provisions for the freed slaves, and its policies included leasing plantations to white people loyal to the North and then coercing freed slaves to sign long-term labor contracts.[12] In January 1865, as the war was drawing to a close, General William T. Sherman had a slightly different plan for resettling freed slaves. His Field Order 15 (appendix 1) decreed that 400,000 acres of confiscated land along the fertile Georgia coast should be set aside for the exclusive use of freed slaves. Each family was to receive forty acres, and the Army was supposed to lend mules for temporary use. Thus was born the phrase "forty acres and a mule." Sherman later said that his plan was designed as a temporary solution to the problem of settling freed slaves and that he did not intend to settle the freed people there permanently. But there was hope for a while that the resettlement might become permanent, allowing freed slaves some real opportunity for both income and, later, education. Such was not to be. President Johnson subsequently revoked the military order and used the Union Army to forcibly evict the freed slaves and return the land to Southern whites.[13]

The transition from slavery to freedom was guided by the Freedmen's Bureau, which Congress established in 1865, shortly before the end of the Civil War. It was charged with preparing the newly freed slaves for their lives as free people and with reestablishing an orderly Southern society. Its missions included establishing a system of free labor in the South, adjudicating claims between blacks and between blacks and whites, educating blacks, and caring for the disabled and sick.[14]

The war left the slaves with nothing but freedom; the Freedmen's

Bureau was supposed to leave them with more, for the Freedmen's Bureau Act promised to help educate and assist the newly freed slaves in economic advancement. Land redistribution was part of the Freedmen's Bureau agenda. The act that established the bureau authorized, perhaps using General Sherman's grant of Georgia land as a model, the distribution of up to forty acres to each freed slave. The bureau was to distribute land confiscated during the war, as well as other land owned by the government.[15] The ideas behind the act were not necessarily compensation for past labor. The goal was forward-looking, trying to make it possible for the freed slaves to be economically self-sufficient.[16] Predictably, the Freedmen's Bureau was unable to complete its grand missions. Soon, Southern state courts reformed their procedures, such as allowing blacks to testify against whites, so that the courts could hear cases that the Freedmen's Bureau had been adjudicating. The bureau's courts had been fairer to blacks than the Southern state courts were, although even its courts frequently dealt harsher penalties to blacks in criminal cases than whites typically received. As the bureau lost jurisdiction over cases, it was also part of reestablishing Southern racial hierarchy in employment. Bureau officials frequently compelled blacks to sign long-term labor contracts, often on unfavorable terms. Even the efforts of the bureau to establish black farmers on their own were undermined by President Andrew Johnson. At the end of the war, the bureau had control of 850,000 acres of land confiscated from Southerners. In early 1865, the bureau rushed to distribute forty acres to the freedmen, but President Johnson rescinded the order and then demanded that the head of the bureau inform the people already on the property that by the time they harvested their crops, they would have to leave the land.[17] The process of moving from slavery to freedom was complex, and in many ways the Freedmen's Bureau prevented gross exploitation. However, the legacy of the bureau is that former slaves frequently ended up working for their former owners.

Still, some members of Congress tried to provide some form of compensation. Representative Thaddeus Stevens of Pennsylvania, one of the most radical members of Congress, introduced a bill in 1867 to condemn Confederate property and provide compensation to freed slaves, in the form of forty acres to heads of households, along with fifty dollars (appendix 2). Stevens saw the plan as serving at least two purposes. First, it would make the freed slaves economically independent.

Second, it would help break down the Southern oligarchy. As Stevens said on the floor of the House of Representatives:

> The whole fabric of southern society *must* be changed, and
> never can it be done if this opportunity is lost. Without this,
> this Government can never be, as it has never been, a true re-
> public. . . . How can republican institutions, free schools,
> free churches, free social intercourse exist in a mingled com-
> munity of nabobs and serfs? If the South is ever to be made a
> safe republic let her lands be cultivated by the toil of the own-
> ers of the free labor of intelligent citizens.[18]

At least part of the bill was justified on the basis of returning a small portion of the value taken from slaves. As Stevens said, the bill "is important
to four millions of injured, oppressed, and helpless men, whose ancestors for two centuries have been held in bondage and compelled to earn
the very property, a small portion of which we propose to restore to
them, and who are now destitute, helpless, and exposed to want and star-
vation, under the deliberate cruelty of their former masters.[19]

Some other radicals, like Senator Charles Sumner of Massachusetts, supported Stevens, but the overwhelming response was one of
opposition to the idea of confiscation and compensation to newly
freed slaves. As Senator Edgar Cowan of Pennsylvania asked, if Sumner's dream of breaking down caste were fulfilled, "Who would black
boots and curry the horses, who would do the menial offices of the
world?" Confiscation, and the remaking of the world that it promised,
failed.[20]

NOT ALL efforts at change were so stillborn. The twelve years (1865 to
1877) following the war, known as Reconstruction, brought changes intended to benefit former slaves beyond the efforts of the Freedmen's
Bureau, with federal legislation that sought to ensure that freed slaves
had equal rights to vote and participate in the economy. The Civil
Rights Act of 1866 required that they be given equal rights to contract.
Other legislation made it a federal crime to interfere with their civil
rights. The Thirteenth Amendment to the Constitution outlawed slavery. The Fourteenth Amendment was designed to ensure that the fed-

eral and state governments treated all American citizens equally, regardless of race; it also authorized Congress to do what was necessary to protect those rights. Finally, the Fifteenth Amendment guaranteed voting rights to male U.S. citizens, regardless of race. Under the protection of federal legislation, freed slaves were entitled to vote, and some entered the legislature.[21] Actions such as the Civil Rights Act of 1866, the Anti–Ku Klux Klan Act of 1871, and the Thirteenth, Fourteenth, and Fifteenth Amendments were part of remaking the U.S. legal framework to facilitate freedom. They were designed to undo slavery and its vestiges and ought to be considered reparations.

However, almost immediately, there were attempts by the former leaders of the Southern communities to wrest back control of the government. Through a combination of violence and "black codes," that mission was accomplished.[22] This was the time of the Ku Klux Klan, and those who dared exercise their rights to vote or to leave their place of employment were subject to harsh reprisals. Throughout the South, small riots forced African American officials from office or prevented them from being elected in the first place. One massacre in New Orleans in 1876, for instance, left more than a hundred African Americans dead. When federal prosecutors attempted to prosecute the murderers, the U.S. Supreme Court limited the scope of the Enforcement Act of 1870, which provided criminal penalties for people who interfered with the right to vote. The Supreme Court held that Congress had no authority to punish such local crimes.[23] Thus was born a doctrine that greatly restricted Congressional power to protect civil rights for the next several generations.

Running parallel to the racial violence were acts of the state legislatures designed to control the newly freed slaves. Instead of assistance in rebuilding Southern society and help for the freed slaves in purchasing property, instead of compensation for their own labor, the former slaves received black codes, which subjected them to harsh penalties for vagrancy and restricted their movement within states.[24] Often former slaves signed long-term employment contracts with their former owners, which limited freed people's rights to work where they wanted and to leave when they wanted. During this era of Jim Crow, Southern whites wrested control from African Americans and created a regime of segregation, of limited voting rights, of limited economic and educational opportunities for African Americans.[25]

CALLS FOR reparations became dormant in years after 1877, as African Americans struggled merely to maintain voting rights and oppose the black codes. As historian C. Vann Woodward has shown in what he referred to as the "strange career of Jim Crow," following the Reconstruction era, oppression through law became harsher.

Under the system of Jim Crow, African Americans had little opportunity for educational advancement, and those who received an education were barred in many places from meaningful employment. In the early part of the twentieth century, Southern states adopted new constitutions designed in large part to solidify Jim Crow rules. The constitutions imposed harsh qualifications for voting, and then the white legislatures prohibited interracial marriage; demanded further separation of the races in streetcars, railroads, education, and other public places; and provided inadequate funding for minority schools. At the local level, housing segregation laws kept African Americans from living in white neighborhoods.[26] Sometimes communities broke into violence. There were periodic riots, in which black communities were destroyed, and more commonly lynchings. There were something like 4,742 lynchings from 1882 to 1968, the date typically given for the end of lynching.[27]

Another important Civil Rights act, the Anti–Klu Klux Klan Act of 1871, provided a right to sue local governments when their officials interfered with civil rights. In a few instances, state legislatures took action to provide compensation for victims of mob violence. For example, the Illinois legislature passed a statute that provided that victims of mob violence had a right to recover a few thousand dollars against the municipality where the violence occurred. The statute seemed to have been designed to encourage municipalities to protect against labor union violence. However, those statutes sometimes provided relief for victims of race riots. After the bloody East St. Louis, Illinois, riot of 1917 and then again after the Chicago riot of 1919, riot victims' families received compensation from the local governments. Those remain some of the few riots for which black victims have ever received compensation.

There was other proposed legislation, such as the Dyer Anti-Lynching Bill, which would have provided a cause of action against municipalities that failed to protect against mob violence, but that bill failed to pass. Table 2.1 summarizes various reparations actions and proposed actions from the Reconstruction era through the early part of the twentieth century.

TABLE 2.1
Eclectic List of Reparations Programs and Proposals, Based in Part on Posner and Vermeule, *Reparations for Slavery*

Program	Year(s)	Maker of Reparations	Recipient	Payment	Total Cost	Cause
Salem witchcraft trials	1725	Massachusetts Legislature	Families of victims	£20	Minimal	Unjust prosecution of suspected witches[a]
Charleston Convent	1834	Massachusetts Legislature	Convent & Catholic church	$0 (proposed)	$0	Mob destruction of Catholic convent[b]
Compensation to D.C. slaveowners	1864	U.S. Congress	Loyal slaveholders	$3,000 per person	<$0.5 million	Emancipation Proclamation
Freedmen's Bureau Act	1865	U.S.	Freed slaves		Unknown	Reconstruction
Anti–Ku Klux Klan Act	1871	U.S.	U.S. citizens	Investigation and act that permitted lawsuits	Unknown	Quasi-governmental actors who deprived citizens of Constitutional rights[c]
Illinois Anti–Mob Violence Law	1887–1919	Illinois Legislature & Illinois municipalities	Riot victims and their families	Up to $5,000 per family member	~$0.5 million	Municipalities failed to protect against violence[d]
Dyer Anti-Lynching Bill	1919–22	U.S. Congress	Families of lynching victims	$10,000 per lynching (proposed)	$0	Rampant lynchings[e]
Indian Claims Commission	1946	U.S.	Native tribes		Unknown	Loss of native lands
Kerner Commission	1968	U.S.		(investigation)	$0	Investigation of urban violence[f]
Alaska Native Claims Settlement Act	1971	U.S. Congress	Native American tribes	Payments to tribes	$962.5 million and 44 million acres of land	Settlement of native claims to Alaska[g]
Civil Liberties Act of 1988	1988	U.S.	Japanese Americans interned during World War II who survived until 1986	$20,000 per person	~$1.65 billion	Internment[h]
Reparations study proposal	1989–present	U.S. Congress	Descendants of slaves	(proposed investigation)	$0	Proposal to study slavery and reparations[i]

Native American Graves Reparation Act	1993	U.S.	Native American tribes	Various	Unknown	Return of tribal property held by government-funded institutions[j]
Apology for Hawaiian annexation	1993	U.S.	Native Hawaiians	(apology)	$0	Annexation of territory in 1897[k]
Apology for sins of racism	1995	Southern Baptist Convention		Apology	$0	Southern Baptist Convention's historical corrections to slavery[l]
Hawaiian Trust Lands, *Ka`ai`ai v. Drake*	1995	State of Hawaii	Native Hawaiians	Settlement of lawsuit	$600 million	Decades-long mismanagement of Hawaiian Homelands Trust[m]
Apology for United Church of Christ's connections to overthrow of Hawaiian government	1996	United Church of Christ	Native Hawaiians	Apology	Approximately $4 million	Church members' complicity in overthrow of Hawaiian government[n]
Mexican land lost	1997–2000	U.S. Congress	Descendants of Mexicans who lost land in 1848	Contemplated action to deal with "lingering inequality"	$0	
Tulsa riot of 1921	1998–2003	City of Tulsa & state of Oklahoma	Survivors of riot	Recommended payment of $20,000 & up	None, but recommended payment of $2 million & up	Destruction of black community by deputized mob[o]
Apology for slavery	1998 & 2003	Presidents Clinton and Bush	Descendants of slaves	Contemplated (apology)	$0	Transatlantic slave trade[p]
Lawsuit for denial of loans to black farmers	1999	Federal government	Farmers denied credit, 1981–96	(lawsuit)	$600 million	Violation of Equal Credit Opportunity Act[q]

(continued)

TABLE 2.1
Eclectic List of Reparations Programs and Proposals (continued)

Program	Year(s)	Maker of Reparations	Recipient	Payment	Total Cost	Cause
Disclosure of insurance for slaves	2000–02	California legislature & insurance companies	Descendants of slaves	(disclosure)	$0	Disclosure of details of insurance policies on slaves' lives[r]
Apology for slave insurance	2000	Aetna Insurance Company		(apology)	$0	Aetna's insurance policies on slaves' lives[s]
Apology for slavery advertising	2000	Hartford Courant	Descendants of slaves	(apology)	$0	Courant's advertising for runaway slaves[t]
Disclosure of companies' complicity with slavery	2002–04	Chicago City Council, Los Angeles City Council, Detroit City Council	Descendants of slaves	(disclosure)	$0	Disclosure of companies' complicity in slavery[u]
Apology for use of slave labor	2004	University of Alabama	Descendants of slaves	Apology	$0	University's ownership of slaves and abuse of slaves by faculty members[v]
University benefit from slave labor	2004	Brown University		Study	$0	Study of university's complicity and benefit[w]

[a]Peter Hoffer, *The Devil's Disciples: The Makers of the Salem Witchcraft Trials*, at 8 (1998).
[b]Theodore M. Hammett, *Two Mobs of Jacksonian Boston: Ideology and Interest*, 62 J. Am. Hist. 845–68 (1976).
[c]17 Stat. 13 (1871): George Rutherglen, *Custom and Usage as Action under Color of State Law: An Essay on the Forgotten Terms of Section 1983*, 89 Va. L. Rev. 925 (2003); see also Eric Foner, *Reconstruction: America's Unfinished Resolution, 1866–1877*, 436–42 (1988).
[d]An Act to Indemnity the Owner of Property for Damages By Mobs and Riots, Laws of 1887 at 237: Act to Suppress Mob Violence, Ill. Rev. Statutes Chap. 38 §§ 512–17; Slanton v. City of Chicago, 130 N.E. 2d 205 (Ill. App. 1955). Payments made to victims of East St. Louis Riot of 1917 and Chicago Riot of 1919. See Alfred L. Brophy, *Reconstructing the Dreamland: The Tulsa Riot of 1921*, at 108 (2002).

[e] *See* Alfred L. Brophy, *Reconstructing the Dreamland: The Tulsa Riot of 1921*, at 108 (2002).

[f] Report of the National Advisory Committee on Civil Disorders (1968).

[g] 43 U.S.C. §§ 1601–1629 (2000); Gail Osherenko, *Indigenous Rights in Russia: Is Title to Land Essential for Cultural Survival?* 13 Geo. Int'l Envtl. L. Rev. 695, 696 (2001); John F. Walsh, *Settling the Alaska Native Claims Settlement Act*, 38 Stan. L. Rev. 227 (1985).

[h] Eric K. Yamamoto et al., *Race, Rights, and Reparation: Law and the Japanese American Internment* (2001).

[i] H.R. 3745, 101st Cong. (1989).

[j] 25 U.S.C. §§ 5001–5013;

[k] *See* 103rd Congress, Joint Resolution, PL 103-150 (November 23, 1993); Eric Yamamoto, *Race Apologies*, 1 J. Gender, Race & Justice 47, 74 (1997); Eric Yamamoto, *Race Theory and Political Lawyering Practice in Post–Civil Rights America*, 95 Michigan L. Rev. 821 (1997). And the apology was cited by Federal District Judge Alan Kay's opinion in Doe v. Kamehameha Schools, 295 F.Supp.2d 1141 (D. Hawaii 2003), which upheld the schools' race-based admissions program. Excerpts from the opinion are conveniently *available at* http://www.ksbe.edu/article.php?story=20050505048114228. The decision was subsequently overturned by the United States Court of Appeals, Doe v. Kamehameha Schools, 416 F.3d 1025 (9th Cir. 2005) and at press time the court is reconsidering the case. See Ken Kobayashi, *Court Gives Hope to Kamehameha Schools*, *available at* http://the.honoluluadvertiser.com/article/2006/Feb/23/ln/FP602230347.html. The case is the subject of a brief discussion at 119 Harvard Law Review 661 (2005).

[l] John Blake, *An Unfulfilled Promise?* Atlanta Journal Constitution, June 14, 2003; Gustav Niebuhr, *Baptist Group Voters to Repent Stand on Slaves*, N.Y. Times, June 21, 1995.

[m] Eric Yamamoto, *Race Theory and Political Lawyering Practice in Post–Civil Rights America*, 95 Michigan L. Rev. 821, 895–900 (1997).

[n] Eric K. Yamamoto, *Rethinking Alliances: Agency, Responsibility, and Interracial Justice*, 3 UCLA Asian Pac. Am. L.J., 33, 39 (1995).

[o] Alfred L. Brophy, *Reconstructing the Dreamland: The Tulsa Riot of 1921* (2002); Alexander v. Oklahoma, No. 03-CV-133 (N.D. Okla. 2004).

[p] Richard W. Stevenson, *Bush, In Africa, Promises Aid but Offers No Troops for Liberia*, N.Y. Times, July 8, 2003; John F. Harris, *Coming out of Africa*, Washington Post A1, April 3, 1998. Neither President Clinton nor President Bush apologized, but both publicly acknowledged the harm of slavery.

[q] Pigford v. Glickman, 185 F.R.D. 82, 85 (D.D.C. 1999). *aff'd*, 206 F.3d 1212 (D.C. Cir. 2000); Charles J. Ogletree Jr., *Repairing the Past: New Efforts in the Reparations Debate in America*, 38 Harv. C.R-C.L. L. Rev. 279 (2003) at 302–03.

[r] http://www.insurance.ca.gov/0100-consumers/0300-public-programs/0200-slavery-era-insur/.

[s] Aetna, slavery reparations issue, *available at* http://www.aetna.com/news/2002/slavery_reparations_issue.html (discussing the 2000 apology and subsequent events); Democracy Now, Pacifica Radio, Aetna Acknowledges Issuing Slave Policies During 1850's . . . Offers Apology, Denies Reparations, *available at* http://www.democracynow.org/article.pl?sid=03/04/07/0227252.

[t] Matthew Kaufman, *The Debt; The Cost of Slavery Was High, but Who Will Pay for It?* Hartford Courant, September 29, 2002; Paul Zielbauer, *A Newspaper Apologizes for Slave-Era Ads*, N.Y. Times, B1, July 6, 2000; Jesse Leavenworth & Kevin Canfield, *Courant Complicity in an Old Wrong*, Hartford Courant, July 4, 2000; Anne Farrow et al., *Complicity: How the North Promoted, Prolonged, and Profited from Slavery* (2006). Some key details are *available at* http://www.insurance.ca.gov/0100-consumers/0300-public-programs/0200-slavery-era-insur/.

[u] John M. Broder, *The Business of Slavery and Penitence*, N.Y. Times, Sec. 4 at 4, May 25, 2003 (mentioning Los Angeles and Chicago City Councils' action to require disclosure of companies' culpability in slavery); Business, Corporate, and Slavery Era Insurance Ordinance, Municipal Code of Chicago, §2–92–585 (2002); *Wayne County Commissioners Pass Slavery Disclosure Ordinance*, Detroit Free Press, May 6, 2004. The Chicago Ordinance has produced disclosure by Lehman Brothers, JPMorgan Chase, and Bank One. *See*, *Company Admits Ties to Slavery; Lehman Brothers News Gives Spark to Reparations Drive*, Chicago Sun 9, November 24, 2003; Fran Spielman, *Bank One "Probably" Dealt with Slave Business*, Chicago Sun-Times, June 24, 2004.

[v] *See*, *e.g.*, Alfred L. Brophy, *University of Alabama Right to Remember and Apologize*, Birmingham News, April 25, 2004; Jay Reeves, *University of Alabama Apologizes for Slavery*, Chicago Tribune 21, April 21, 2004.

[w] Ruth J. Simmons, *Facing Up to Our History of Slavery*, Boston Globe, April 28, 2004; Pam Bellack, *Brown University to Examine Debt to Slave Trade*, N.Y. Times, March 13, 2004.

In the late nineteenth and early twentieth centuries, there were periodic calls for reparations. In the early 1890s, Walter R. Vaughan drafted a bill, which was introduced to the U.S. House of Representatives, to provide fifteen dollars per month to former slaves.[28] A few years later, Reverend Isaiah H. Dickerson and Mrs. Callie D. House established the National Ex-Slave and Mutual Relief Bounty Pension Association. It was premised on the idea that former slaves, like Union and Confederate soldiers, deserved a pension.[29] In 1915, Cornelius J. Jones, a Washington, D.C., attorney, filed suit in federal court to recover the taxes paid on cotton produced with slave labor.[30] Somewhat later, Marcus Garvey—called by one reparations proponent "the twentieth century's greatest advocate for human rights, equal rights and reparations for the Africa"[31]—established the United Negro Improvement Association (UNIA). He sought payments for descendants of slaves as part of the "back to Africa" movement. As Adjoa Aiyotoro, a leader of the reparations movement, has written recently, the UNIA was more successful than the National Ex-Slave and Mutual Relief Bounty Pension Association "in large part because it spoke to getting away from a government that had oppressed so brutally and had then refused to implement reparative remedies—to make peace with the past."[32]

But most of the energy was devoted to getting basic equal treatment. The times were such that reparations for past injustice were not the most pressing issue; merely stopping unequal treatment was more urgently needed. The National Association for the Advancement of Colored People (NAACP), founded in 1909 in the aftermath of the horrible riot at Springfield, Illinois, spent much of its energy fighting against gross unfairness in the legal system. This organization was remarkably effective at fighting housing segregation ordinances. The U.S. Supreme Court struck down a Louisville zoning ordinance that mandated segregation in housing in 1917; in 1915, it struck down a voting registration law that essentially prohibited African Americans from registering to vote; in 1914, it struck down a railroad segregation statute that permitted unequal accommodations for African Americans. The victories continued—slowly—but there was so much work to be done to get equal treatment that few could think about reparations.[33] At points in the Progressive era, some black writings saw the Civil War as a form of atonement. Roscoe Dunjee, who served on the national board of the NAACP in the 1930s, wrote in terms reminiscent of President Abraham Lincoln's Second Inaugural Address:

> The slave-holders of the Old South could find eloquent arguments to justify an unrighteous system through which they could amass great wealth and live in ease and luxury, but there came a day of reckoning and for every drop of sweat and blood that the humble black slaves poured upon the soil of the cotton fields, there flowed a drop of white blood upon the battlefield as an atonement for the enormous crime that had been committed against an innocent people. "God is not mocked, whatsoever a man soweth, that shall he also reap."[34]

Still, such forward-looking writers as W. E. B. DuBois reminded their readers that the legacy of slavery had never been eradicated. DuBois's history of Reconstruction chronicled the shifting fortunes of African Americans and the ways that the black codes left them with little opportunity.

As attention shifted to obtaining equal treatment, there was no opportunity to ask for reparations. Such a request would have been fruitless; courts were unreceptive to them, and there were more pressing problems. There were other claims to be made, though. Relying on state statutes that provided a cause of action for victims of mob violence, a few African American victims of the Chicago and East St. Louis race riots obtained compensation. But for the large-scale crimes, for the people who had themselves been slaves, nothing happened.

Then, in the years after World War II, Congress and the federal courts became dramatically more receptive to requests for relief from discrimination. Many factors account for the changing attitude of the federal government. Some are noble: African American soldiers who fought in World War II earned the respect of the rest of the country. Having just defeated Nazi racism and totalitarianism, many Americans wanted to wipe out the Jim Crow system.[35] Television brought home the images of discrimination and made people in other parts of the country aware of gross mistreatment in the Jim Crow South. There were other, less lofty reasons why Civil Rights gained momentum. There had been a growing doctrine within the judiciary that each person is entitled to equal treatment. Then there were political and economic reasons as well: African Americans were beginning to vote in increasing numbers, in both North and South, so politicians had to pay more attention to them. African Americans' increasing economic power increased the costs of discrimination against them. Finally, the transportation revolution made it more difficult to maintain segregated facilities.

The initial phase of the Civil Rights movement focused on trying to ensure equal treatment rather than repairing past damage. President Truman desegregated the military; then the Supreme Court issued its *Brown v. Board of Education* decision in 1954. The Civil Rights Act of 1957 promised certain limited rights. Still, the courts were taken up with cases figuring out what equal treatment might mean, as they slowly desegregated public facilities, public parks, and schools. There were substantial questions about what that integrated world might portend, in both the black and white communities. In Little Rock, Arkansas, for instance, where the schools were desegregated in 1957, some members of the black community worried what integration would do to the community's schools and teachers. Would there still be opportunity for black students to achieve in integrated schools?[36]

Then came the Civil Rights Act of 1964, the Voting Rights Act of 1965, and the Great Society, all designed to end racial injustice, as well as to help reconstruct the lives of all poor Americans. That Civil Rights legislation put power into the hands of those who had suffered. For example, the Civil Rights Act of 1964 creates a right to sue businesses that discriminate in the provision of public accommodations, such as restaurants and hotels. The Great Society was not styled as a form of reparations; the rhetoric surrounding its passage was of building something for the future, a spiritual renewal. It was forward-looking;[37] it sought to harness the power of the government to build something more positive for the future, as has the Homestead Act of 1862, as had the New Deal of the early 1930s, and as had the GI Bill of 1944.[38] For a time, the Civil Rights movement celebrated its triumph. And still there were periodic calls for discussion of reparations. Many of the reparationists who seek wholesale redistribution of wealth take inspiration from Martin Luther King's prescription in *Why We Can't Wait* that there be reparations.[39] As Yale Law Professor Boris Bittker said, "in proposing a 'Bill of Rights for the Disadvantaged,' Martin Luther King, Jr., argued that '[t]he moral justification for special measures for Negroes is rooted in the robberies inherent in the institution of slavery.'"[40] And so, reparations talk resurfaced periodically.

The modern reparations movement is often said to have started in 1969, when James Forman made a demand to the congregation of the Riverside Heights Church, situated between the Columbia University campus and Harlem, for $500 million from white churches and synagogues as a down payment on reparations.[41] He defiantly stated:

> We are therefore demanding of the white Christian churches and Jewish synagogues which are part and parcel of the system of capitalism, that they begin to pay reparations to black people in this country. We are demanding $500,000,000 from the Christian white churches and the Jewish synagogues. This total comes to 15 dollars per nigger. This is a low estimate for we maintain there are probably more than 30,000,000 black people in this country. . . . Fifteen dollars for every black brother and sister in the United States is only a beginning of the reparations due us as people who have been exploited and degraded, brutalized, killed and persecuted. Underneath all of this exploitation, the racism of this country has produced a psychological effect upon us that we are beginning to shake off. We are no longer afraid to demand our full rights as a people in this decadent society.[42]

Forman was breaking away from the early Civil Rights movement— that of the post–World War II era, which rested on the idea that integration was the paramount goal of constitutional law. Truman's 1948 executive order that integrated the military and *Brown v. Board of Education* were premised on the belief that the government should not be permitted to draw distinctions based on race; it was part of an ethic of individualism that people should be treated as individuals by the government, not as members of a group. Novels such as Ralph Ellison's *Invisible Man* illustrate that theme.

Yet, as 1960s Civil Rights advocates saw the limits of the Civil Rights movement, some began to speak a different language—one of Black Power and autonomy. The realization of key Civil Rights goals, such as the Supreme Court's expansion of the principle that federal, state, and local governments could not discriminate on the basis of race, was followed by federal Civil Rights legislation (mentioned previously) that prohibited much private discrimination as well, along with President Lyndon Johnson's Great Society program and the origins of race-based set-asides in education and employment.

Although Great Society programs helped in reducing the poverty rate among African Americans, by the late 1960s, there was frustration that change was not happening fast enough. The assassinations of Robert Kennedy and Martin Luther King in 1968 and the riots that followed, as well as the election of President Richard Nixon later that year, signaled declining confidence in the Civil Rights movement and the idea of integration. Ideas that emphasized not integration but empowerment of the black community were growing in popularity. Forman's demand for restitution both illustrated and contributed to that movement. His black manifesto drew substantial attention, including responses from many churches, and within a few months, discussion had migrated well beyond the churches, which were the original audience for the manifesto. The discussion led to many of the same questions that the more recent reparations movement has faced. As Robert Lecky and H. Elliott Wright wrote in 1969, the concept of reparations raises "a host of thorny issues." Those issues, in 1969 as well as now, include:

> Who pays? Who gets (after all, some blacks are affluent)? Who administers? What programs and channels would be most helpful? What responsibility would well-off whites have for still worse-off blacks after a set sum was paid? What would be the implications for race relations?[43]

Lecky and Wright presciently observed that "there is no reason to believe" that those questions' "importance has passed or will soon fade."[44] How right they were. It is significant, indeed, that the questions at the center of the reparations debate in the 1960s are still the questions that motivate us more than thirty-five years later.

Forman was not the only instigator of the calls for reparations, but he has been remembered as the most famous proponent. For a time, Forman's claims, which grew out of the Black Power movement of the late 1960s, received attention. Forman drew a serious response from Yale University Law Professor Boris Bittker, whose *The Case for Black Reparations* still remains one of the leading explorations of reparations.

Bittker used Civil Rights law as a framework for analyzing the mistreatment of African Americans in both the era of slavery and Jim Crow. What distinguishes Bittker from other, more recent, reparations advocates is that he sought to apply well-known legal principles to the case of black reparations. He made an intriguing legal case for holding the federal and state governments legally liable in court, assuming suspension of the statute of limitations. (As discussed in substantial detail in chapter 5, the statute of limitations requires lawsuits to be brought within a fairly short time after a harm has occurred. In most cases, it is between two and six years, depending on the type of case involved.) He concluded that the barriers to recovery for slavery were probably insuperable but that for more recent racial crimes—such as the maintenance of unequal schools—the law ought to provide a remedy. Bittker's abandonment of claims for slavery has the virtue of pragmatism. Still, Bittker left many critical legal issues unaddressed, such as standing and statutes of limitation, as well as critical issues including sovereign immunity. Bittker's book is perhaps best viewed as an attempt to use legal doctrine to provide guidance in making a case for reparations to a legislature, rather than a court.

But Bittker was not writing a brief in a legal case; he was writing a brief in a moral case. Bittker simply used civil rights law as a framework to suggest moral culpability. Others have followed Bittker's lead, trying to construct their utopian plans with a precision that is more usually seen only once a plan is firmly in place.[45] Bittker then placed the issue of reparations into a larger context, comparing it with other social programs, so that the comparative advantages of reparations might be judged against other ways of spending the federal government's limited resources. He concluded that although lawsuits would not be effective ways of recovering for past wrongs because the statute of limitations bars them, Congress ought to act to repair some of the damage. Bittker's analysis looked to the harm African Americans suffered, rather than to the contributions they made during the era of slavery and Jim Crow, in determining entitlement.[46]

Needless to say, a lawsuit for reparations for harms that occurred in the 1860s or before is going to be quite difficult. Such a result made sense in 1973, when many of the harms of Jim Crow were more readily identifiable than today and when the legal system holding Jim Crow in place had so recently been dismantled. Despite attention from Bittker and others, Forman's movement did not go far. For a time, the Civil Rights movement focused its energies elsewhere: on cementing its victories in the Voting Rights Act, the Civil Rights Act of 1964, the Fair Housing Act of 1968, and affirmative action in employment and education. Yet in recent years, attention has turned back to reparations. The next chapter takes up the recent movement and its relationship to reparations precedents throughout American history and throughout the world. When Derrick Bell, one of the leaders of what would soon be known as the critical race theory movement, reviewed Bittker's *The Case for Black Reparations*, he concluded pessimistically that "legal analysis cannot give life to a remedial program that must evolve from the perceptions of those responsible for the perpetuation of racism in this country."[47] Professor Bell may be correct in concluding that the impetus for reform must come from outside the judiciary, for as the reparations advocates predicted, courts have not been receptive to reparations claims. Nevertheless, on occasion, courts can present the opening wedge for presentation of reparations claims. Bell's prediction came true in the short term. From Bittker's book until the mid-1980s, talk of reparations for slavery was sparse. But there were other movements for reparations. Those movements, for Native Americans, Japanese Americans, Holocaust victims, and others, are part of the reparations movement. They also serve as models and as motives for the black reparations movement.

Reparations to Other Groups

Recent Reparations Precedents and the Age of Apology

Other racial groups, such as some Native American tribes and Japanese Americans interned during World War II, received reparations. The Native American reparations began in 1946, the year after World War II ended, and Japanese Americans received limited reparations in 1948. But most of the reparations for Native Americans and Japanese Americans took place in the 1970s and 1980s. A look at those precedents—of Native American, Japanese American, and even black American reparations—discloses that reparations are more common than one might initially think. Table 2.1 gives an eclectic listing of what one might consider reparations: payments from the government to repair for past injustice. The table, which is based in part on a table presented by Eric Posner and Adrian Vermeule in the *Columbia Law Review*, might be expanded many times, but it may suffice to convey the sense that in many times in the past, state and federal governments have used their vast power to improve the lives of those injured by the government's acts, as well as others.

The Examples of Native American and Japanese Americans

The expanded view of reparations, as including programs designed to repair past damage, suggests that such programs have been common in American history. Table 2.1 includes a series of reparations proposals and programs, such as apologies, truth commissions, civil rights legislation, community-building programs, and payments to individuals, in U.S. history. Two reparations movements in recent history have received particular attention as precedent for black reparations: payments and property settlements with Native Americans and with Japanese Americans interned during World War II. They are worth exploring in a little depth.

In the 1970s, the movement for reparations to Native Americans was coming of age. Like blacks, Native Americans have been making claims for reparations—or restoration of their property—for generations. In 1863, Congress passed its first statute that allowed Native Americans to petition the Court of Claims when they had a complaint against the federal government based on a treaty violation. In the following eight decades, Congress occasionally passed special legislation allowing tribes to sue for property losses unrelated to treaties. It was not until 1946, however, that Congress made major steps toward hearing Native claims, with passage of the Indian Claims Commission Act. The commission was designed to consolidate and adjudicate Natives' claims against the federal government. Much of the impetus for the act was the desire to consolidate claims and streamline the procedures for determining claims, as well as offering tribes an economic incentive for following government policy. Congress also recognized the moral claims that Natives had—and provided that the commission could hear claims that had a moral basis only, not just those based on legal claims.[48] The commission would, Secretary of Indian Affairs John Collier hoped, "add to the tribal assets and reflect the country's renewed

commitment to treating Indians fairly."[49] The moral claims provision
has been used relatively infrequently, and a 1954 Supreme Court decision restricted the commission to hearing claims of recognized tribes.
However, the commission has represented for decades a commitment
to at least hearing claims of Natives (mostly to property), even if it
rarely does something about them.

The largest single payout of reparations in U.S. history came in
1971, in the Alaska Native Claims Settlement Act of 1971,[50] which provided Alaskan tribes with nearly $1 billion, along with the return of 44
million acres of land. It was motivated in large part by politics: Alaska
Natives had a plausible claim to land that was crucial to the completion of the Alaska pipeline. So, as happens so often, Congress joined
the moral and political issues and provided money and certain land to
Native tribes in exchange for their claims to other land. The form of
reparations is important as well; the tribes, rather than individual
members, were given money, which was designated for economic development. The Alaska Claims Settlement Act was, thus, part of the
emerging belief of the late 1960s and early 1970s that poverty might be
effectively dealt with by institution building, rather than by transfers to
individuals. Reparations to Native Americans have been limited,
though Natives have received more in what one might call reparations
than any other single group.

There have been other important programs, as well. The Native
Graves Repatriation Act, passed in 1992, requires the return of human
remains to tribes from institutions that receive federal funding, such as
museums, in exchange for continued funding. This provides a different
form of relief, the return of "property" to the descendants of its original
owners. And there have been a series of lawsuits providing for return of
parcels of land, such as the Black Hills litigation in South Dakota.[51]
Those are isolated cases, however, and the largest case of Native
American reparations, the Alaska Claims Settlement Act of 1971, is now
more than thirty years old. Yet other legislation, such as the Alaska
Claims Settlement Act and Great Society programs, provides for direct
and huge transfer payments, either to communities or to individuals
and sometimes to both. The wide-ranging programs, which span the
history of the United States, testify to the frequent presence of reparations programs in state and federal legislation.

Perhaps the best-known case of reparations is the Civil Liberties Act of 1988,[52] which provided compensation to Japanese Americans interned during World War II. In early 1942, President Roosevelt ordered the relocation of Japanese Americans from the West Coast. In accordance with his order, Japanese Americans were interned. Many had to sell their homes and businesses at well below market value; still others turned their property over to friends, who held it for them until the war was over. In 1948, after the war ended, Congress provided limited compensation.[53]

But the 1948 act provided compensation for only a fraction of the actual loss of property, and it offered no official apology. For decades, Japanese Americans struggled for more justice than the 1948 act had provided. Japanese Americans had begun in the late 1970s to seriously question their treatment by the United States government during World War II. New documents came to light, aided by the work of lawyer Peter Irons, who later wrote a book documenting the ways that the U.S. government exaggerated the threat that Japanese American citizens posed during the war. When the United States argued the constitutionality of the internments in the federal courts during World War II, it failed to disclose evidence that showed there was little threat. With that evidence, the convictions were overturned in 1982; then a lawsuit was filed to recover damages for the internment. That research in turn motivated a series of lawsuits, which are discussed more fully in chapter 5. The lawsuit was ultimately dismissed based on the statute of limitations.[54] The courts were, as one could easily have predicted, unlikely bases for proceeding.

Thus, in 1985 the Japanese Americans who had been interned forty years earlier were left with no avenues for relief from the courts. They did, however, still have the opportunity to press their case in the U.S. Congress. And lobbying then turned to Congress, which held extensive hearings, beginning in 1986. Congress has the power—which it often exercises—of passing legislation to aid people who have been victims of government or who have some special claim to relief. For two years, Congress considered a bill to grant compensation to the people interned. The centerpiece of the $1.6 billion act, signed by President Ronald Reagan, was a payment of $20,000 to every Japanese American (and some Native Alaskans) interned during the war who survived until 1986. The act also made an official apology and provided money for education about what happened during the internment. It thus linked truth commission, apology, and payments to individuals. The act was part political compromise—it was an issue of extreme importance to the wealthy and powerful Japanese American community—and part act of contrition by the U.S. Congress. The act was the culmination of a decades-long struggle to recognize the injustice of internment. The political stars had aligned. Congress took action for a large but limited class of claimants. According to the Office of Redress Administration, which was established in the Justice Department to administer the Civil Liberties Act of 1988, of the approximately 1.2 million people who were interned, something like 82,219 received compensation.[55]

The Civil Liberties Act had to deal with many problems in determining remedies, including who would receive compensation and for how much. The internments damaged people in many ways. Those interned lost property at the time of internment and suffered for years away from home. How, one wonders, does one compensate for that? Had the lawsuit been successful, it is likely that the people interned (or their family members, if they had died) would have had claims both for property lost (or sold at fire-sale prices) and for internment. Had Congress tried to establish such a compensation scheme, there would have been enormous problems in proof. How do you demonstrate the value of property lost more than forty years ago? Individuals would also have received widely divergent payouts. Those who had lost more property would have received more money than others. Moreover, there might have been widely different figures even for the period of internment. Presumably, some people suffered more than others during internment. To avoid those problems of proof—but also to limit dramatically the size of the compensation—Congress developed another scheme. It gave a flat payout of $20,000 to every person who had been interned *and* who was still alive in 1986. The Civil Rights Act incorporated two principles, then: a flat fee, which treated everyone's loss as the same, and a requirement that the person had to be alive at the time the act was proposed.

Those principles are central to many reparations plans; they have powerful motives behind them. The requirement that victims still be alive helps to ensure that the people most directly affected receive compensation. It poses problems with fairness, of course. Many descendants of those interned suffered, because their families had less money than they would have had without the internment. It is hard to say that the harm ended with the people who were interned. However, Congress judged that the limited budget for reparations would best be spent on those who were still alive. Limiting payments to survivors meant that money went to the most directly affected; it avoided difficult problems of ascertaining which people who were not interned should receive money.

Fixed sums offer a series of advantages: They reduce problems of proof, and they offer certainty in terms of liability. They also pose significant problems in fairness, however. Particularly when the sum is fixed at a small amount, such as $20,000 per survivor, the money is at best a token to go along with the government's apology. No one thinks that the amount would make whole those individuals who lost their property or that the money would begin to compensate for relocation and years in detention camps. Nevertheless, legislative reparations programs — as opposed to judicial ones — often attempt to fix a set dollar figure, which is a token of what was lost, rather than attempt to make someone whole, based on an individualized calculation of what was lost.

International Examples: Reparations
for the Holocaust and Apartheid

The movement for redress of historic injustices is not limited to the United States. There is, in fact, lively discussion about reparations for crimes that took place outside the United States. Sometimes that movement uses U.S. courts. The best-known example is the lawsuits filed in the mid-1990s to hold companies liable for benefiting from the Holocaust, including Swiss banks, which paid money that was held by the banks to family members of victims. There have been lawsuits, discussed in chapter 4, against companies that used slave labor. Some lawsuits asked for the return of artwork taken during World War II. Similarly, victims of torture abroad have sometimes employed the Alien Tort Claims Act to bring suit against their torturers in U.S. courts.

The Holocaust has generated substantial litigation in the United States, as well as political negotiations for reparations. In the mid-1990s, victims of the Nazi Holocaust began seriously pursuing claims with some success in U.S. courts.[56] The best-known litigation in the United States was against Swiss banks, which held assets owned by Holocaust victims. The banks refused to return deposits to family members unless they produced documents, such as account books and death certificates. In the wake of World War II, neither were available. So the assets sat in Swiss banks for decades. As a result of litigation in U.S. federal court in Brooklyn, New York, followed by pressure from U.S. politicians, the Swiss banks agreed to a settlement of $5 billion, which capped the banks' liability and established a plan for asserting claims.[57] Professor Burt Neuborne of New York University Law School, a central figure in the Holocaust litigation, identified four key types of lawsuits: banks that refused to return assets of victims; banks that knowingly profited from the Nazi "Aryanization" program, which required non-Aryans to sell their property at well below market value; claims against insurance companies that failed to honor life insurance policies on Holocaust victims; and claims against German companies for the use of slave labor during the war.[58] Others have asserted similar claims. For example, French victims of the Holocaust have recently won a preliminary round in the courts for return of gold taken from them.[59] There have also been limited suits for return of stolen art.[60]

The fall of the Berlin Wall led to compensation for those whose families lost property when the Communists took control after World War II. In East Germany, many families received land that had been taken in the 1940s. As with much Holocaust litigation, the key there was restoration of property, rather than compensation for the value of the use over the intervening forty years or compensation for harm to individuals. When there was property that could be returned, it was returned. There was no action for payment for damage done to humans, because the repair was based on the idea of restitution. When we are talking about injuries to humans, it is difficult to see what can be restored.

Much of the movement for redress has taken place entirely outside the United States, of course. The best-known movement is South Africa's Truth and Reconciliation Commission (TRC), which the South African government created in 1995 as a way of grappling with that country's legacy of state-sanctioned violence during the era of apartheid. The TRC offered immunity for those who testified about past crimes. It was based on the premise that it was difficult, if not impossible, to prosecute those past crimes but that reconciliation might be facilitated if people who had committed crimes confessed them. The confessions also held out the promise of giving family members of victims some closure. They might, then, know something more about how their family members died and see the true story of what happened known. Such were the noble purposes behind the TRC. The literature on South Africa's experience is enormous. Much of it questions how effective the TRC has been, for the TRC has offered little more than truth and precious little reconciliation.[61] However, it must be judged in light of the limited opportunities that were available. Opportunities for criminal prosecutions were indeed limited, as were the government's financial resources to compensate for past crimes.[62]

Other nations have gotten into the business as well, from New Zealand, which is revisiting its troubled history of taking land from the native Maori people,[63] to Canada, which has provided compensation to its citizens of Japanese ancestry who were interned during World War II, to Japan, which is revisiting its own crimes during that war. For decades, Korean women who were used as sex slaves by Japanese soldiers during World War II kept quiet.[64] The problem was enormous. Perhaps as many as 60,000 young women, who were euphemistically called "comfort women," were kept in slavery for years during the war. The abuse they suffered was awful, and the humiliation kept them from coming forward for decades. Slowly, mostly after 1980, a few women began talking. Then, beginning in December 1991, after decades of denial by the Japanese government, a few women filed suit against Japan.[65] Just a few plaintiffs, facing an uphill battle, were able to win modest compensation and later, with pressure from South Korea, to compel an apology from the Japanese prime minister. That acknowledgment and then apology led to further, albeit modest, efforts to compensate those who were still alive.

The movement for truth and reconciliation commissions is continuing to grow. In 2004, a TRC endorsed by the United Nations in Sierra Leone recommended reparations payments to families of that nation's bloody civil war, which began in 1991.[66] And other commissions have appeared in Uganda, East Timor, Ghana, and Nigeria, among many others.[67] Those international movements came as the debate over the U.S. history of race discrimination was changing.

The Age of Apologies and Recent Reparations
Running parallel to those developments in the international scene during the 1990s were a series of developments in the United States. The election of William Clinton in 1992, who was known for his empa-

thy with the American people, marked the switch to an age of apology, in which many groups sought and received apologies for a diverse set of past grievances. President Clinton apologized for, was part of apologies for, or discussed apologizing for slavery,[68] the genocide in Rwanda,[69] executions of civilians during the Korean War,[70] U.S. support of Guatemala's military while it committed genocide,[71] medical experiments on African Americans at Tuskegee,[72] radiation experiments,[73] and the deprivation of native Hawaiians of their land.[74]

Given that broad set of apologies, some questioned whether they were genuine, and their value even if they were genuine. The apology for the failure to intervene to stop the Rwandan genocide, which took place while President Clinton was in office, seemed a particularly hollow apology. The close connection between commission of the wrong (the failure to act to protect against genocide, which left something like a million people dead) and the apology made it look as though the people offering the apology must have known that their actions were wrong at the time yet did not care. Because the apology was not linked to anything more concrete in terms of atonement, it looked even hollower. Moreover, while some apologies were for long-past events, with the primary meaning an expression of compassion for the victims and their families (such as the land and sovereignty grab in Hawaii), the ethnic conflict that led to the genocide in Rwanda might—indeed, probably will—recur somewhere in the world soon. An apology that suggests that its makers learned an important lesson and are committed to never repeating that mistake might have great meaning. There was little confidence, however, that policy makers in the United States had genuinely resolved not to stand by while genocide occurred again. (This feeling seemed confirmed when Clinton's successor, President George W. Bush, who had supposedly promised, in the margins of a report on the Rwandan genocide, "not on my watch," was criticized for not intervening in a similar genocide in Sudan that did happen on his watch.) Other apologies were, however, linked to something more tangible. The men in Tuskegee, Alabama, whom Clinton apologized to, were victims of a U.S. Public Health Service medical experiment on the effects of untreated syphilis, and had already received compensation through a lawsuit in the 1970s. They had not, however, received an apology.

Those public apologies from the president were joined with apologies from other groups as well. In 1995, the Southern Baptist Convention, which had split from the American Baptist Convention in the 1840s over the issue of slavery, apologized for the sins of racism. The Presbyterian General Assembly and Presbyterian Church in America both followed suit a few years later,[75] as the Disciples of Christ have joined the call for a national slavery apology.[76] The United Church of Christ apologized in 1993 for its involvement in the 1893 overthrow of the Hawaiian monarchy and the establishment of U.S. control over Hawaii. That apology was accompanied with the transfer of land on five major islands, along with several million dollars given for both Native Hawaiians and for the churches' traditionally Hawaiian congregations. That apology was part of the basis for the U.S. Congress' 1993 joint resolution that recognized and apologized for the overthrow of the kingdom of Hawaii. More recently, universities have begun to revisit their past. The first was Yale University, which was inspired by a report released by several graduate students in the fall of 2001. The report explores Yale's connections to slavery in the money the university received and the colleges and buildings named after prominent slaveholders (such as John C. Calhoun, who led the nullification movement in South Carolina in the 1830s and was a prominent pro-slavery theorist at his death in 1850).

In 2003, Brown University President Ruth Simmons composed the Slavery and Justice Committee to study Brown's connections to slavery and to make recommendations regarding the memorialization of slavery on the Brown campus.[77] Even at liberal Brown, however, there was immediate controversy.

And as the Slavery and Justice Committee's work is showing, Brown University has an exceedingly complex relationship to slavery. Its grand University Hall was built in the 1770s, in part using slave labor. The Browns, for whom the school is named, were Rhode Island merchants. Some members of the family made money in the slave trade; others, including Nicholas Brown, whose contribution of $5,000 in 1804 led to the renaming of Rhode Island College as Brown University, were not slave traders.[78] Moreover, Francis Wayland, Brown's president from 1827 to 1855, was a prominent antislavery advocate. He vigorously debated slavery with South Carolina minister Richard Fuller through a series of letters.

Thus, the great Brown University profited from the rich Rhode Island community supported in part by the slave trade and trade in the products of slave labor. Yet, as the Civil War approached, Brown was a vehicle for urging abolition of slavery.[79]

Even in the South, schools are revisiting their past. In the spring of 2004, following a contentious debate that captured the attention of the state's talk radio stations and newspapers, the University of Alabama faculty senate apologized for the university's use of slave labor and for the faculty's role in beating slaves owned by the university. In the fall of 2005, the University of North Carolina archives presented an exhibit on the university's connections to slavery and there is talk in the spring of 2006 from students and faculty of asking for apology from the University of Virginia.

The request for apologies continues elsewhere as well. In early 2004, Senators Brownback (R, Kansas), Campbell (R, Colorado) and Inouye (D, Hawaii) introduced a joint resolution (appendix 7) in the U.S. Senate to recognize U.S. mistreatment of Native Americans and to apologize for that mistreatment.[80] And in the summer of 2005, the U.S. Senate passed an apology for its predecessors' failure to pass antilynching legislation.[81]

There has been other action, too. Representative John Conyers of Michigan has proposed a bill to study the effects of slavery at every Congress since 1989. His bill, which is reprinted in appendix 3, has never gotten out of committee, but at some point, Conyers's bill is likely to receive at least a hearing. In fact, as Republicans look for wedge issues in the coming years, the possibility of support for reparations by Republicans in Congress seems to be growing. What better way, one might ask, to drive white voters—who almost uniformly dislike reparations talk—away from the Democrats than by allowing more discussion of reparations?[82] Alternatively—and perhaps more optimistically—members of both parties may see further reparations talk as a way of appealing to African American voters. Such, at least, is the speculation about the recent apology by members of the U.S. Senate for their predecessors' failure to pass antilynching legislation.[83]

It is in state legislatures and city halls around the country that reparations have most vigorously been advocated in recent years. During the 1990s, state historical commissions in Florida and Oklahoma, respectively, investigated the Rosewood Massacre of 1923 and the Tulsa race riot of 1921. The Florida legislature even set aside approximately $2.1 million for descendants of the massacre. The Oklahoma legislature apologized but did not pay money to riot victims. That led to a lawsuit, which was dismissed in March 2004. The dismissal, which was affirmed by the U.S. Court of Appeals in September 2004, marks the end of the road for Tulsa riot victims. But there may yet be lawsuits tried in other jurisdictions for racial violence that took place during Jim Crow.

The California legislature has gone the furthest of any state in reparations actions. It passed a statute (appendix 4) requiring insurance companies to disclose their involvement with slavery—by searching their records and disclosing the names of the slaves whom they had insured, as well as the names of the slaves' owners and their location. The California state insurance commission Web site has a database containing all the information it has received so far. It is an important source of information and an elegant testimony to the lives and work of people whose names have been forgotten. That Web site discloses that many of the slaves whose lives were insured worked in such hazardous occupations as mining.[84]

California also passed a similar statute requiring insurance companies to disclose the policies they wrote in Europe from 1920 to 1945. Some of those policies were cashed in by Nazi Germany on behalf of Holocaust victims. In the spring of 2003, the U.S. Supreme Court struck down that legislation as an interference with the president's power involving foreign businesses. Another California statute was struck down in the spring of 2003. That one permitted U.S. soldiers who had been held as slave laborers in Japanese prison camps during World War II to recover against the companies for which they had worked. The U.S. Court of Appeals held that the statute was barred by treaty with Japan. Given California's active involvement in reparations legislation, one wonders how long it will be until the legislature passes a statute giving the descendants of slaves the right to sue companies for benefits retained from slavery.

The city of Chicago, following the lead of California, passed an ordinance (appendix 5) that requires businesses to search all available records and disclose their relationship with slavery—whether they owned slaves or profited from slavery—as a condition of contracting with the city.[85] The Chicago ordinance, which has now been copied by Los Angeles and Detroit, has already produced several disclosures that remind us of the often-hidden connections between the past and the present (see chapter 6). Chicago Alderman Dorothy Tillman, the author of the ordinance, stated the purpose: "America has to acknowledge that its power is built on the backs of slaves."[86]

There are now requests for investigations into specific racial crimes, such as the Wilmington, North Carolina, riot of 1898; the forced sterilization of welfare recipients in California and North Carolina; and the Greensboro, North Carolina, execution of peaceful demonstrators by the Ku Klux Klan in 1979. It seems likely that those investigations will grow, as will prosecutions of racial crimes. The 2002 prosecution of the last of the survivors who bombed the Sixteenth Street Baptist Church in Birmingham, Alabama, in 1963 is one example of the revival of prosecutions for past crimes. The June 2005 conviction of Edgar Ray Killen for his role in the 1964 murders of three civil rights workers, Andrew Goodman, James E. Chaney, and Michael H. Schwerner, is yet another recent reminder that the process of revisiting the past continues in criminal courts around the country.[87]

And the quest for lawsuits that can overcome typical objections and problems such as the statute of limitations continues. One avenue that has received some attention is a claim against corporations for recent denials that they participated in slavery. That suit, not for reparations itself, would assert a claim for recent deception. Another, which has received no publicity yet, draws on the long-forgotten right of access to a graveyard by descendants of people buried in the graveyard. Thus, descendants of slaves buried on a plantation could file a lawsuit to have access to the plantation graveyard. No money would change hands, but there could be great symbolic significance to descendants visiting their ancestors. It would remind everyone of the multiple connections between past and present.

At local as well as national levels, reparations talk still grows, for there is an increased awareness and focus on the present effects of past pain. It has also given legitimacy to claims that someone (usually the government) should apologize and then pay.[88]

PART II

Reparations Ascendant

The Recent Renascence of Reparations

Debate and Refined Reparations Theory

3

The Modern Black
Reparations Movement:
Why Now, Why, and What?

WHY IS it that we are talking about reparations now, 140 years after slavery ended? A series of factors have come together to lead to serious discussion of reparations for slavery in the last few years. First, as we discussed in chapter 2, African Americans have seen reparations paid to other groups, such as Native Americans, Japanese Americans, and victims of the Nazi Holocaust. Thus, given the focus on apologies and reparations for other groups, many are led to ask, When will the descendants of slaves receive their due? Perhaps more important, however, is the rapidly decreasing commitment to affirmative action in the legislatures and the courts. As a result, some people have begun to try to shift the nature of the debate over race and the legacy of slavery and Jim Crow to thinking about compensating descendants of slaves for their labor and redressing the current effects of slavery, as well as discrimination in the twentieth century.[1]

Why?

The Material Bases

When reparations advocates make their case, they begin by talking about the gross differences in wealth, income, and educational achievement between blacks and whites in the United States today. The bare numbers are stark. The poverty rate for African Americans in 2004 was 24.7%. The poverty rate is near its lowest point ever, but still nearly one in four African Americans lives in poverty.[2] Children have it even worse: 33.6% of African American children in 2004 lived in poverty.[3] By comparison, a significantly lower percentage of non-Hispanic whites (8.6%) lived in poverty in 2004; 10.5% of non-Hispanic white children in 2004 lived in poverty.[4] The median income for African American families in 2004 was $30,134; for non-Hispanic whites, it was $49,061 50% higher than for African Americans.[5] In 2000, the median income for African American married couples was $50,749 and for non-Hispanic white couples it was $62,109, closer together.[6]

If we take a picture of the economic status of African Americans compared with whites, the telling data are the overall median incomes. The most recent data disclose that the median income of African Americans is less than 62% that of non-Hispanic whites. The data are even starker when we compare the wealth—as opposed to income—of blacks and whites. According to Melvin Oliver and Thomas Shapiro, whose 1997 book, *Black Wealth/White Wealth*, is dedicated to exploring the effects of race on wealth, nearly a quarter (23.7%) of whites have a net worth of more than $50,000, while only 3.3% of blacks have that much net worth.[7] On the other end of the spectrum, 63% of blacks have a negative net worth, and 28% of whites have a negative net worth. Those figures are illuminating for several reasons. They point out how many Americans—white as well as black—struggle financially and how we need to be concerned for a significant percentage of the population. But they also point out how much worse economic life is for blacks than for whites.[8]

Such evidence of inequality could easily be multiplied across an entire spectrum. In terms of educational achievement, 88% of non-Hispanic whites have high school diplomas and 27% have college degrees, while 77% of non-Hispanic blacks have high school diplomas and 15% have college degrees.[9] The story for health care is similarly bad. The infant mortality rate for black babies, for instance, is more than twice the infant morality rate for white babies.[10] Such figures, suggesting that we inhabit two separate nations, to borrow a phrase now common in political debate, serve as one pillar of the movement for reparations.

Another pillar of the case for reparations is the legacy of slavery—with its brutalization of humans, the generations of forced (and uncompensated) labor, rape, destruction of families, deprivation of even the right to an education, whippings, and torture—and the legacy of Jim Crow, which denied the right to vote and limited educational, employment, and housing opportunities. It is depressing to dwell on those legacies.[11] Even opponents concede, as they must, the horrible nature of slavery and the gross injustices of the Jim Crow system.[12]

Reparations supporters also point to wealth created by blacks for the benefit of whites. They assert that wealth has been retained by whites and point to the harm to blacks imposed by slavery and Jim Crow. Supporters emphasize the benefits conferred by blacks on whites through slavery and Jim Crow and the harm done through the institution of slavery and the period of Jim Crow discrimination to blacks. Those are the main bases that supporters employ as a justification for reparations.

The discussion of reparations is expanding well beyond the idea that reparations are based on the disparity of income, educational opportunity, and achievement; on the centuries of brutalization under slavery; and on decades of state-enforced segregation in schools, in public accommodations, and in employment. Now the arguments are focused on a spectrum of complex moral issues. How might one identify the appropriate recipients of reparations? Who would pay? Is there some continuing debt or other obligation? Why should people who committed no wrong be responsible for paying reparations? Will reparations make racial reconciliation more difficult by angering payers?[13]

That material disparity between blacks and whites has a long history; it is nothing new. So, one wonders, why is reparations talk so popular now? What about contemporary politics made reparations talk grow so much in the 1990s and early 2000s? Why, in short, are we talking about reparations now?

There are several main reasons. The discussion of the history of reparations in chapter 2 shows several of them. Awareness of past tragedies and their impact on the present has led to a renewed focus on tragedies. And that focus on the past has led to an expansion of apologies. At the same time, other members of certain groups have been successful in obtaining reparations, such as Native Americans, Japanese Americans, Holocaust victims, and victims of the Armenian genocide. Those are all positive precedents that push the reparations debate forward by example. There has also been a growing realization that the promise of the Civil Rights agenda has not been fulfilled. The popularity of affirmative action is in decline. Recent court cases have brought important elements of it into serious question. At the same time that realization came, there was the development of critical race theory (CRT). The CRT movement, as it is known, studies the importance of race to American society and seeks ways to address racial inequality.

Decline in Affirmative Action

Beginning in the late 1960s, as some in the Civil Rights movement were beginning to make more radical demands—such as claims for reparations—there was a countermovement that opposed affirmative action. Those counterforces began to gain substantial strength in the Supreme Court, and a series of opinions called into question the constitutionality of race-based programs. One of the best-known cases was the 1978 decision in *Bakke v. California Regents*. It upheld a policy under which certain spots in the medical school class of the University of California, Davis, were reserved for minority students. However, the badly fractured court could not decide on the basis supporting the program. Four members of the court thought that race-based set-asides were unconstitutional; four thought they were permissible, because they were designed to redress past discrimination and because they were limited. Justice Lewis Powell provided the fifth vote to uphold the admissions policy, but he cautioned that race ought to be only one factor. At best, affirmative action was permissible in limited circumstances.

A series of other decisions further clarified the boundaries of race-based affirmative action. The opinion of Chief Justice Warren Burger upholding limited affirmative action in the 1980 case of *Fullilove v. Klutznick* suggested that affirmative action had won a significant place in constitutional law. Burger upheld a provision of the Public Works Entitlement Act of 1977, which required that at least 10% of the value of the contract went to "minority business enterprises." Burger observed that the program was limited in scope and that the requirement could be waived when it was impracticable.[14] Burger looked to the history of the act and found that it was designed to eliminate the "perpetuation of the effects of prior discrimination which had impaired or foreclosed access by minority businesses to public contracting opportunities." Moreover, the program did not allocate money "according to inflexible percentages solely based on race or ethnicity." In 1984, in *Firefighters Local Union 1784 v. Stotts,* the Supreme Court upheld a decision by the city of Memphis to lay off black workers with less seniority than white workers—in keeping with the city's seniority plan. The black workers argued in essence that, had there not been discriminatory hiring in the past, the white workers would not have had the amount of seniority that they did. *Stotts* has come to stand for the proposition that it is inappropriate to displace white workers with seniority over black workers.[15]

A principle was emerging that the government could take limited race-conscious action but that it could not displace incumbent workers and that the action had to be taken to make limited remedies of past discrimination. That was confirmed in 1986, when the Supreme Court struck down a layoff plan devised by the Jackson, Mississippi, Board of Education. The plan called for the layoff of white teachers with more seniority than minority teachers, when following a strict seniority system would have reduced the percentage of minority teachers in the school system.[16]

Thus, in the mid-1980s, just as there was increasing pressure to do something about Japanese American internment, other decisions were drastically limiting the power of the government to take race-based action. In 1988, in *Richmond v. J. A. Croson Company,* the Supreme Court struck down a program established by the city of Richmond, Virginia, that required 30% of construction contracts be set aside for companies owned by racial minorities. That decision limited state governments' power to places where there was evidence of discrimination in the specific location in the past. After *Croson,* race-based affirmative action was permissible only in cases where it serves a compelling governmental interest and when it is narrowly tailored to further that interest.[17] The Supreme Court requires that any racial classification— which is presumably what reparations would be—must meet "strict scrutiny."[18] To satisfy strict scrutiny—which the Supreme Court has emphasized is strict in theory, though not fatal in fact[19]—Congress must show that the program meets a compelling governmental interest and that it is narrowly tailored. To show that the program is compelling probably requires some important governmental interest—such as repairing past discrimination. As the Supreme Court has repeatedly recognized, governmental bodies may take action to respond to past discrimination.[20] The problem is defining "compelling governmental interest" and what kind of evidence would show the pattern of discrimination in the past.

To show that the program is narrowly tailored requires showing that the program is aimed at remedying discrimination against African Americans in the past in the specific location and of the specific type being remedied. *Croson* identified several types of evidence that would support a limited race-based affirmative action program: systematic exclusion from the construction industry and a significant statistical disparity between the minority contractors qualified to receive contracts and those who receive them.[21] The latter test sets a high standard—and suggests that the court wants a close connection between the past discrimination and the remedy being sought. Many people might have been excluded (or discouraged) long before they became contractors and, therefore, were eligible to be counted in the pool of potential bidders, yet the Supreme Court was unwilling to speculate further into past discrimination.[22] That is part of their focus on "narrowly tailoring" the remedy to fit the past discrimination.

Croson applied only to state governments; for several years, there remained substantial question about whether the same standard applied to the federal government or whether the federal government might have broader power to take race-based action. Those urging that the federal government had broader power pointed to the Fourteenth Amendment. They said that Section Five of the amendment gives Congress the power to make sure that the guarantees of equal protection and due process are fulfilled. So, the argument goes, Congress may make findings about what laws are necessary to ensure the equal protection of the laws. Those hoping that Section Five would be interpreted broadly, to give Congress extra power to take race-based action, were disappointed in 1995, when the Supreme Court decided *Adarand v. Pena*.[23] It applied the high standard articulated in *Croson* to the federal government. Afterward, a race-based set-aside established by any government unit—municipal, state, or federal—had to show compelling government interest and narrow tailoring, which made race-based affirmative action difficult.

The attack on affirmative action continued in the 1990s in the lower federal courts as well. There were decisions in several circuit courts that limited the scope of race-based programs in college and graduate school admissions. Moreover, the attack continued in state legislatures, too. Proposition 209 in California, passed in 1995, prohibited the state from taking race into account in hiring and school admissions. In that context, many sought a different dialogue for race and racial justice.[24]

The Supreme Court's June 2003 decision in *Grutter v. University of Michigan* may signal a change in the requirement that reparative action must be linked to harm. Indeed, by finding that diversity itself is a compelling interest, *Grutter* produces an independent ground for race-conscious action that is completely separate from remedying past discrimination. Justice O'Connor's inclusion of a time limitation on the race-conscious action (she suggests twenty-five years) is particularly puzzling in this context. While it pays homage to the Court's previously announced requirement that race-conscious action have a definite stopping point, it is unclear where that limitation comes from. There is no reason why the race-conscious action should last twenty-five years, as opposed to ten or fifty or one hundred years. Moreover, if diversity itself is a compelling interest, then one wonders why there is a time limitation. However—and assuming that we can rely on the Supreme Court's statement that diversity, as opposed to remedying past discrimination, is now a compelling interest—that opens up great possibilities for race-conscious action in school desegregation.[25]

Grutter may represent a reversal of the trend that led to *Missouri v. Jenkins*. *Grutter* rejects the requirement of previous cases, like *Croson*, that the government attempt to find nonracial ways of achieving its purposes before it takes race into account. In the case of *Grutter*, that meant that the University of Michigan did not need to try to find a nonracial way of achieving diversity. *Grutter* thus supports a broad program of race-based action, even if not tied specifically to past harm.[26] The larger effect of *Grutter* may be to shift dialogue away from reparations and more toward consideration of race as part of a campaign for diversity. It remains to be seen what *Grutter* does to the reparations debate. Perhaps, in proclaiming that diversity is a goal, our society will move away from consideration of the past and the history of racial crimes and discrimination.[27] Or perhaps it will reinforce consideration of race throughout American politics. Or perhaps *Grutter* marks one of the last cases that will uphold race-conscious affirmative action; it may be that it is limited to elite universities.

There are other important implications of *Grutter* for reparations. It revitalizes race as a category of legal analysis and restores (or further establishes) discussion of race to the center of contemporary American law. But is there less need for discussion of reparations, with its requirement of demonstrating how past harm has an effect on people today, now that there is an independent basis for race-conscious action? Reparations may continue to be a way of justifying affirmative action, but now that diversity opens up a separate rationale, there is less need for talking about it. Moreover, the people who most need reparations—and the people it would help the most—may not be the same people who receive preferential treatment through diversity programs, especially at elite universities. So academics and others continue to search for a new way of talking about racial inequality's origins and what to do about it.

Critical Race Theory and the Emergence of Reparations Theory

Intellectual dialogue around reparations grew out of discussions of what to do about the end of the Civil Rights movement and the decline of its successor, affirmative action. The ideas that were contributing to the intellectual movements important to reparations were critical legal studies and critical race theory. Critical legal studies, which began to emerge in the late 1970s, developed a vocabulary and literature that is important in reparations theory. The critical legal studies movement focused on rethinking common assumptions about law and politics. It popularized the idea that politics and political choices are central to law. By the mid-1980s, the critical legal studies movement had gained great intellectual credibility at the elite law schools, but it was a movement headed mostly by white males. And it was having trouble sustaining interest, for once people accepted the central tenet of the movement—that political choices are central to law—the movement had been unable to produce scholarship that used those insights for political activism. Much was learned from the critical legal studies movement, but what would be done with that learning? Indeed, a central critique of the movement was that it failed to turn intellectual insight into political action.

From the remnants of the critical legal studies movement, critical race theory emerged. CRT, as it is known, contributed an interest in activism that was frequently missing from critical legal studies scholarship, and it was driven frequently by minority law professors who were bringing their insights to legal theory. It showed the importance of ethnic identity and groups and joined critical legal studies' concern for the relationship between politics and law with an understanding that racial issues frequently underlie the decisions of legislators, judges, and prosecutors. Critical race theory emphasized the distinctive political identity and political goals of racial groups, such as African Americans, Hispanic Americans, and Japanese Americans.

The multicultural ethic that emerged from the 1960s and came into legal theory in the 1980s changed the traditional story of immigration from one of a melting pot in which every group assimilated into one (and needed no special recognition in law) into a story of a patchwork, where groups maintained their own separate identities and had their own agendas. Perhaps the most important article that linked those new insights with the emerging reparations talk in the African American community is Georgetown University Professor Mari Matsuda's 1987 article "Looking to the Bottom," in the *Harvard Civil Rights–Civil Liberties Law Review*.[28] Matsuda's article appeared right when a separate group of scholars, focused on race, was emerging from the critical legal studies movement. Her article, thus, signaled the emergence of critical race theory, as it also established reparations as a key part of the agenda.

Matsuda, joined by such other progressive legal scholars as Richard Delgado, established that critical race theory was more than groups of law professors who enjoyed "trashing" law, as many charged of critical legal studies at the time. It was a movement that could draw inspiration from workers and minorities and might make law responsive to them. Matsuda suggested that law should draw insights from those at the "bottom of the well." And she linked an academic's attention to racial groups with a social activist's attention to political solutions, which went beyond lawsuits. Matsuda's great insight was that of reparations. She uses reparations for slavery as an example of an idea born in the minds of the dispossessed, who call for some sort of economic justice. Matsuda develops an argument that reparations claims should be considered as claims of a group of victims against a group of perpetrators, instead of individual victims against individual perpetrators, which is how courts typically view claims for reparations. Perhaps most important, she began to give the idea intellectual respectability. By talking seriously about reparations, she made the case seem plausible. Matsuda first, though, identified four key arguments against reparations:

1. That there are factual justifications or excuses for mistreatment
2. That it is difficult to identify perpetrators (or people who are currently responsible for the perpetrators' acts) and victims
3. That there is an insufficient connection between the harm and the claim
4. That calculation of damages (or fashioning of another remedy) is difficult[29]

Matsuda focused much of her analysis on the second problem: the identification of victim and perpetrator groups. She addressed a classic problem: that law typically grants relief to individuals when they show they have been harmed. It is much harder for groups to make out claims; true, class action lawsuits allow a class of people—who can demonstrate close connections—to recover after a single lawsuit. But classes are viewed with great skepticism in modern American legal thought. She suggested some forms that reparations might take and sketched a legal argument for them, trying to fit reparations arguments into a traditional legal format. Her ideas were general, as one would expect from a germinal article. She suggested what reparations might look like: that they should be forward-looking. Obviously, they could not repair the damage for people who are already dead; instead, drawing upon well-established principles from antitrust cases, they should try to identify groups of people who have been harmed. Then the remedy should try to make better-off the group of people who had been harmed, even if the specific group members who had been harmed could not be identified or made whole. The classic example of this in the antitrust context is consumers who have been harmed because they have been overcharged. Sometimes it is too costly or indeed even impossible to identify the people who have been overcharged. Instead, a typical remedy in an antitrust case is to require the people who have overcharged to lower their prices to future consumers. The idea is that, on average, justice is done; consumers as a class receive back what was wrongfully taken, and the misbehaving business disgorges the money it wrongfully took. A similar idea is behind the school desegregation cases, which are discussed at more length at other points in this book.

Matsuda was building on others who were talking with increasing fervor about group identity and asking for equal treatment across groups. The debate turned to questions of the utility of reparations, how to achieve racial equity, and what is owed.[30] Matsuda thereby linked traditional legal doctrine with radical reparations arguments. Her article brought the subject of serious reparations talk to law journals. The intellectual movement for reparations was moving.

Reparations proponents, then, set a broad agenda of justice, which involved wholesale redistribution of wealth. Along the way, they established more modest goals of demonstrating the contributions of African Americans to social and economic growth and the injustices they suffered. The proponents hope to educate the public about those contributions and harms. The goals are wealth redistribution, education, and justice.

Legal Scholarship on Reparations

Thus, with Matsuda's work and the other emerging precedents, the stage was set in the early 1990s for serious exploration of reparations for slavery in the legal literature. The first law review article to address that issue squarely and exclusively was Vincene Verdun's 1993 "If the Shoe Fits, Wear It: An Analysis of Reparations to African Americans," in the *Tulane Law Review*.[31] Verdun's article set out a general case for reparations based on moral and political, more than legal, grounds. She divided the world into holders of the dominant (antireparations) and African American consciousness. The dominant view derives from the legal system's (usual) requirement that there be an identified victim and an identified wrongdoer. Verdun critiqued the "dominant" perspective as providing far too little liability, for it prevents courts from imposing remedies on those who are the beneficiaries of past discrimination.[32] Affirmative action decisions—tracking that dominant perspective, albeit not following it completely—have required a close tailoring of race-conscious remedies to past discrimination in a specific location. The implications of affirmative action and desegregation decisions are discussed more fully later, when we contemplate the constitutionality of reparations.[33] Verdun's focus on the African American consciousness—which is part of a much larger debate over the persistence of African values—focuses on what she identifies as values of "collectivism and communalism."[34] Those values lead to the conclusion that the community should help repair the damage imposed on African Americans by slavery and decades of Jim Crow.[35] Verdun did not distinguish between harm caused by the government and that caused by private discrimination. She concluded with a sweeping statement about society's continuing liability for racism: "Because society perpetuated and benefited from the institution of slavery, all of society must pay."[36]

Just a few months after Verdun's article appeared, Rhonda Magee published in the *Virginia Law Review* "The Master's Tools from the Bottom Up: Responses to African-American Reparations Theory in Mainstream and Outsider Remedies Discourse," which aimed at both clarifying the case for reparations, based on the historical evidence of government-sponsored mistreatment of African Americans in slavery and the era of Jim Crow, and placing it in a context of contemporary American law.[37] Like Verdun, Magee was skeptical of the possibility of lawsuits but discussed the case for them. Magee placed most of her hope in the case for reparations through legislatures. Yet Verdun and Magree also illustrated cracks within the reparations movement—for they looked to rather different goals.

Magee used law as a framework for evaluating reparations. Like Matsuda and Verdun, Magee explored the differing conceptions of fairness of those in the mainstream and of outsiders. But Magee also focused on the differences between outsiders. Some, like Marcus Garvey and his descendants, advocate a nationalist perspective, which urges separatism of African Americans and European Americans. Others urged integration. Magee portrayed reparations as a third way, which is part of achieving a "multicultural balance," what Magee called "cultural equity."[38] Magee went far toward envisioning what a world of cultural equity might look like—and the role of reparations as part of that world. She called for a renewed focus on education and for nurturing awareness of African American contributions to American economic and cultural development. Affirmative action and reparations are both part of that program, for the wealth redistribution they effect increases African American participation in politics and leads, one would predict, toward economic and social equality.[39] Magee provided an important justification of reparations as more than a replacement for affirmative action. She saw reparations as a key component of a program that integrates African Americans more fully into American politics. Implementation of reparations, she concluded, "simultaneously acknowledges official responsibility, promotes economic and cultural self-sufficiency, and relinquishes to African-Americans a measure of control over the implementation of the remedy."[40] Magee sought what she identified as a "utopian ideal"[41] that dismantles what she identified as a pervasive ethic of white supremacy.[42] Magee attacked, as do many critical race scholars, the idea of color blindness. She argued that courts' adherence to color-blind principles hinders remedies that "eliminat[e] internalized racism"—and, one presumes, redistribute wealth along racial lines.[43] Magee aimed not so much at suggesting new uses of old doctrine as at a systemwide critique of liberalism in American law.

One can gauge Magee's mission in part by comparison with other law review articles written in the 1990s. In 1999, Tuneen Chisholm, then a student at the University of Pennsylvania, published "Sweep around Your Own Front Door: Examining the Argument for Legislative Reparations for African Americans."[44] A comparison of Magee's and Chisholm's work suggests the different rationales for reparations. Chisholm bypassed discussion of reparations through the courts. She argued that the legislature should, as a matter of distributive justice, reallocate money to African Americans. Where Magee saw reparations as part of achieving a Great Society, Chisholm saw them as part of justice for generations of undercompensated labor. But, significantly, she also saw them as part of a movement, ultimately, toward a race-neutral society. More recent writers see reparations as enabling blacks to have a separate society.

The single most important article in modern reparations theory was Professor Robert Westley's 1998 "Many Billions Gone: Is It Time to Reconsider the Case for Black Reparations?"[45] Westley's article took its title from a James Baldwin essay, "Many Thousands Gone," about the slave trade.[46] Westley made out the moral case for reparations in the broadest terms then available. He surveyed the horrors of slavery and the ways that even after slavery ended the system of segregation systematically disadvantaged African Americans in job and educational opportunities, in voting rights, and even in obtaining financing for housing. Discrimination by the Federal Housing Authority in funding for housing is often cited as evidence of the federal government's culpability in the Jim Crow system: In the years after World War II, when home ownership by whites was dramatically expanding, due in large part to the FHA's underwriting of mortgages, black home ownership did not increase so drastically. The FHA engaged in "redlining," drawing lines in red on maps of residential real estate that marked the less desirable areas. The FHA would not underwrite mortgages in the areas in red.[47] Those discriminatory practices, which were in part a response to consumers' wishes, illustrate some of the choices made by government that in turn left many minorities with little opportunity or ability to acquire homes. Those who already owned homes in redlined areas saw their property values decline while homes outside the red lines increased in value.[48]

Westley's article also provides a more detailed picture of what those who see reparations as part of a wholesale remaking of America want. He aims at establishing a "legal norm reflecting and refining the interests and perspectives of the subordinated."[49] He seeks a "committed, concerted, and visionary appeal."[50] Westley sees the movement for black reparations as part of a larger movement that must take account of reparations to other oppressed groups. In fact, he admits that other groups, like Native Americans, may have an even better claim on reparations than do blacks.[51]

Westley sees distinct advantages to group-focused remedies, which would provide for the development of institutions. Individual compensation would not. "Additionally, beyond any perceived or real need for Blacks to participate more fully in the consumer market—which is the inevitable outcome of reparations to individuals—there is a more exigent need for Blacks to exercise greater control over their productive labor— which is the possibility created by group reparations."[52] Even though there would be only limited payments to individuals, Westley sees money as the central element of a reparations plan. Compensation must be significant, so that it is clear that there is a commitment to repairing:

Sufficient, in other words, to reflect not only the extent of un-just Black suffering, but also the need for Black economic inde-pendence from societal discrimination. No less than with the freedmen, freedom for Black people today means economic freedom and security. A basis for that freedom and security can be assured through group reparations in the form of monetary compensation, along with free provision of goods and services to Black communities across the nation. The guiding principle of reparations must be self-determination in every sphere of life in which Blacks are currently dependent.[53]

Westley concludes with an optimistic—though vague—assessment that reparations will bring equality to blacks:

[F]or those who long for the millennium in which Black equality with whites ceases to be the American dilemma and becomes the American reality, reparations contain within them at least the promise of closure. The closure afforded by reparations means that no more will be owed to Blacks than is owed to any citizen under the law. . . . Once reparations are paid, Blacks will be able to function within American society on a footing of as volute equality. Their chance for public happiness, as opposed to pri-vate happiness, will be the same as that of any white citizen who currently takes this concept for granted because the public so ut-terly "belongs" to him, so utterly affirms his value, his humanity, his dignity and his presence.[54]

Westley's article marked a key turning point in the reparations debate, for he established the case for reparations as more than a claim on the legislature. He phrased it as payments owed to African Americans. Soon others took Westley's idea and popularized it.

The Expanding Circle of Reparations Talk

Professor Westley provided the seed of the idea that reparations are owed, not just morally but legally. He inspired in turn major sections of Randall Robinson's book *The Debt: What America Owes to Blacks,* published in January 2000.[55] Robinson, whose advocacy organization, TransAfrica Forum, had been at the center of movement in the 1980s to free South Africa from apartheid, sparked a national debate on reparations. Robinson's best-selling book had as its thesis the idea that African Americans contributed to the building of America, received minuscule compensation, and thus were owed compensation, hence the title, *The Debt*. His book describes the differential between black and white America in psychological as well as economic terms. Robinson sees many costs to African Americans of the legacy of slavery—broken hopes, broken families, a cycle of poverty that is enormously difficult to escape from.

Robinson, like Harvard Law School Professor Charles Ogletree and Robert Westley, focuses his attention on the poorest African Americans. The critical issue is to aid the most disadvantaged, the people who have been left furthest behind. As Robinson says, affirmative action "programs are not *solutions* to our problems." He recognizes that they are too little and that they are not aimed at the most impoverished:

> They are palliatives that help people like *me*, who are poised to succeed when given half a chance. They do little for the millions of African Americans bottom-mired in urban hells by the savage time-release social debilitations of American slavery. They do little for those Americans, disproportionately black, who inherit grinding poverty, poor nutrition, bad schools, unsafe neighborhoods, low expectation, and overburdened mothers.[56]

Money is important, obviously, because cash payments are one way to move out of poverty. However, an important part of Robinson's reparations movement goes beyond money. Robinson sees an important goal—and maybe the most attainable one—as spiritual growth. Even if Congress never paid a penny in reparations, Robinson sees great promise in the ability of reparations talk to bring about psychological change. He concludes *The Debt* with this prayer:

> We must do this in memory of the dark souls whose weary, broken bodies endured the unimaginable.
> We must do this on behalf of our children whose thirsty spirits clutch for the keys to a future.

This is a struggle that we cannot lose, for in the very making of it we will discover, if nothing else, ourselves.[57]

Robinson represents one strand of reparations thought: that the basis for reparations is the degree to which African Americans have enriched American society. There is much to be said for that; under even conservative calculations, the value of slave labor—with interest—is enormous. Running parallel to the lawyers' writings on reparations were works by economists, such as Richard America, which attempted to put a dollar figure on what is owed.[58] Then activists and some philosophers began talking less in legal terms and more in moral ones.[59]

After *The Debt* appeared, reparations talk grew dramatically. There were more than three times the number of stories on reparations in major newspapers in 2000 as there were in 1999.[60] The talk was of grand visions, of major changes in U.S. social policy, in a renewed understanding of history. Newspapers asked hotly contested questions: Who should receive reparations? Should they be paid to groups or individuals? What form should they take: cash, community-building programs? What are the goals? Moderate groups saw reparations as part of basic fairness but wanted integration; radical groups saw reparations as part of a separatist movement.

Professor Manning Marable of Columbia University is representative of those who think of reparations in grand terms. He sees the goal as justice and equity. People such as Marable see reparations as a movement to reconceptualize politics and society. They want an America that builds the African American community, that recognizes the African American contributions, that is freed of the legacy of disadvantages suffered by African Americans. In essence, they ask for society to be as it might have been without state-sponsored or state-allowed slavery and later discrimination. In summary, Marable writes, "white Americans, as a group, continue to be the direct beneficiaries of the legal apparatuses of white supremacy, carried out by the full weight of America's legal, political, and economic institutions. The consequences of state-sponsored racial inequality created a mountain of historically constructed, accumulated disadvantage for African Americans as a group."[61] Marable grimly concludes that "America's version of legal apartheid created the conditions of white privilege and black subordination that we see all around us every day. A debt is owed, and it must be paid in full."[62] Marable is aiming at the wholesale remaking of American institutions, which he sees as premised on and structured around white supremacy.[63] In an important talk at Columbia Law School in 2003, he stated that "the goal of the black freedom movement is freedom. Reparations are part of that movement." In contrast to many in the Civil Rights movement of the 1950s and 1960s, the goal for Marable is not integration. "Integration," Marable said, "is only a tool to freedom." "The two things we've never had are freedom and justice." What is a black theory of justice? "Black people as a whole are in a hole they will never get out of." What they need to address, in Marable's mind, are the material differences. And reparations are a way of maneuvering, to address those material differences.[64]

Other reparations proponents have vaguer, but similar, goals. One theme that arises frequently in the literature is the "breakdown of white privilege." It entails a whole host of other assumptions, probably including the redistribution of property, so that it is distributed equally on a per capita basis among racial groups. Or, as one writer has recently summarized, the opposition to reparations comes in large part because it is about breaking down privilege:

> More than any other remedy, reparations transforms the material condition of recipients.
>
> Moreover, it connotes culpability: for a majority that rejects group hierarchy, harm, and responsibility, reparations is a radical redistribution of wealth, rather than a disgorgement and reallocation of an unjust acquisition, that exacerbates unrest. Reparations thus yields resistance, backlash, and "ethnic elbowing." As it would strip their racial privileges along with their currency, reparations is opposed by all but the most altruistic whites.[65]

There is a considerable debate that has yet to take place on the value of white privilege. What does that mean? How is it measured?[66] What is the value of the privilege for white people living in poverty or who have no college education or who are above the poverty line but are trapped in low-paying jobs? For example, one wonders what privilege is possessed by the 7.5% of white Americans living in poverty, the 9.4% of white children who live in poverty?[67]

Others more radical have followed in the wake of Robinson, Ogletree, Matsuda, and Westley. Lee Harris, writing in 2001, for instance, took a cue from the creation of Israel. He suggested a radical model for reparations: creation of a separate political state for African Americans.[68] Harris acknowledged the role that black nationalism plays in his version of reparations. With Harris providing an important and concise statement for the movement, the question of the reparations movement was becoming, as Professor Roy Brooks said, a question of integration versus separation.[69]

But the movement was also going in other directions. Some began to focus more on racial reconciliation, picking up on a theme of Professor Eric Yamamoto's 1999 book, *Interracial Justice: Conflict and Reconciliation in Post-Civil Rights America.*[70] Adjoa Aiyetoro, a leader of N'COBRA: the National Coalition of Blacks for Reparations in America, has spoken and written extensively on the reparations movement. Much of her work relates to raising consciousness about reparations issues. Because of that, Aiyetoro's work involves advocating a broad and flexible agenda, which can change as the reparations movement evolves. Where such academics as Westley have suggestions for specific plans, Aiyetoro establishes grand goals: "to stay visible and increase that visibility, to posture ourselves to be a part of the discussion that will more than likely take place behind the scenes on the form reparations should take and to assure that a package of reparations and not appeasement is developed, and to stay [to] principles, demanding accountability to African descendants."[71]

The most complete case to date on the moral basis for reparations is Roy Brooks's *Atonement and Forgiveness: A New Model for Black Reparations.* Brooks presents a moral case that looks to a world that does not exist right now. Brooks hopes for a world where "the government and the descendants of slaves can reach racial reconciliation through moral reflection rather than political confrontation."[72] Brooks makes his detailed case for reparations on a twofold argument. First, he notes that slavery denied African Americans life and liberty, as well as the opportunity to acquire wealth to give to their descendants. Thus, it impoverished people at the time and successive generations. Second, even after slavery ended, the period of Jim Crow prevented African Americans from fully participating in the acquisition of education and wealth.[73] One might reasonably add to that argument that there were unequal burdens placed on blacks. Those burdens meant that even as blacks had the opportunity to acquire some wealth, many had fewer opportunities than other people. Thus, the federal and state governments have culpability for their participation in slavery and Jim Crow. Then others, those who did not themselves decide to enslave or participate in the Jim Crow system, are beneficiaries of a system in which whites could rise economically and educationally even when blacks could not.

Brooks's case is thought provoking. Yet, as he acknowledges, we are a long way from the world he envisions. There is little interest among white Americans in atonement; indeed, there is little sense among them that there is anything to atone for.

So we have many goals of reparations. Some of them are corrective, to correct for past injustice. Others are distributive, to redistribute wealth and political power.[74] Some seek interracial justice and peace, others redistribution of privilege, even a separate state for African Americans. Still others have such modest goals as teaching about the connections of the past to the present, to illuminate the many ways in which past discrimination continues to have an effect today. There is the hope among reparations proponents that, once those connections are clearly established, there will more readily be action to overcome that past. It is becoming difficult to answer the question "What do reparationists want?" because they have so many different—and perhaps even contradictory—goals.[75]

Of course, as talk of reparations has escalated, those opposed to reparations have responded. We look at the main arguments against reparations in the next chapter.

4

Against Reparations

As REPARATIONS talk has grown, so has opposition to reparations. Arguments for reparations for slavery and its claims for an accounting of past injustice, for apologies and truth commissions, for reconciliation of decades-old debts and forward-looking relief, and for group-based relief represent yet another front on what has been called the "culture wars" of the 1990s and 2000s. The case for reparations rests on how the past is viewed and what one believes should be done about it. Indeed, the reparations discussion taps into decades of debate over how to deal with inequality in American society. Should we try to ensure equality of outcome or equality of opportunity? Is racial progress best achieved by demanding equal treatment through the courts or by a gradual process of accommodation? By having a reckoning with slavery and the legacy of Jim Crow or by focusing with single-minded devotion on the present? At the beginning of the twentieth century, the debate on these issues was between Booker T. Washington and W. E. B. DuBois. More recently, it has been between public intellectuals such as reparations opponents John McWhorter and Ward Connerly and proponents Charles Ogletree and Randall Robinson.

The Arguments against Reparations

The most famous statement of the arguments against reparations comes from David Horowitz, who took out a series of advertisements in college newspapers in the spring of 2001 entitled "Ten Reasons Why

Reparations for Slavery Are a Bad Idea and Racist, Too." His ten points are:

1. There Is No Single Group Clearly Responsible for the Crime of Slavery
2. There Is No One Group That Benefited Exclusively from Its Fruits
3. Only a Tiny Minority of White Americans Ever Owned Slaves, and Others Gave Their Lives to Free Them
4. America Today Is a Multi-Ethnic Nation and Most Americans Have No Connection (Direct or Indirect) to Slavery
5. The Historical Precedents Used to Justify the Reparations Claim Do Not Apply, and the Claim Itself Is Based on Race Not Injury
6. The Reparations Argument Is Based on the Unfounded Claim That All African-American Descendants of Slaves Suffer from the Economic Consequences of Slavery and Discrimination
7. The Reparations Claim Is One More Attempt to Turn African-Americans into Victims. It Sends a Damaging Message to the African-American Community.
8. Reparations to African-Americans Have Already Been Paid
9. What About the Debt Blacks Owe to America?
10. The Reparations Claim Is a Separatist Idea That Sets African-Americans against the Nation That Gave Them Freedom[1]

Others have made more modest, and perhaps more persuasive, cases against reparations. Probably the best way to address the multitude of arguments against reparations is to classify them according to broad categories and then to explore the nuances of each category. The arguments may be broken down into four main categories:

1. Those asked to pay have no liability, because compensation is immoral or compensation was never due.
2. Compensation has been made.
3. Compensation is impracticable or politically unworkable.

4. Reparations are divisive and focus attention on the past rather than the future.

We shall take up each of those arguments in turn.

No Moral (or Legal) Liability

It appears that the type of argument that has gained the most attention—and is advanced most seriously against reparations—is that the people currently asked to pay had nothing to do with the injustices of the past. This argument draws on a popular thought in the United States—and Western culture more generally—that liability should attach to fault, that people should receive punishment (or rewards) based on their personal culpability. Carried to an extreme, that argument concludes that there is culpability only for the harms one causes, that there is no general societal culpability, and that there is no culpability for the crimes of predecessors.

The principle that one should pay only for the harms one causes—or benefits from—has great resonance as long as we are talking about lawsuits. A bedrock principle of American law is that defendants are not liable unless they have some culpability—that is, unless they caused a harm (or in rare instances benefited, even if they did not cause the harm). Antireparationists use that principle when speaking about legislative reparations as well. Two University of Chicago Law School professors, Eric Posner and Adrian Vermeule, have provided a comprehensive investigation of the moral issues regarding culpability and reparations. They argue that there are two primary bases to justify reparations: compensation for past harm caused by the people asked to pay and restitution of benefits held by the people asked to pay.[2] Many antireparationists look past the federal and state governments, which would be making the payments, to the people who fund those governments—the taxpayers.

In the context of reparations for slavery, then, one needs to assess whether there is culpability among the individual taxpayers or whether they have retained some benefit. Here, then, is a critical question for reparations debate. How much do we abide by the formula that it is immoral to ask someone to pay who does not have culpability or a benefit? How much are benefits retained? Have there been sufficient benefits to blacks that harm has been more than offset? How much are the individual taxpayers culpable for the benefits that are retained?

Of course, we see legislatures—even courts—acting on ideas of general culpability in many places. There are many crimes committed by government officials that lead the entire community to be liable for the actions of those officials. As the Rodney King verdict illustrates, there is already a lessening of the connections between wrongdoer and payer. After King obtained a damages verdict against the Los Angeles Police Department officers who assaulted him, that verdict was satisfied by the taxpayers of Los Angeles. Very few taxpayers were actually responsible for the crime, but they had to pay for the crime. Many antireparationists probably object to taxpayers paying for the King verdict as well, citing the taxpayers' lack of culpability. But American law has worked out the general principle that taxpayers are liable for the acts of government officials acting under color of law. And corporations—which are really a collection of individual shareholders—are liable for the acts of their employees. In cases of environmental pollution, companies (meaning their shareholders) are frequently held liable for decades following the pollution. For example, in 1994, Mobil Oil Company was held liable for polluting the waters of the little town of Cyril, Oklahoma, as early as the 1940s. It is likely that none of Mobil's shareholders had any direct culpability for the actions of the company's officers who decided to pollute in the 1940s, yet the shareholders had to pay.

So it is reasonable—in fact, corporate liability is premised on the idea—that shareholders, even those who had no direct influence on the decisions, have to pay. In the United States, culpability attaches even without fault in many instances. It is natural to expect that corporations— or government bodies—will have liability for the decisions they made, sometimes decades ago.

But antireparationists say that even though in some cases there is continuing liability, the taxpayers are the people who will have to pay. And many of those individual taxpayers have no culpability. Where is the fairness in asking people whose ancestors were not even in the United States in the period of slavery (or maybe even in the period of Jim Crow) to pay reparations for crimes occurring in that time? David Horowitz phrased the argument in this way:

The two great waves of American immigration occurred after 1880 and then after 1960. What rationale would require Vietnamese boat people, Russian refuseniks, Iranian refugees, and Armenian victims of the Turkish persecution, Jews, Mexicans, Greeks, or Polish, Hungarian, Cambodian and Korean victims of Communism, to pay reparations to American blacks?[3]

Moreover, other people beside the U.S. government have culpability for slavery, such as African nations themselves.[4] Those are powerful arguments, if it is correct that the taxpayers are indeed innocent.

Closely allied to the argument of innocence is the claim that no benefit has been retained. How much is owed—or how much benefit we need to pay off the debt—varies based on which theory for reparations is applied: Are we seeking only to pay off the benefits that have been conferred by slaves on the rest of American society, or are we seeking to pay for all the harm that slavery did to the slaves and their descendants?

Reparationists have two responses. First, governmental bodies, like corporations, have a continuing existence. Governments are liable for the judgments issued against them—and, unfortunately, they have to satisfy those judgments with taxpayer money. New immigrants take their new government subject to the liability existing at the time. We all take America with the good and the bad at the same time. There are a lot of opportunities here; so there are some disadvantages.[5] Reparationists' second response is more general. It denies that the people who are claiming innocence actually are innocent. As Professor Ogletree has recently phrased it, "while black folks were sitting at the back of the bus, generations of white immigrants go straight to the front."[6] Now, it is substantially debatable how much privilege some immigrants received, particularly those from southern Europe, Asia, and the Spanish Americas. But the point is important and worthy of significantly more study. If currently living whites are beneficiaries of past discrimination against blacks, then convincing claims of innocence are hard to make. Someone may be the beneficiary of a system of discrimination, even if he had no role in setting up that system. But there is yet another response to claims that those who are descended from subsequent immigrants are free from liability. Those who come to the United States take it, one suspects, with all of the liabilities as well as the benefits. As citizens, we all are entitled to the huge benefits of citizenship; those benefits come with certain liabilities as well. In this case, some of the liabilities may be repairing the past damage that was done by the U.S. federal and state governments.[7]

It is at this point that the debate runs up against strong elements of national ideology: Americans believe they are where they are today because of their own hard work and innate talent, rather than the good fortune of their birth; they believe that the United States is a meritocracy. That is an issue on which we need further debate, but at present it appears that the truth is somewhere in the middle: Undercompensated black labor and lack of opportunities made it possible for whites, even those whose ancestors came to the United States after the era of slavery ended, to advance more quickly than they otherwise would have. It is likely—indeed, hard to dispute—there is some privilege retained to the present day. On the other hand, it could be said that white immigrants had to take the least desirable jobs and that the salaries for those jobs were considerably depressed by competition with low-paid (or, in the slavery era, unpaid) black labor.

There is yet another way that antireparationists argue that there is no liability: there is no (or little) continuing effect of slavery. Reparations proponents commonly argue that reparations are for the continuing effects of slavery and Jim Crow. Adjoa Aiyetoro, for instance, has said, "We're not raising claims that you should pay us because you did something to us 150 years ago. We are saying that we are injured today by the vestiges of slavery, which took away income and property that was rightfully ours."[8] Yet antireparationists frequently maintain that the current inequality in wealth is due to black culture, not the legacy of slavery. Journalist Walter Williams, like many antireparationists, places blame on single-parent black households:

> Illegitimacy among blacks today is 70 percent. Only 41 percent of black males 15 years and older are married, and only 36 percent of black children live in two-parent families. These and other indicators of family instability and its accompanying socioeconomic factors such as high crime, welfare dependency and poor educational achievement is claimed to be the legacy and vestiges of slavery, for which black Americans are due reparations.[9]

Yet Williams points out that a high incidence of single-parent families is relatively recent; in 1940, for instance, fewer than 20% of black children were born into single-parent families. Herbert Gutman's *Black Family in Slavery and Freedom* found that in Harlem between 1905 and 1925, 85% of black children lived in two-parent families.[10] "The question raised by these historical facts is: If what we see today in many black neighborhoods, as claimed by reparations advocates, are the vestiges and legacies of slavery, how come that social pathology was not much worse when blacks were just two or three generations out of slavery? Might it be that slavery's legacy and vestiges have a way . . . of skipping generations? In other words . . . the devastating 70 percent rate of black illegitimacy simply skipped six generations—it's a delayed effect of slavery?"[11] That is a central argument among reparations opponents and critics of the Great Society programs of the 1960s more generally.[12]

It is important to try to separate the effects of slavery and Jim Crow discrimination from other causes in determining the current wealth gap between blacks and whites. Obviously, that is central to the case for reparations. If slavery has no lingering effect, then there is no reason to try to repair it.[13] But we do not need to think about generation-skipping effects to link the current sad condition of the black family to slavery. The family structure is only the latest manifestation of a social policy, born in the years after the Civil War, that did not seek to help blacks move into the mainstream of the American economy and education system. Even though current U.S. social welfare policy has good intentions—which we can hardly say of the policy in the years before World War II—it is designed to discourage two-parent families. It makes sense to consider the current policy as a vestige of the era of Jim Crow, which was necessary because of the limited economic opportunities of the Jim Crow era. It is reasonable to consider the problems with single-parent black families as yet another legacy of slavery and the neglect during the Jim Crow era and as the result of lack of job opportunities.[14]

Compensation Has Been Made

The next most popular argument is that reparations have been paid—in the form of Great Society programs, such as the war on poverty and affirmative action, as well as welfare.[15] And are not reparations being paid right now through welfare? Why is that not enough? That is an important—and reasonable—question. As journalist Walter Williams has said, "today's blacks benefited immensely from the horrors suffered by our ancestors. . . . In fact, if we totaled the income black Americans earned each year, and thought of ourselves as a separate nation, we'd be the 14th or 15th richest nation. Even the 34 percent of blacks considered to be poor are fairly well off by world standards. Had there not been slavery, and today's blacks were born in Africa instead of the United States, we'd be living in the same poverty that today's Africans live in and under the same brutal regimes."[16] Michael Levin argues that the disproportionate of blacks as welfare recipients is not evidence of the need for reparations but evidence that there is a transfer from whites to blacks of $75 billion a year.[17] There are some important questions about how much the United States owes to descendants of slaves. Even more so, antireparationists argue that the opportunity to live in the United States has itself more than offset the harms.

To answer that, one needs to ask, What is the basis for reparations claims? If the claim is against the U.S. government for unpaid labor—and only unpaid labor—then it is natural to ask how much the slaves' descendants have received from the U.S. government in the form of welfare payments. It is possible that the compensation that has been paid will, on average, compensate for the unpaid labor. But one must remember that welfare is not a race-based program; everyone who meets the eligibility requirements receives assistance, regardless of race. Why should we consider welfare payments as paying down the debt? Perhaps because we lump all debts and all payments together. When reparationists are arguing that what is owed is based on undercompensation for labor, as Richard America does, then it is important to talk about the compensation that has already been paid. Perhaps it is right to add in welfare payments—or costs spent on affirmative action—as a way of offsetting some of the debt. This is an area in which we need substantial additional work to explore the value that slaves contributed to the American economy and how much of that value is still retained, as well as how much value has been returned. At this point, it is impossible to make even rough guesses about how the balance sheet stands—and that is due to the failure of either side to seriously address this issue. The only person who has even attempted to compute the value of the slave labor to the United States, Richard America, has made no effort to provide for an offset. Those who argue that welfare has paid the debt make no effort to identify the size of the welfare payments that should be counted as offset or to compare that value with the amount blacks contributed without compensation in the eras of slavery and Jim Crow, to say nothing of whether those benefits have been retained. Reparationists argue that welfare is not compensation but itself an effect of the legacy of Jim Crow and governmental policies that encouraged welfare dependency rather than independence.

Reparationists, by their frequent reference to ideas of "unjust enrichment," have brought on the comparison of how much has been contributed and how much has been paid. However, most reparationists compute what is owed based not on uncompensated labor alone. The huge gap between black and white economic and educational achievements stands as testimony, for them, to the legacy of slavery and Jim Crow discrimination. That gap testifies to the continued harm—which, tragically, as happens so often, is greater than the value retained. If we view the amount owed as not just the amount of value contributed but as also including the harm imposed by slavery and Jim Crow, it is self-evident that full reparations have not been paid, for the gap in wealth between blacks and whites testifies to the lack of full reparations.

But there are two related questions: how much wealth slaves' descendants would now have, even if their ancestors had been paid, and how much wealth descendants of slave owners and those who benefited from slavery would have. Antireparationists argue that the amount of money passed down from the slaves to the next generations would have declined.[18] Perhaps the amount of money held by those who benefited from slavery has declined, but perhaps there are continuing benefits. Similarly, one wonders whether other people have superior claims to that same fund. That is, are there other people who are more closely linked to harm than slave descendants?[19]

There is, moreover, the question of equal treatment. One of the great principles of American law is the equal protection principle, which requires that similarly situated people be treated alike. Have people who are making reparations claims been treated differently— and worse—than others? If there has been unequal treatment, then that is a separate basis for reparations. The issue ought not to be how people would be living if their ancestors had not been brought to the United States—or freely immigrated—but how they are treated relative to other people here. Although David Horowitz is fond of pointing out that the average yearly income in Benin is less than $1,000, that has little relevance to how people are treated in the United States. Sure, life is better than it would be in another country, but the relevant comparison group is other citizens of the United States. The fact that voting rights were denied to serfs in Russia does not mean that people of Russian descent in the United States are not entitled to vote or that they do not have a claim if they are denied the right to vote.

THERE ARE other ways of paying the debt, though, beside cash payments. Part of the argument that reparations have been paid is the assertion that the Civil War paid that debt. Some Lincoln scholars are particularly active in advancing the argument that the Civil War was part of abolishing the debt to African Americans.[20] Those who view the Civil War as an expiation of American guilt over slavery draw on Lincoln's second inaugural address, in which he wonders whether the war will continue until "all the wealth piled by the bond-man's two hundred and fifty years of unrequited toil shall be sunk, and until every drop of blood drawn with the lash, shall be paid by another drawn with the sword."[21] Perhaps, Lincoln told the country, such exaction would be necessary. He hoped that we might "achieve and cherish a just, and a lasting, peace, among ourselves."[22] Roscoe Dunjee, editor of Oklahoma City's *Black Dispatch* newspaper, had a substantially similar attitude in the 1920s. He believed that the violence of the Civil War was atonement for slavery, as well as divine retribution for it: "God is not mocked, whatsoever a man soweth, that shall he also reap," he wrote in an editorial after paraphrasing Lincoln's address.[23]

David Horowitz's formulation is that white Christians began the antislavery movement, which ended more than two millennia of slavery.[24] That interpretation leaves a great deal out of the historical record, of course. The Christian nations of Western Europe and North America contributed to the market for slaves; they provided an incentive for African nations to enslave Africans, and then those Western countries participated in "one of the greatest crimes in history."[25] To credit the United States with abolishing slavery does, well, not quite wipe the slate clean, for there would have been no need for abolition of slavery in the United States unless it had been imposed by law here. Even if we say that the United States fought a war to free slaves—which only begins to describe the Civil War—we cannot ignore why that war was necessary.

An important—and related argument—is that reparations will not work. In short, spending money on reparations is counterproductive. This is premised on the belief that money spent on the Great Society was ineffective in reducing poverty and may even have been counterproductive. This is a critical issue and is, indeed, central to the reparations debate. Will money spent on reparations make racial equality more likely? Reparations skeptics point to several key pieces of data. The most frequently used evidence is that the poverty rate among black families declined dramatically, from nearly half (48.1%) in 1959 to under a third (27.9%) in 1969, before the major redistribution plans of the Great Society could have had much effect.[26] Reparations skeptics point out that the poverty rate of blacks continues to shrink. In 1999, the rate of black families in poverty was 21.9%. (For purposes of comparison, the rate of white families in poverty was 15.2% in 1959 and 7.3% in 1999.)[27] Much of that differential rate is attributable, so the argument goes, to the difference in marriage rates between whites and blacks. As Professor Keith Hylton of Boston University Law School has argued, "If black families below the poverty line had the same marriage rate as white families below the poverty line in 1999, the general black poverty rate would be 12.3%, nearly half the 22% reported for that year."[28] He might have gone on to add: "and fairly close to the 7.3% reported for white families."

We need to determine with much greater precision than we have the connection between slavery and Jim Crow discrimination and their legacy's effect on the contemporary black community. If the gap in economic achievement is due to factors within the black community, rather than the legacy of slavery and Jim Crow—and those factors are not themselves attributable to slavery and Jim Crow—then reparations ought not to be paid for them.

Reparations Are Divisive

Despite the marked socioeconomic progress black Americans have made in this country over the past half century, the reparations movement, at bottom, encourages minorities to believe that they are really lost souls. The leaders of this movement do not talk about how such a distant crime has led to specific damages in the present lives of most minorities. For them, feelings of victimization in general, not damages in the specific, are the point. So they fervently maintain that all full-grown, capable minorities ought to blame the missed opportunities of their lives on the slavery that transpired centuries ago, as though their pains were interchangeable with those endured by slaves.[29]

The final group of arguments against reparations is at the center of the culture wars. How one feels about reparations rests in large part on how one views American history and the future. There are several parts of that conflict. First, how much of the gap between African American and white economic and educational achievement is due to a legacy of slavery and Jim Crow? That is, how much has history left an imprint of inequality on current society? Second, what is the best way of addressing that gap? That is, is racial equality best achieved through reparations payments or in some other way? Third, what, if anything, ought to be done to achieve racial reconciliation? How does one value truth commissions, and does one believe that racial reconciliation can take place without a remedy? They revolve around the belief that reparations talk divides the country along racial lines. By talking about the past—and by focusing on past injustices—blacks alienate themselves from the rest of the country. Reparations talk leads blacks to see themselves as victims who deserve government payments.

Within the genre of "reparations are divisive," there are several subcategories. First is that blacks have a cult of victimhood. Perhaps the best-known proponent of the cult of victimhood theory is Professor John McWhorter of the University of California, Berkeley. Even talk of reparations or the sins of the past causes African Americans to lose focus on the task at hand: gaining an education and rising economically.

The second subcategory is that focusing on the injustices of the past alienates blacks from American society at a time when they should be focusing on the benefits that American society has to offer. This is central to the culture wars; we have heard versions of this same argument since at least the Vietnam War era, when those who criticized the United States were told they were being un-American. The argument is, in essence, that it is more productive to spend time focusing on the benefits that blacks have by virtue of U.S. citizenship than on the injustices they have suffered.

The third subcategory is that reparations talk divides people along racial lines. It makes blacks think that whites as a group are their oppressors; it makes whites who have no responsibility for the sins of the past feel like oppressors, and it plays on feelings of guilt. That division falsely (in the minds of reparations opponents) continues the harmful focus on race. At a time when the government—and everyone else—should be moving toward a color-blind society, reparations talk reemphasizes race. It reestablishes racial divisions that we are eliminating (or at least ought to be eliminating). As Vanderbilt University Professor Carol Swain wrote in her 2002 book, *The New White Nationalism in America*, "Current reparations talk inflames the white electorate, undermines the bridge-building process across racial lines, fuels white nationalist sentiments, and is insufficiently targeted in its aims to help those members of minority groups who are most in need."[30]

That debate over reparations turns on more important moral issues, such as who should pay for the legacy of slavery and Jim Crow. On moral issues, as on legal ones, Americans often emphasize personal fault. The opposition to reparations may be yet another remnant of Puritan thought in American culture.[31] Whatever the origins, the emphasis on personal moral culpability for failure parallels American law's liberalism, which seems to deny remedies unless a victim can trace with great specificity an identifiable perpetrator.[32] Each generation, it seems, must stand on its own—or at least is not liable for the debts of the previous generation, even if it is entitled to the benefits bequeathed to it by the previous generation.[33] In the context of reparations for slavery, there are two ideologies working in tandem to limit public support. The first is racism. The second is the idea that each person must succeed or fail based on his or her own merit.[34] The morality of intergenerational liability has great importance for discussions of reparations for slavery. Estates law, which is the area of law most directly concerned with issues of intergenerational liability, limits liability to the value of the estate at the death. Perhaps even more important, once an estate is distributed, it is virtually impossible to reopen issues of liability.[35]

The issue of reparations is, of course, controversial in large part because it is about the redistribution of wealth and power.[36] More than a century ago, the issue of property and race was framed in the form of abolition of slavery. Abolitionist Ralph Waldo Emerson recognized that opposition to slavery confronted that sacred American value: support for property.

> Every reform is only a mask under cover of which a more terrible reform, which dares not yet name itself, advances. Slavery & Antislavery is the question of property & no property, rent & anti-rent; and Antislavery dare not yet say that every man must do his own work, or, at least, receive no interest for money. Yet that is at last the upshot.[37]

Slaveholders' claims to property were critical to the development of constitutional law and political theory in the years leading into the Civil War.[38] But the sanctity of property was by no means limited to the South.[39] The antirent movement that Emerson referred to was a movement by tenants in upstate New York to acquire the right to purchase the land they held on long-term leases. The movement evoked bitter conflict—and occasionally armed conflict—in the New York courts and legislature. Those arguing in favor of property rights frequently invoked the fear of antirentism as a talisman to ward off the encroachment of public rights on private property.[40] And so the issue is the same today: The question of whether reparations are to be paid has important implications for the redistribution of wealth in the United States. It implicates—as did slavery—other issues of humanity and the efficient use of human capital. But for the people in Congress who must decide on reparations, the current distribution of property is critical, just as arguments regarding workers' rights in businesses implicate those questions.[41]

Ideas such as self-reliance hold great appeal for Americans; they are often closely tied with more traditional conservative arguments against the redistribution of wealth. Emerson captured those arguments in his essay "The Conservative":

> "Touch any wood, or field, or house-lot on your own peril," cry all the gentlemen of this world; "but you may come and work in ours, for us, and we will give you a piece of bread."

And what is that peril?

Knives and muskets, if we meet you in the act; imprisonment, if we meet you afterward.

And by what authority, kind gentlemen?

By our law.

And your law—is it just?

As just for you as it was for us. We wrought for others under this law, and got our lands so.[42]

Emerson was merely presenting the argument of conservatism, but many others believed in the importance of opposing redistribution of wealth and power. Speaking to the Harvard Phi Beta Kappa Society shortly after the Fugitive Slave Act of 1850 was passed, as abolitionists were urging Americans to refuse to abide by the law, law professor Timothy Walker warned about the dangers of reform:

We cannot, indeed, change the past,—that is for ever immutably fixed; but we can repudiate it, and we do. We can shape our own future, and it shall be a glorious one. Now shall commence a new age,—not of gold, or of silver, or of iron, but an age of emancipation. We will upheave society from its deepest foundations, and have all but a new creation. In religion and politics, medicine and law, morals and manners, our mission is to revolutionize the world. And therefore we wage indiscriminate war against all establishments. Our ancestors shall no longer be our masters. We renounce all fealty to their antiquated notions. Henceforth to be old is to be questionable. We will hold nothing sacred which has long been worshiped, and nothing venerable which has long been venerated. These are the glad tidings which we the reformers of the age, are commissioned to announce.[43]

Nevertheless, others in antebellum America recognized, with Emerson, the role that claims to "vested rights" played in stopping reform. George Bancroft, one of the parents of the discipline of American history and an important advisor to President Andrew Jackson, delivered a Fourth of July oration on property rights. He critiqued the Whig Party for its adherence to property:

This system regards liberty as the result of a bargain between the government and the governed; and as measured by the grant. The methods of government being once established are fixed forever. . . . Instead of saying, it is Right, it says, It is established. . . . You will further perceive, that this system of an original compact is hardly but one step of an advance towards a truly liberal system. It regards every injustice, once introduced into the compact, as sacred; a vested right that cannot be recalled; a contract that, however great may be the pressure, can never be canceled. The Whig professes to cherish liberty, and he cherishes only his chartered franchises. The privileges that he extorts from a careless or a corrupt legislature, he asserts to be sacred and inviolable. He professes to adore freedom, and he pants for monopoly.[44]

Ralph Waldo Emerson's twentieth-century namesake Ralph Waldo Ellison addresses these same concerns in his posthumously published novel, *Juneteenth*. The novel revolves around an African American jazz musician-turned-minister, Alonzo Hickman, who raises a boy, Bliss, of ambiguous racial heritage (though he is probably white). That boy was born to a woman who had falsely accused Hickman's brother of rape. Hickman takes in the woman and her child when she has nowhere else to turn.[45] The boy later runs away and becomes a race-baiting politician, Senator Sunraider. Yet, somehow, the lessons that Sunraider learned as a child seep through, and—in his last speech in Congress—he addresses the connections between past injustice and the future. Sunraider asks, "How can the many be as one? How can the future deny the Past? And how can the Light deny the dark?"[46] Ellison is addressing the question, which he had explored in his essays as well, of how the contradictions of American society—for instance, of how much of what African Americans contributed to the building of America could be so completely dismissed from the myths of America's founding—can be reconciled. Sunraider warns about the need to confront those contradictions and to work them out:

Our forefathers then set our course ever westward, not, I think, by way of turning us against the past and its lessons, although they accused it vehemently—for we are a product of those lessons—but that we should approach our human lot from a fresher direction, from uncluttered perspectives. Therefore it is not our way, as some would have it, to reject the past; rather it is to overcome its blighting effects upon our will to organize and conduct a more human future. . . . Our sense of reality is too keen to be violated by moribund ideals, too forward-looking to be too long satisfied with the comforting arrangements of the present, and thus we move ever from the known into the unknown, for there lies the more human future, for there lies the idealistic core.[47]

Ellison identified—through Sunraider—the need to remake Americans' understanding of the contributions of African Americans to America and to make sure that (at least in the future) that understanding is part of the reconstruction of the world.[48] Yet Ellison knew that reconstruction was a long way off. What is more common is for the "winners of a given contention . . . to concern themselves with only the fruits of victory, while leaving the losers to grapple with the issues that are left unresolved."[49] That is the issue that we all face in considering reparations for slavery. It is a struggle in which everyone must be involved, for it implicates the redress of past injustice and the construction of something better for the future. It is also a part of the American creed, for it is a problem of creating a just society.

All of this points up the cultural wars at stake over reparations. They are not just about redistribution of wealth, although they certainly are controversial for that reason alone. Reparations—and the apologies that surely precede them—are but a microcosm of how we view U.S. history. Do we see the United States as a place of plentiful opportunity, where people can go as far as their ability and energy will take them, or as a haunted landscape full of oppression? Do we view the chasm between black and white wealth in this country as the fault of blacks and the Great Society, which intervened in the mid-1960s to destroy black families and the economic progress they were about to make? Or do we view it as a legacy of past state-sponsored discrimination and racial crimes? That self-image—and the accompanying narratives we tell ourselves about how we view our own accomplishments (I'm wealthy and well-educated because of my merit, not because of the fortunate circumstances of my birth, or I'm poor and poorly educated because of a racist society, not because of my lack of ability or motivation)—carries powerful weight.

Are Reparations the Best Way of Overcoming the Past?

One question that is rarely discussed in reparations literature—but one that is, nevertheless, critical—is, Are reparations the best way to spend society's limited resources? There might very well be better uses for the money. When we think of the limited resources that the federal and state governments have to spend, we must ask whether repairing those long-distant harms are the best use of resources. That is part of a cost-benefit analysis, which must involve looking at other programs and the good that can come from them. There is simply nowhere near enough money to compensate everyone for every past harm, so we must be selective in choosing the past harms—if any—that we will repair. Why should we spend money on one particular set of past harms? Reparations advocates will have to establish a convincing case for each past crime. This is part of a request that every claimant on public money is expected to bear; it is also one that few are able to make persuasively.

Part of the decision about whether to advocate reparations turns on how much they will benefit us—and how much benefit we could get by spending our efforts elsewhere. Perhaps reparations should focus most on the people who are most in need right now, and in that formulation, it looks less like reparations and more like general social welfare programs.

The Utility and Disadvantages of Reparations

Much of the utility of reparations is obvious. They offer hope of realizing the contributions that African Americans have made to American economy and society, as well as the disadvantages they have suffered; they offer the hope of restoring justice, to the extent that can be done, for some of the worst crimes of history; and they hold out the promise of helping us all build a better future, together. Looked at from the black perspective, they also promise to repair past damage, incorporate blacks more fully into the benefits of American society, and let everyone know that the crimes and sacrifices—the history of brutalization that is so important a part of American history—have been remembered. For whites, reparations promise some closure, some sense that injustices have been corrected, and—perhaps most important—an opportunity to improve the entire community. We can, one hopes, all move away from the centuries of human suffering and wasted opportunities with a commitment to improve the future. We can struggle for the future to overcome the past, to paraphrase Ralph Ellison.

But there are significant costs to reparations. They may tend to temporarily divide people along racial lines; recalling past tragedies is, indeed, painful. Even more than recalling past tragedies, however, reparations will require the government to draw further lines on the basis of race, for many separationists see reparations not as a way of achieving integration and a color-blind society but as a way of achieving further race-conscious action.[50]

Eric Yamamoto is one of the rare reparationists who takes seriously the disadvantages of arguing for reparations. He acknowledges the potential of reparations to lead to feelings of victimology and political backlash.[51] Victimhood is not just a mind-set, however. There are other problems associated with it. Reparations talk can be distracting. It may cause people to focus on past injustice when their energy should be focused somewhere else. And yet, reparations talk can actually be forward thinking, by creating a more equitable distribution of property that looks more like what the distribution would be like without the legacy of slavery and Jim Crow.

It may also lead to increased division in society. When many people think we ought to be moving in the direction of a color-blind society, reparations talk makes that difficult, or at least it raises the prospect of a continued focus on race. At the same time, two groups of commentators—reparationists and some conservatives—see reparations as a way of ending the significance of race. For reparationists such as Rhonda Magee Andrews—the author of one of the most important articles ever written on reparations—the prospects of reparations offer the hope of someday, perhaps someday soon, ending the legal significance of race. We may be able to get to the point where the damage has been repaired. Then, as Magee Andrews argues in a recent path-breaking article, "The Third Reconstruction," maybe we can move to a focus on helping those in the community who need help the most.[52] The center element of attention will be need. There are also conservatives, with whom Magee Andrews shares little in philosophy, who see reparations as a way to end the focus on race. Once there is a reckoning, the reparations can be paid, and the government will then stop paying attention to race. There will be no more affirmative action or other race-conscious actions. However appealing such a world may appear, as a simple solution to age-old problems, reparations are unlikely to offer that kind of closure. Difficulties of racial equality are unlikely to be solved overnight.

The reparations movement may end with some further recognition of the role of slavery and Jim Crow in American history. There may also be payments to a limited class of identifiable victims and perhaps payments to aid those most in need. There may never be a complete accounting of the costs imposed by hundreds of years of forced labor and decades of gross discrimination in voting rights, education, and employment. This may be yet another instance in which African Americans will have to be content with not what is just but with the knowledge that they have contributed yet again to the enrichment of American society, though they have not received adequate compensation for their labor. And perhaps that makes this one of the greatest of American stories: people laboring to benefit others, building and enriching the community for the benefit of everyone. That may also be the best ground for continued advocacy of reparations: that we all have a shared future and if the many are to become as one, to paraphrase Ralph Ellison, then the community must work together. The tragedy that is the legacy of slavery is a problem that visits us all and will continue to do so until it is overcome.

PART III

Implementing Reparations

Reparations Practice

5

Evaluating Reparations Lawsuits

IN THE United States, lawsuits are often the signifiers of social revolutions. We see lawsuits at the beginning of movements and at the end of them, as well. We see lawsuits when a movement is first gaining momentum, for people turn to courts to work out their claims and to gain statements of their rights. And we see lawsuits again at the end of social movements, when other methods have failed. This happened during the long struggle for civil rights in the twentieth century. A key strategy of the National Association for the Advancement of Colored People (NAACP) through much of the twentieth century rested on education and lawsuits. Beginning in the 1910s, the NAACP frequently pursued litigation as a way of challenging unfair practices, such as zoning that prohibited blacks from living on the same blocks as whites; the grandfather clause, which allowed anyone whose ancestors were allowed to vote in 1865 (before blacks obtained the right to vote) to register, while subjecting others to ridiculously difficult literacy tests; and unequal accommodations on railway cars. The NAACP won all three of those cases in the 1910s. And their victories continued, though slowly, into the 1940s and 1950s, as the Supreme Court freed black men convicted through laughably biased trials and as it built a series of decisions that required states to provide equal—even if separate—schools. All of that led to the *Brown v. Board of Education* decision, which prohibited segregation in public schools.

The reparations movement has also seen lawsuits, though what is most noticeable about them is how few have been successful. The first slavery reparations lawsuit, for taxes the federal government made off cotton grown and picked by slaves, was dismissed in the 1910s. That trend has continued. In January 2004, a poorly conceived slavery reparations lawsuit, which garnered much attention, was dismissed. In March 2004, the courts dealt a more significant blow to reparations lawsuits. A federal trial judge in Oklahoma dismissed what was perhaps the best case for Jim Crow–era reparations, a lawsuit brought by Harvard Law Professor Charles Ogletree on behalf of victims of the Tulsa riot of 1921. And yet, as the reparations movement gains momentum, we are likely to see more reparations lawsuits, even though they face high hurdles. This chapter discusses the requirements for a successful suit, as well as past suits and ones that may someday be filed.

Requirements for a Lawsuit

The U.S. courts are designed to handle only limited claims. Those are claims by plaintiffs against other defendants for very well-identified harm. Plaintiffs and defendants may be individuals, governmental bodies, or businesses. In each case, the plaintiff must identify some legal right that has been violated by the defendant and the ways that violation has led directly to harm to the plaintiff. To succeed on a lawsuit for reparations, plaintiffs have to show that they (or someone for whom they hold the right to sue) were injured, that the injury was caused by some person who had a duty to not injure that person, and that said injury resulted in damage. Courts typically adjudicate claims between a plaintiff (or group of plaintiffs) and a defendant (or, in very limited circumstances, a group of defendants). Of course, all of this must have happened within the statute of limitations. That is, suit must be filed within the usually short period of time that plaintiffs are given to file their lawsuit.[1] Those are tough hurdles, to say the least.

Lawsuits limit in dramatic ways who may seek relief and the means they may use to do so. This chapter explores the possibilities and limitations of lawsuits. We will be talking about each of the elements of a lawsuit, identifying (1) plaintiffs; (2) the basis for action, including the harm imposed on the plaintiffs; and (3) the defendants themselves, as well as (4) statute of limitation issues.

Problems with Identifying the Plaintiffs

Some claims are just difficult to fit within a traditional legal framework; slavery reparations are some of those claims. Courts typically deal with claims by well-identified victims against well-identified wrongdoers.[2] Reparations lawsuits are often of a different type, setting a class of victims against a class of descendants of perpetrators, current beneficiaries of past injustice, and others.[3] The lawsuits frequently pose a claim of a group, loosely defined by relation to those enslaved, against the entire society. Such claims are hard to put into a legal framework, though there have been some thoughtful attempts to do so in recent years.[4]

To have a successful claim, plaintiffs must show that they were caused injury. Unless plaintiffs can show that the defendant caused them some particular injury, they will not have what courts call "standing." To have "standing," plaintiffs must allege that they have suffered some particular injury by the defendant. In the case of slavery reparations lawsuits, plaintiffs must link themselves to some ancestor who was enslaved by a defendant. Reparations claims sometimes fit within that framework. There may be identifiable victims and perpetrators, as there were when Japanese Americans interned during World War II (unsuccessfully) sued the federal government in the early 1980s. But reparations suits rarely present such clean claims. Often, the perpetrators cannot be identified with specificity, or they do not exist anymore. Take war crimes, for example, where it is frequently impossible to identify who committed the crimes, although a group that committed the crime may be identified. At other times, the victims are also difficult to identify; who, precisely, are the victims of Jim Crow legislation, one must ask?

We can identify a significant number of people who have been harmed, but the Supreme Court typically requires some showing of close connection between those who were harmed and those receiving a remedy.[5] At the risk of belaboring the obvious, the harms of slavery were enormous. Even a short catalog includes sexual exploitation (including rape), physical and emotional abuse, kidnapping, destruction of families (such as the sale of children away from their parents, separation of parents, and denial of the right to marry), child labor, social stigmatization, and denial of freedom of speech and opportunity for education and religious instruction. Still, it is difficult to identify how people who are alive today have been harmed by specific defendants.

There are two possible ways of suggesting how currently living people have been harmed by slavery. First, subsequent generations have suffered because they are descended from people who were harmed. The current generation would argue that they have suffered because their ancestors were injured and that led to diminished opportunities and to other harm, which continue to have an impact. This is similar to "loss of consortium" claims filed by families of people who have been killed or injured. Second, subsequent generations might claim for harm to ancestors. But the generations born after slavery have also suffered independent harm: They have been subject to the segregation of the Jim Crow era, such as separate, inferior schools, limited employment opportunities, limited (and in many cases nonexistent) voting rights, and segregated and inferior housing.

The list of Jim Crow crimes is long and continued until very recent years. Many locate the end of the Jim Crow era in the mid-1960s, with the passage of the Civil Rights Act of 1964, the Voting Rights Act of 1965, and the Fair Housing Act of 1968. Those acts assured formal equality, but economic equality has not been reached yet. Reparations proponents argue that the effects of slavery and Jim Crow continue to the present day. Segregation mandated by law has been eliminated, they acknowledge. But then they ask, Does that elimination only lead to a myth that there is no longer a problem?

Formulating a legal claim requires linking past victims with people who are making a claim in the present—or what one might call present victims of past discrimination. One legal scholar links those people by arguing that victimization itself is racial: "Each specific act of oppression against a minority group reinforces, entrenches, and promotes the assumption that non-whites are different and appropriately treated as different."[6] Therefore, an appropriate response is to treat racial identity as a substitute for individual victim identity.[7] An important element in the expansion of the conception of victim and perpetrator identity is psychological harm, which leads to conceptions that groups are the appropriate way to classify victims.[8] Reparations proponents also use more tangible factors to link victims together as groups, such as low economic status and lack of property.[9] Courts have sometimes adopted such arguments in school desegregation cases. Courts are reluctant to adopt such an approach for perpetrator identity, however.[10]

Perhaps the plaintiffs could be people who are descended from slaves, as well as those who were alive and suffered during the era of Jim Crow, but those plaintiffs will have to show how they were harmed, by identifiable defendants, within the statute of limitations.

Finding Defendants Who Caused Plaintiffs Harm

Lawsuits require that plaintiffs demonstrate that a defendant (or defendants) caused them harm in a way that was illegal. The plaintiffs must appear before a court within the "statute of limitations"; that is, within a relatively short period of time after the harm has been caused.[11]

Even if we can identify specific plaintiffs who have been harmed by slavery, we must link them to specific defendants, for the victims must make a claim that asks for money from people who committed some wrong, or who at least inappropriately benefited from some wrong. Unfortunately, few corporations from the era of slavery are still in existence, and there are, obviously, no individuals who are still alive who committed wrongs. Thus, the claims against defendants are most likely to be in the form of claims against people who benefited from slavery. Here again, we run up against the problem that there must be some specific action taken by the defendants who harmed the plaintiffs. Many people have benefited from injustices committed in the past, yet there is no remedy against those beneficiaries. Sometimes there can be claims by plaintiffs against those who are unjust beneficiaries of past harm. Hence, there have been attempts to sue the few corporations that trace their origins to the era of slavery. The problems with that approach are explored in depth later in this chapter.

Yet even if the courts do not recognize the closeness of the connections, because they demand that particular plaintiffs identify particular defendants, many victims draw connections between past wrongdoers and people in the present. It seems that few deny that there are connections between past wrongdoing and present harm (though recognition of that fact may be more prevalent among victims than among descendants of perpetrators), but the problem becomes putting that connection into some framework that law recognizes. At a general level, there are connections between past harm and present inequality. Hypothesizing a legal theory that requires payment from those who are the beneficiaries of past injustice is going to be difficult, however.

Linking Plaintiffs to Those Injured

Closely related to the difficulty of identification of victims and wrongdoers is the requirement that there be a sufficient connection between past wrong and present claim.[12] That is, there must be a showing that the plaintiffs were injured by the defendants. In some instances, courts are willing to relax the usually strict connection between past wrong and present claim. In environmental law, for instance, a present owner of property may be liable for reclamation costs, without regard to fault.[13] However, even in those instances, there is a connection between the past wrong and the individual asked to pay— that person is the successor to title to property. If subsequent purchasers can demonstrate they took extraordinary steps to investigate the property before purchasing it, they can claim status as an "innocent owner" and escape reclamation costs.[14]

Georgetown University Law Professor Mari Matsuda offers an alternative test for gauging the relationship between past wrong and present claim. She proposes that victim status continue as long as "a victim class continues to suffer a stigmatized position enhanced or promoted by the wrongful act in question."[15] Matsuda suggests that the statute of limitations is extended for as long as there is a group that is suffering harm, which is potentially generations. Such creative lawyering poses interesting ways of viewing the past; it has not yet been recognized in the U.S. courts, however.

The Most Difficult Hurdle: The Statute of Limitations

Finally, there are enormous questions about such typical legal problems as statute of limitations, finding a claim, and computation of damages.[16] Difficulty in determining relief, as the U.S. Supreme Court has frequently pointed out, should not bar relief.[17] Maybe it is hard to prove the amount of harm that the plaintiffs have suffered, but they may still be entitled to some relief. Yet, the difficulty of figuring remedies, such as who is entitled to reparations and the form they will take (such as individual payments), pales by comparison with the other issues, such as identifying proper defendants and overcoming the barriers of the statute of limitations and locating a substantive claim. How, one wonders, can plaintiffs come into court in 2006 and ask for relief for a claim arising before 1865? And, given that slavery was legal before 1865, how can there be relief for harms imposed during the era of slavery?

The bases for statute of limitations defenses are not well explored. Most commentators are content to say something along the lines that there should be repose at some point so that institutions, corporations, and people can move forward. Repose is a relatively weak argument when weighed against the argument that there was never an opportunity—during the statute of limitations—to challenge the defendants or hold them accountable.[18] Statutes of limitation also preserve against the need to defend against stale claims, an argument that has been made recently in the wake of old claims asserted in sexual abuse cases. A court weighing a statute of limitations claim may want to take into account the quality of evidence in deciding whether to toll. A court should consider, then, a series of factors: the availability (or unavailability) of relief at the time of the racial crime, the identity of the victims (and whether they are still alive), the identity of defendants, the significance of the crime, the continuing impact of the crime on victims, and the quality of evidence.

Other Hurdles: Identifying Damages and a Theory of Harm—The Debt–Unjust Enrichment Model and the Tort Model

What is emerging in legal scholarship on reparations are several key conclusions. First, reparations claims through the courts are going to be extremely difficult. Second, there are multiple approaches to evaluating reparations claims. Proponents of reparations more readily see harm to entire groups and want to repair the economic and psychological harm. They seek a whole new system that radically redistributes property and therefore economic and political power. Those later claims, which have to be addressed through legislation, are discussed in the next chapter. The legal system recognizes much more limited principles for tracing harm. There must be some way of tracing who caused harm and who is harmed and of measuring that harm, according to a "cause of action." That is, plaintiffs must identify that the law recognizes that they have a right to relief.

Substantive Bases for Considering Slavery Reparations?

A key problem for a lawsuit for slavery reparations is locating a substantive basis for suit—in essence, finding some harm that is going to be recognized by a court today. The problem is particularly acute because slavery was legal at the time, so we are asking a court to go back and impose liability where there had been none before. Or, as Boston University Law Professor Keith Hylton says, in a critique of slavery reparations lawsuits, "there is no getting around the fact that any attempt to apply tort law to slavery means applying today's law to an institution that existed within the law a century and a half ago."[19] Sometimes courts impose liability after the fact, but at the very least, a corporation or government would argue that it is unjust to impose liability for acts that were legal at the time.

One can conceptualize two bases for lawsuits for slavery. Under one model, plaintiffs can recover the benefits they conferred on another. That model is known as the "unjust enrichment" model, because it seeks to identify the value of benefits that have been "unjustly" retained. To take a simple example, the unjust enrichment value in slavery is measured by the value of services that slaves conferred on their owner. Unjust enrichment provides a relatively small measure, however, because it allows recovery of only the value of benefits conferred.

The second basis is called "tort"—the name given to general wrongs. Assault, for instance, is a tort, which allows the person assaulted to recover for all the harm imposed by the assault, such as lost wages while recovering, medical expenses, pain and suffering, and punitive damages. The key difference between the two types is that tort suits allow someone to recover for all the harm suffered, whereas "unjust enrichment" suits allow someone to recover only for the amount of money that has been unjustly taken and is still retained. In essence, the difference is between the harm to one person and the benefit to the other. Harm almost always is greater than benefit.

A tort claim for harm is the most promising in terms of measuring the basis for recovery, because it is likely to be larger than a claim for unjust enrichment. A tort suit could be phrased in two ways: as claim on behalf of the slaves themselves, for the harms of slavery—of forced labor, assault, battery, sometimes rape—or, alternatively, as a claim by the slaves' descendants for the harms to their ancestors, which have injured them. That later basis is similar to the claims filed by family members for "loss of consortium" when a spouse or parent is injured.

The most frequently discussed basis is suits for harms against slaves themselves. What would the claims be, then? What are the harms that slave owners imposed on slaves? There were multiple torts: assault and battery, conversion of property, false imprisonment. Perhaps there might also be a claim against states for permitting slavery. The states established the legal framework that permitted their exploitation. They established laws with the understanding that particular people would be enslaved, separated from their families, and denied education; just about everything that can be done to destroy a person's humanity was contemplated or mandated by the laws of the slave states.[20]

Yet, any suit faces the hurdle that slavery was legal; indeed, that it received state sanction. It would have been laughable for a slave to file a suit in the antebellum era to recover for the evils of slavery, precisely because slavery was state-sanctioned. Does that mean, however, that there could be no retroactive liability imposed once slavery ended? One of the virtues of lawsuits is that judges can impose retroactive liability, more easily than could a legislature.

There is a second, much larger measure of recovery, the tort model. It allows a plaintiff to recover for harm that has been "proximately" caused by the defendant. The tort model, which is the most common model for recovery, is based on the idea that slaveholders committed "torts" against slaves. Those torts include assault, rape, and false imprisonment. Courts recognize that once a tort has been committed, a plaintiff is entitled to recover for all the harm that is caused by the tort. Thus (and again suspending such problems as statute of limitations and such confounding issues as whether there is a cause of action, given that slavery was legal at the time), plaintiffs who are descended from a slave might assert tort claims on their behalf against a defendant corporation that enslaved their ancestor. The measure of recovery would be whatever harm was "caused" by the enslavement.

Further Complications with the Tort Model:
Damages and Plaintiffs

Reparations lawsuits are part of a larger movement with many goals, including bringing attention to the contributions that African Americans made to the American economy and society, for which they received too little compensation, and correcting that unjust undercompensation. The movement for reparations for Jim Crow—the period between the end of Reconstruction and the beginning of the modern Civil Rights movement, when African Americans were subject to state-sponsored discrimination in education, housing, employment, and public accommodations—is aimed at the entire system of racial crimes during that era. Legislatures and municipalities passed acts that limited voting rights, provided grossly disproportionate funding of schools, and mandated racial segregation in housing and on streetcars. Then private actors followed and limited employment opportunities. Together, that led to dramatically limited economic opportunity for African Americans. A parallel community developed, sometimes with benefits for those segregated, but most often with low wages, long hours, and little opportunity for advancement.

Calculating the Harms to Slaves

The problem becomes even more complex when one considers subsequent generations. Descendants of slaves who sue stand in essence in the shoes of their ancestors. They can assert, one supposes, at least the same claims their ancestors had, in the nature of a "survival action." (Survival actions allow victims' estates to sue for harm they suffered while alive.) Thus, the descendants of enslaved people might be able to "stand in the shoes" of their ancestors and sue for the harms those ancestors suffered. Then it becomes a question of how to measure damages. Certainly, the harms to the slaves were enormous. But can we recover for the harms to the subsequent generations? Are harms to children recoverable?[21] Would that analogy allow people who were not born at the time of the torts to recover? People who were not born to the immediate tort victims? Or might those remote descendants even have an independent claim? There is no direct relationship between the descendants and the defendants; nevertheless, there is harm. Might there be a claim—as some descendants of people who ingested harmful medicine have asserted—against the original tortfeasors?[22]

Just trying to frame the claims makes for a lengthy thought-experiment, for what we have to do is create a line of causation, linking past harm to present conditions. Then we have to fit that line of causation into a framework that courts will be willing to recognize, given their proclivity to limit compensable harm to that proximately caused by the harm.[23]

Perhaps we would consider the harm of the tort of slavery as continuing down to each generation for which one could prove damage. That is, even though the harm took place in 1850, there may be continuing harm. That raises huge problems of proof. It also leads to the question of whether the harm is caused by slavery or by subsequent discrimination during the era of Jim Crow. Are those subsidiary claims? The cause of action might be in the name of the original enslaved person, with descendants entitled to bring action in the nature of a survival action.

Professor Hylton advances the possibility that slavery "may not have been as harmful as many have asserted." Hylton points to *Time on the Cross*, the work of economic historians Robert Fogel and Stanley Engermen, published in 1974. That book became one of the most hotly contested works of history in the 1970s. They argued, in essence, that slavery was economically viable and that slaves were—relatively—well treated. The point is that "if Fogel and Engermen are correct, slavery's victims would be unable to prove that they suffered substantial damages."[24] But Hylton's real argument, I think, is that slavery did not lead to the vast differentials of wealth and educational achievement between the black and white communities today. Instead, I imagine, he blames subsequent events, perhaps Jim Crow, although the typical argument among reparations opponents is that black culture is to blame. Opponents of reparations, such as John McWhorter and Stephan and Abigail Thernstrom, point to the high rate of single parents as a critical explanation for differential wealth achievement.[25] There is substantial question about the continued impact of slavery. Here, tort law might provide a helpful framework for evaluating causation. What percentage of the harm, one might ask, is caused by slavery, as opposed to other, intervening causes? Of course, some people might be able to overcome the harms of slavery; others might not be able to.

If we consider that there might be a separate action—something independent of a survival action—then we need evidence for causation.

How much did the institution of slavery affect not only the people who were in it but also their descendants? For purposes of considering tort law as a basis for a lawsuit, I think there is ample liability. But this question of linking past torts to present harm is critical if we think of tort law as an analogy. Here we need systematic research that links current harm to slavery. The legacy of slavery on African Americans is one of the most hotly contested issues throughout the social sciences from the 1940s, when Gunnar Myrdal published *An American Dilemma*, through today. Those questions are susceptible to no easy answer. One might compare Stephan and Abigail Thernstrom's *America in Black and White: One Nation, Indivisible*, which blames African American culture, not American society, for the chasm between white and black economic status,[26] with Douglas Massey and Nancy Denton's *American Apartheid: Segregation and the Making of the Underclass*. Massey and Denton's book, while not as comprehensive in scope as the Thernstroms'—it focuses on housing segregation—lays much of the blame on factors external to the African American community. *American Apartheid* concludes that "racial segregation—and its characteristic institutional form, the black ghetto—are the key structural factors responsible for the perpetuation of black poverty in the United States."[27] As we explore the legacy of slavery in current inequality, we can apportion damages based on how much we determine that slavery has led to that inequality.

So we are faced with the question of whether tort law would provide compensation for harm to subsequent generations or only to the generations of enslaved people, and whether subsequent generations could recover. Could there be a recovery for such "derivative claims"? One might think of analogies to such cases as *Ryan v. New York Central Railroad*, which is a favorite of torts casebooks. In that case, a railroad engine threw off sparks, which burned first one house . . . and then a whole bunch of others. That is a case about a judicial doctrine that limited liability of an industry that we wanted to promote. The New York Court of Appeals considered distinguishing cases where fire was caused by negligence—as in that case—and cases where fire was set intentionally. Perhaps people who commit intentional torts should have greater culpability for the harm they cause than those who are merely negligent. The court rested on another distinction, though, that the destruction of the first house was "the ordinary and natural result of its being fired." It thought that the destruction of the other houses was "not a necessary or a usual result." Moreover, imposing liability would potentially ruin any defendant:

> In a country where wood, coal, gas, and oils are universally used, where men are crowded together into cities and villages, where servants are employed, and where children find their home in all houses, it is impossible, that the most vigilant prudence should guard against the occurrence of accidental or negligent fires. . . . No community could long exist, under the operation of such a principle.[28]

Ryan is frequently criticized because it made the poor people who lived along the railroad bear the costs of development. All of this suggests that we can impose a different set of standards if we view the equities differently—if, for instance, we do not want to protect the institution of slavery.[29]

Some courts are willing to impose liability in the absence of a statute, and legislatures frequently imposed liability by statute.[30] All of this suggests that it is not unreasonable to impose liability for torts associated with slavery. We can safely say that even at the time, law protected masters' interests in slaves' lives, for owners had a cause of action for someone who killed their slave.[31] So it is not much of a leap for us to then recognize a cause of action that protects the slaves' interest in their own lives.

But the larger point is not just that tort law in the nineteenth century was narrow and generally unprotective of individuals rather than property claims.[32] It is certainly correct, of course, that it is unclear how much slavery, as opposed to other factors, hindered individuals and led to the current chasm between African American income and white, non-Hispanic income. That's a topic that needs a whole lot of evidence and discussion—and one that receives attention in the next chapter.

Unjust Enrichment and Slavery Reparations

There is yet another basis for slavery reparations lawsuits: unjust enrichment actions.[33] Where tort actions allow plaintiffs to recover for the wrong that they have suffered, unjust enrichment allows plaintiffs to recover for the benefits they have given other people. Thus, reparations proponents frequently speak about the benefit that slaves conferred on the United States—and ask for the return of that benefit.

Reparations advocates frequently speak in terms of a debt analogy. Randall Robinson frames his book *The Debt*, the leading statement on reparations, around the idea that African Americans are owed a debt by America for generations of uncompensated labor:[34]

> Through keloids of suffering, through coarse veils of damaged self-belief, lost direction, misplaced compass, shit-faced resignation, racial transmutation, black people worked long, hard, killing days, years, centuries—and they were *never* paid. The value of their labor went into others' pockets—plantation owners, northern entrepreneurs, state treasuries, the United States government.[35]

Joe Feagin's recent book, *Racist America*, likewise argues for reparations based on unjust enrichment.[36] He focuses on the benefits that African Americans conferred on American economy and society[37]—and then argues for reparations from the benefited group (whites) to the harmed group (African Americans).[38] Yet some opponents of reparations, such as David Horowitz, argue that slavery is—on balance—a benefit to African Americans.[39] That question is related to the idea that African Americans are owed a debt for their centuries of uncompensated and undercompensated labor.

There are some conceptual problems with the talk of debt as a measure of reparations for slavery, problems needing serious attention. Horowitz points out some of them.[40] The debt talk derives from unjust enrichment doctrine, which quite reasonably requires that people (or corporations) must disgorge money that in equity belongs to someone else. It requires little abstraction to conclude that money that was unjustly earned from slave labor ought in fairness to be paid to the slaves whose labor was stolen through violence. During the era of slavery, courts routinely recognized that property rights in labor lay at the center of the institution.[41] And, while judges did not recognize that slaves had an ownership interest in their labor, they recognized that when an owner's interest was interfered with, that owner had a claim. In one remarkable Alabama opinion, for instance, an owner who rented out his slave asserted an unjust enrichment claim against the renter when that person used the slave for services beyond the contract![42] Thus, it makes conceptual sense to talk in terms of unjust enrichment, if we can show that enrichment has been retained.[43] So there are two key requirements: that there be a benefit that is *still* retained and that the benefit is unjust.

Yet even if one can overcome the significant problems of tracing and doctrines of limitations, there are the significant problems of computing the debt and of figuring whether the enrichment has already been disgorged. Remember here, when we are talking about a debt, we are dealing with quasi-contract principles. It is a question of how much benefit has been conferred—and is still retained—by the people who are disgorging the benefits. On the benefit side is the labor conferred by the slaves and the economic explosion that labor made possible.[44] Much of that debt may have been paid by the Civil War—by Northern expenditures and by destruction of Southern wealth. Horowitz sees that as a straight cancellation of the debt. But the issue may be substantially more complex than that. It is not clear that the Northern costs of the war should be considered as a payment on the debt; moreover, the war fueled further economic development in the North. Perhaps most important, the federal government may not be entitled to an offset of the costs of the war, given that the war ended the harm of slavery that the federal government had authorized and helped to keep in place. Is someone entitled to the costs of stopping slavery if they were responsible for it in the first place? Other questions include: What do we make of the benefits from the Civil War? Do they increase the debt owed to slaves, because without slavery there would have been no war and hence no stimulus to the economy? Perhaps. But then what do we make of the costs of the war to the North? Do they count against the debt? And what does one make of the arguments that there have been forms of reparations, such as the Great Society, New Deal, and, more recently, affirmative action? Has compensation equal to that taken already been paid?[45] Finally—and even though this is a distasteful (even revolting) argument if we are talking about unjust enrichment, as opposed to a moral obligation to repair damage—there is a question of whether, when one offsets the benefits, African Americans are better off because of the institution of slavery.[46] An analogy beyond that of debt may be needed; at the least, there has to be more precision in the discussion.

Unjust enrichment theory is an important—and often overlooked—basis for asserting a claim. However, it carries with it substantial limiting principles. And in situations such as slavery, where tracing the wealth created by the institution presents an almost insuperable task, it may make sense to adopt other analogies. Perhaps a better way of thinking about reparations is as another case of the government's obligation to assist in repairing the lives of people who have been harmed or, as an analogy to a tort case, where there is no need to trace benefits conferred (and still retained) and benefits received. On that argument—of the need to repair damage that is still affecting people today—Horowitz has less to say, other than that life is good enough right now.[47]

While it is understandable to say—as reparations proponents frequently do—that the rest of society is "unjustly enriched" by the fruits of slaves' labor,[48] we have to look closely to know how much slaves' labor continues to benefit us today. In essence, can we say that we are unjustly enriched by the slaves' labor so long ago? And was the taking of the slaves' labor unjust (from a legal standpoint) in the first place? As the American Law Institute's draft of the *Restatement of Restitution (Third)* points out, there are "numerous cases in which natural justice and equity do not in fact provide an adequate guide to decision."[49] Moreover, there is a question whether the fact that slavery was legal at the time prevents us from going back and addressing the labor that was taken from the slaves. The critical question then becomes, Was there an "adequate legal basis" for taking the labor?[50]

The *Restatement* provides a limited basis for determining when benefits are conferred without adequate basis. One might argue that the benefits were conferred under duress, which left the taker without title.[51] Alternatively, one might conclude that the benefits were obtained by tort, such as conversion or trespass.[52] In both cases, one confronts the problem that slavery was recognized as legal. One fears that a court approaching a claim of unjust enrichment will conclude that during the period when slavery was recognized as legal in the United States, the benefits extracted from enslaved people are not recoverable in restitution.

However, there is some recent precedent to suggest that courts will look beneath a transaction to ask whether it is "legal" in some fundamental sense, rather than merely recognized as "legal" temporarily. In *Altmann v. Republic of Austria*,[53] the Ninth Circuit revived a claim for six Gustav Klimt paintings that had been essentially stolen from a family during the Holocaust. Though the actions might have been "legal" under the existing regime, the court concluded they were not entitled to be treated as legal under international law. Therefore, the heirs of the people from whom the property was taken *might* assert an unjust enrichment claim for their return. Similarly, in the case of slavery, an unjust enrichment claim is particularly compelling. Because unjust enrichment focuses on a benefit—or tangible property—that is still retained, there is a connection between past wrongdoing and present benefit that is much easier to see than in many reparations cases. Moreover, the moral claim that one person has some property that rightfully belongs to another is easier to establish than a claim that taxpayers who may have no benefit and who took no part in the wrongdoing must pay. There are two critical problems with an unjust enrichment claim for slavery: first, that slavery was legal; second, that the claim can be asserted now, so many years later.

The first defense—the legality of slavery—requires a court to recognize as legal a system that has been rejected and was subject to challenge at the time. Those working within—and accepting—the Southern legal system recognized property rights in humans as the basis for the slave system. What is asked for now is merely an accounting of the benefits of that labor. In some ways, the legality of slavery—the recognition that slaves produced something valuable—is made the basis for a claim.[54]

It is not outlandish to make a claim for what everyone understood was property. At the time, when someone else took slaves' labor from their owners without permission, those converters were liable. Why should we not now recognize the slaves' rights in their own labor, at least to the extent that their labor continues to provide benefits in 2006? Even if a court is unwilling to impose a quasi-contract basis of recovery, because it applied the rule that slavery was legal, it might be willing to use restitution as a *measure* of recovery for torts associated with slavery, such as assault. In that case, restitution might provide a measure of recovery and a means for doing so, even though the substantial basis is in actuality a claim in tort.[55]

The unjust enrichment rationale is particularly complicated because it deals with rights to some identifiable property. There are two claimants; often both are innocent, but we are trying to apportion property to one or the other. There are particularly strong equities when we are dealing with the current possessor who is a gratuitous beneficiary of the original wrongdoer. The statute of limitations does not offer so strong a support when you are contemplating disgorging a benefit from someone who has received it unjustly. So if there were still slaveholders alive, the case against them is compelling. In a manner of speaking, there are still some who hold from slaveholders, because there are some people who are gratuitous beneficiaries of those slaveholders.[56] Here tracing is important, because that allows us to follow assets into a new form—the "innocent" beneficiary of another's wrong. When we have a beneficiary of a gratuitous transfer (such as something passed down within a family), there is at least the possibility of treating that beneficiary as standing in the shoes—and taking the property subject to the same obligations—of the grantor.[57]

Altman points up the utility of an unjust enrichment claim, particularly where there is identifiable property: one can trace that wrongfully acquired property through other hands, even those of subsequent innocent purchasers. So, although I recognize that such a claim is fanciful and requires a suspension of the statute of limitations, we might conduct a thought-experiment along the following lines:

1. Labor of enslaved people was unjustly converted and used to build a plantation home or some other tangible property that continues to this day; that labor can then be traced into a new form—the plantation house.
2. Particularly in cases where the property is gratuitously transferred, there is a claim between descendants of the enslaved people and the current possessor of the property.
3. Even in cases where the property has been sold, the people whose labor was converted might have a claim against the subsequent purchaser.

Sample Damages Formulas

If there is going to be a tort claim that seeks to compensate for the harms of slavery to subsequent generations—that is, unless we are going to limit the recovery to damages to the immediate victim and then not permit consideration of harm to subsequent generations—

then we need to prove with specificity how slavery affected each subsequent generation. That will make for some pretty interesting trials. So let me suggest what the models of liability might look like in a suit by descendants of enslaved people, for slavery imposed on their ancestors, in ascending magnitude:

1. In unjust enrichment, for the benefits ancestors conferred on others, which are still retained
2. In the nature of a survival action, damages are calculated according to the damage done to their ancestors
3. In the nature of loss of consortium claim (or other claim for loss of family services), damages are the harms that slavery imposes on the subsequent generations, which involve proof of damage due to torts of slavery

The differences between those three measures are dramatic. If we limit damages to the first measure—unjust enrichment—then plaintiffs will recover only the amount of money that was unjustly taken from their ancestors *that is still retained*. Thus, unless we can trace some property that still benefits a defendant, there can be no recovery. The second measure—that of the harm to ancestors—offers a medium recovery, for it allows a recovery of the enormous damages to enslaved ancestors, although it provides nothing for the descendants who were not enslaved. Still, those descendants are likely to have suffered from the effects of slavery. The third measure, then, would provide for recovery of the harms suffered by descendants of slaves that can be traced to slavery. Those harms might include lack of opportunity, a home filled with violence learned under slavery, and lack of education, religion, and hope.

There is a problem in calculating the harm of slavery—how much the institution of slavery is continuing to have an effect on living people. One way to investigate the effects of slavery is to look at the current gap between African American and white income. Let me suggest this as a basic measure for damages: The measure of the harm to each individual slave is the difference between the average income of that slave's descendants and the average income of white Americans. Or perhaps that might be discounted some, to account for causes other than slavery that might account for a descendant's poverty. That formula would offer a starting point for a compensation scheme, but it does not necessarily work justice for individuals, for it offers no compensation to those descendants of slaves who earn above the average white income, regardless of how much they were injured by the institution of slavery. The formula offers a starting point for thinking about measuring harm; it cannot account for harm in each case. One might, of course, explore other formulas: The harm is the difference between a descendant's income and the amount necessary to reach the poverty line. That would offer a much more modest accounting of the damage, though it would also focus the government's limited resources on those in the worst financial plight.

A formula that takes account of only differences between income of African Americans and whites cannot, of course, address the host of other legacies of slavery and Jim Crow—decades of undercompensated labor, lost educational opportunities, and the lack of hope that derives from these. The list of harms is nearly interminable, one supposes. However, the difference in current income is something that is easily measured and is—reparations proponents will argue—a continuing harm of slavery, which ought to be addressed.

But no matter what basis one proposes for a lawsuit for reparations, we still face the problem of statutes of limitation. It is, quite simply, going to be enormously difficult to file a suit that gets over that limitation. There are, doubtless, some cases to be made. Take the case of art created by slaves. In New York State, a claim for the return of personal property (such as art) does not begin to run until the owner makes a request for its return. New York applies that rule to protect owners of stolen art; they cannot lose their property merely because a thief (or someone who purchases from a thief) hides the property for a few years. Perhaps the descendants of a slave who created art could make a claim for its return against the museum where the art is housed. That will be difficult for two reasons: first, because it may be quite hard to prove who is the appropriate descendant who has the right to make a claim, and, second, because the slaves who created art did not have a property right in its creation. Nevertheless, a court faced with claimants who can link themselves to the creator might be willing to consider the slave the owner of the property at the time it was created. All of this is open to speculation, at any rate.

But in each case, it is going to be difficult, and lawsuits are, at best, going to provide only limited opportunity for recovery. They will be, most likely, the vanguard of a movement for reparations. As we move closer in time to the present, however, there are better opportunities for lawsuits. Perhaps lawsuits for Jim Crow crimes will have an easier time overcoming statute of limitation defenses. And so we can now turn to Jim Crow lawsuits, to discuss what they might look like, what they would have to prove, and how they might overcome the statute of limitations.

Previous Reparations Lawsuits

Japanese Americans

Before the Civil Rights Act of 1988 provided reparations for internment, Japanese Americans filed a lawsuit against the federal government for internment. The district court in the District of Columbia dismissed that suit on statute of limitations grounds, and then the Court of Appeals reversed.[58] The case for tolling the statute of limitations turned on the doctrine of fraudulent concealment, which tolls the running when the defendant has fraudulently concealed the facts that constitute the basis of the action *and* the plaintiff could not have discovered those facts through reasonable investigation. The U.S. Supreme Court held that the claims for taking of property had to be heard in the U.S. Court of Appeals for the Federal Circuit,[59] and on remand, the Federal Circuit agreed with the district court's conclusion that the statute of limitations had already run. In short, it believed that the plaintiffs could have discovered the facts that led to their suit, even though the Justice Department had hidden evidence that the internment was unnecessary.[60] The problems with use of the courts are illustrated by Judge Robert Bork's dissent from a denial of rehearing in the District of Columbia Circuit Court: "justice according to morality is for Congress and the President to administer, if they see fit, through the creation of new law."[61] Even after Congress passed the Civil Liberties Act of 1988, which provided $20,000 in compensation to Japanese Americans interned during World War II, traditional legal principles barred some victims of wartime discrimination from recovering.[62]

Holocaust-Era Litigation

Several high-profile cases involved Holocaust-era crimes. The most famous is the litigation against Swiss banks, which refused to return deposits placed by Holocaust victims before World War II. That was a particularly clear case, because the banks still existed and could be shown to have retained assets of Holocaust victims. The lawsuit presented a pretty straightforward case of trying to return assets to the rightful owners. Yet even that litigation faced significant problems with the statute of limitations. Perhaps surprisingly, the plaintiffs in the Swiss banks case overcame an initial motion to dismiss—a preliminary procedural motion. Plaintiffs showed that they had made constant demands for return of assets, which were denied by the banks, which demanded proof of deposits. Such proof was impossible, for records had been destroyed during the Holocaust. Moreover, the banks had refused to allow claimants to search bank records. Thus, plaintiffs showed that they had been vigilant in trying to get their assets and that the banks had frustrated the attempts. The initial success on the motion to dismiss signaled that the plaintiffs had raised significant questions, although they were still a long way from victory in court. So plaintiffs brought considerable political pressure in New York to settle the claim. Following threats that New York State would boycott doing business with the Swiss banks, they agreed to a settlement of approximately $1.25 billion.[63] The settlement was more about politics than about law and an important reminder that to succeed, reparations advocates will need politicians behind them.

The Swiss bank settlement is the best known of the Holocaust-era lawsuits, but there have been several other types of Holocaust litigation. Following the success of the Swiss bank litigation, there have been successful claims against Austrian banks and for bank deposits stolen from French victims of the Holocaust. In the latter case, *Bodner v. Banque Paribis*, decided in 2001, found on a preliminary motion that the plaintiffs had raised sufficient questions to allow the case to go forward to "discovery."[64] That would allow plaintiffs to conduct thorough investigations of the French banks' records. At that point, as happened in the Swiss bank litigation, the French banks wanted to settle, which they did for approximately $172.5 million.[65]

Whereas the Swiss banks settlement is about returning assets to descendants of depositors, there has also been substantial litigation to return art to descendants of owners. Some of those lawsuits have been successful because they seek the return of specific property. The statute of limitations does not present as large a problem with artwork as with other types of property, because of a doctrine discussed earlier in this chapter that says the statute does not begin to run against personal property until the identity of the possessor is known. Because artwork can be easily hidden for extended periods of time, claimants can sometimes successfully assert claims many decades after the art has been taken.[66]

The California legislature came to the rescue of some Holocaust-era victims with its 1998 statute, the Holocaust Victim Insurance Act. It gave California courts jurisdiction over claims that Holocaust-era insurance had not been paid, invalidated forum selection clauses in insurance contracts that would require filing a lawsuit in a jurisdiction chosen by the insurance company, and extended the statute of limitations until 2010. Another statue, the Holocaust Victim Insurance Relief Act of 1999, required insurers doing business in the state to disclose all policies they and their affiliates wrote in Europe from 1920 to 1945.[67] That statute was struck down in 2003 by the U.S. Supreme Court as an interference with the president's foreign affairs power.[68] Efforts to settle the claims arising from insurance policies have been relatively unsuccessful, although a small number have been settled.[69]

As Holocaust lawsuits move away from seeking return of specific assets or personal property, they face much longer odds, and several other Holocaust-era lawsuits have been somewhat less successful. In 1999, several cases seeking compensation from private companies and from Germany for their benefit from slave labor were dismissed.[70] Yet, shortly after those cases were dismissed, German companies acting in conjunction with the Germany government—and under political pressure from New York politicians—agreed to a settlement of something like $5.2 billion, to pay those who had worked as slave laborers at concentration camps.[71]

Perhaps the most successful recent reparations litigation dates from the Armenian genocide of the early twentieth century. Family members of the Armenian genocide settled a case in July 2004 with New York Life for approximately 2,400 life insurance policies written on Armenians living in the Ottoman Empire. Following the genocide of

1915, the policies, some of which were written as early as 1875, were not paid. Around 1918, the Turkish government made a feeble attempt to recover for the people it had killed, arguing that because there were no identifiable heirs that the proceeds should be paid to the government. But they were never paid, and little was known about the policies until the California legislature passed the Armenian Genocide Insurance Act.[72] The act specifically contemplated lawsuits against insurance agencies by heirs of policyholders and suspended the statute of limitations.[73] The settlement provided $20 million, of which $11 million was for heirs of the deceased, $4 million to the plaintiffs' attorneys, $3 million to educational and social welfare organizations, and $2 million to administer the settlement.[74] As with other reparations movements, the payment is relatively small compared with the damage done. *Armenian Weekly* editorialized shortly before the settlement was announced, "We must be careful to note the order of difference between payments owed to individuals and the far broader reparations due the Armenian nation as a result of the Armenian Genocide." Moreover, the payments came from a private insurer, rather than the government responsible. "Although the New York Life case is an unprecedented effort to achieve justice for the victims of the Armenian Genocide and their heirs, it must be noted that the insurance provider is the one being asked to pay, whereas the restitution and reparations for the Genocide are the obligation of the Turkish state."[75]

Other Reparations Litigation

In rare instances, the courts are a viable means to suit and sometimes settlement. The *Ka`ai`ai v. Drake* case in the Hawaii state and then federal courts settled for more than $600 million for beneficiaries of the Hawaiian Homelands Trust, established in the 1920s. The state had, for more than twenty-five years, used trust land for people other than the beneficiaries of the trust, then had refused to allow beneficiaries to participate in the task force to resolve the dispute. As public attitudes shifted in Hawaii, the legislature moved to abandon an initial plan to settle the case for $39 million and instead paid $600 million in the early 1990s. In *Drake* there were clear beneficiaries and well-established misdeeds by the state in administering the trust. In other cases, there may be a successful suit where there are identifiable victims and identifiable perpetrators, and the suits are brought shortly after the events occur. In the spring of 2002, for instance, a federal court in Georgia held a Bosnian war criminal, who had resided in the United States, liable for torturing four Muslim prisoners.[76] Similarly, Holocaust victims have been able to overcome initial statute of limitations defenses and are able to fit their claims into traditional modes of individual victims versus defendant corporations. In other cases, they have asserted specific claims for identifiable property or specific torts.[77] The question that must be addressed is how much slavery and Jim Crow lawsuits can fit into those models.

Slavery and Jim Crow Reparations Lawsuits

Cato v. United States

In recent years, the U.S. courts have reviewed several slavery reparations claims. Unsurprisingly, every one of those claims has been dismissed. A series of claims were filed in northern California in 1994;[78] the opinion of the U.S. Court of Appeals for the Ninth Circuit in one of those suits, *Cato v. United States*,[79] is the leading judicial statement on reparations for slavery. It is a remarkable opinion in many respects, partly because it takes seriously reparations claims and partly because it is so dismissive of them.[80] Cato sought $100 million for a series of crimes, including

> forced, ancestral indoctrination into a foreign society; kidnapping of ancestors from Africa; forced labor; breakup of families; removal of traditional values; deprivations of freedom; and imposition of oppression, intimidation, miseducation and lack of information about various aspects of their indigenous character.[81]

The court considered ways to remake those allegations into a claim against the federal government or, perhaps more accurately, reasons that no suit could be sustained for the federal government's role in slavery.

First, the court addressed the federal government's sovereign immunity. The court concluded that the Federal Tort Claims Act waived immunity only for actions occurring after 1945. The court rejected the argument that the Thirteenth Amendment, which abolished slavery, provided a basis for recovery.[82] The court also addressed the statute of limitations. Cato argued that constitutional claims should never be subject to the statute of limitations, using an analogy to Native American claims. The court distinguished those claims, where the statute of limitations is tolled for decades, even centuries, because the tribes have both a treaty relationship and a relationship as trust beneficiaries with the federal government.[83] Cato also argued that continuing discrimination retolled the statute of limitations; the court merely concluded that continuing discrimination did not provide an independent statutory basis for suit.[84]

Other recent claims for reparations for slavery in other contexts have fared poorly. In May 2001, the U.S. Court of Appeals for the Seventh Circuit, for instance, rejected a claim of a person enslaved in a Nazi concentration camp.[85]

Then California passed a statute to assist U.S. soldiers who had been held as slave laborers in Japanese prison camps during World War II to recover against the companies for which they had worked.[86] The U.S. Court of Appeals for the Ninth Circuit held the statute was barred by treaty with Japan. World War II veterans who had been enslaved as prisoners of war and forced to work for Japanese corporations lost in the Northern District of California in 2000, because the 1951 treaty with Japan waived those claims.[87] More recently, the claims of foreign nationals suing federal court have also been dismissed, based on the statute of limitations.[88] In October 2001, the District Court of the District of Columbia dismissed a complaint brought by "comfort women"—more accurately described as sexual slaves—who were forced to labor for the Japanese military during World War II. That complaint, too, was dismissed because of sovereign immunity, which had not been waived under the Foreign Service Immunities Act.[89]

Cato and the other slavery cases show just how perceptive scholars are who talk about the inability of judicial doctrine to address reparations claims. Even though Cato wanted reparations for a series of acts, many of which were only tangentially related to the federal government, the court considered only the federal government as a defendant. It could not even consider the possibility that there might be other defendants—or other modes of approaching the problem. It acknowledged that Cato wanted broad relief. In its one-paragraph treatment of her request for an apology, for instance, the court cited its earlier discussion of Cato's lack of ability to "seek relief premised on the stigmatizing injury of discrimination in general."[90] And that is appropriate, of course; the court is established to hear discrete claims.

In re African American Descendants' Lawsuit

Other cases have reached similar results. The lawsuit filed by Deadria Farmer-Paellmann in 2002 in federal court in Brooklyn, against corporations that were in existence (or are successors to companies that were in existence) during the era of slavery and that profited from slavery, presents yet other questions.[91] The suit was styled as a class action, on behalf of people descended from slaves, against CSX, Aetna, and FleetBoston, which are all successors to companies that were in existence and allegedly profited from the institution of slavery. One wonders whether the lawsuit might be more viable if the class were people descended from the people who worked for (or were bought and sold or whose life was insured by) the defendant companies. Because the companies continue in existence, there is at least the possibility that they are subject to suit. The two major problems are locating a substantive basis and overcoming the statute of limitations, of course. As to substantive basis, the most commonly cited bases are unjust enrichment and tort. Because judges at the time recognized that violence lay at the heart of slavery and the judges willingly embraced that violence, it may be difficult to successfully sue in tort. Perhaps that is a case where the change in law could have been anticipated and, in the spirit of enterprise liability, a court might choose to impose retroactive liability on a corporation, though that is going to be a significantly uphill struggle.[92]

Unjust enrichment provides an alternative substantive claim. The typical elements of an unjust enrichment claim include the allegations (1) that the person seeking compensation furnished services that were accepted by the person charged, (2) that the person seeking compensation expected compensation, (3) that the person charged had reasonable notice that compensation would be expected, (4) and that retention of the benefit would constitute unjust enrichment. An unjust enrichment claim is less likely than a tort claim to be barred by a claim that slavery was legal at the time, although it's likely that a court might not find that the bases for unjust enrichment are met in instances where a corporation profited from the trade in slaves or from insuring them. It seems questionable whether slave owners had notice that they would be expected to pay for the services they took from the slaves. In the case of corporations that profited from insuring slaves, I think the connection between slavery and unjust enrichment is even more attenuated.[93] The claim for unjust enrichment will be strongest where the fruits of a slave's labor are retained. In that case, which will be admittedly very rare, there is a compelling moral claim that someone has retained property that rightfully belongs to another. Yet, the statute of limitations continues to pose a significant problem.

Following the March 2002 filing in federal court in Brooklyn, Deadria Farmer-Paellmann, the lead plaintiff, filed other suits around the country. Those cases were subsequently brought together in January 2003 in a federal court in Chicago, in a procedure commonly used when cases raising similar issues are filed throughout the country. At the end of July 2003, all the defendants together filed a "joint motion to dismiss." This joint motion is the most comprehensive legal response yet available to slavery reparations claims. It advances four main claims: (1) that the plaintiffs lack standing, (2) that the statute of limitations bars claims, (3) that the claims are barred by the political question doctrine, and (4) that the plaintiffs have not alleged facts sufficient to support a cause of action.

In January 2004, the federal court adopted much of the defendants' argument and dismissed the case. The opinion, which has attracted substantial attention, is likely to signal the end of the recent attempts to obtain large-scale reparations for slavery through the courts. The opinion dismisses the suit because of a lack of connection between plaintiffs and defendants.[94] The court went on to state that the dispute is inherently political and one that is not subject to resolution by a court. These kinds of claims are best heard, the court argued, by legislatures. It also found that the suit was barred by the statute of limitations.

Indeed, Deadria Farmer-Paellmann framed the lawsuit in a way that created problems. There is no evidence linking her to any of the behavior of any of the defendants. Hence, she had problems with "standing." At the very least, a court would demand that the plaintiffs show a connection between the people harmed by the defendants' predecessors and themselves. In essence, one might reasonably demand that the plaintiffs show some connection between the defendants' predecessors and their predecessors. Yet, this problem of connecting plaintiffs to people harmed might be cured fairly easily by identifying people who are descended from those who were employed as slaves by the defendant companies and their predecessors. It ought to be a relatively simple task to locate the living descendants of people who worked as slaves for companies that are still in existence. The task will be educational, because it can illustrate the continuing connections between past and present. Indeed, the previously discussed California legislation that required insurance companies to disclose the names of slaves insured by them is premised on precisely that idea. But even once we link currently living people to those who labored as slaves, we still have the problem of finding a basis for suit and an enormous problem with the statute of limitations.

A more credible suit would have located the descendants of slaves who worked for CSX's predecessors or whose lives were insured by Aetna. At least that much will be necessary, because courts are established to hear discrete claims by one party against another. That, of course, is the problem when one then tries to talk about lawsuits for reparations. There are certainly some that have a chance of success. It appears as though Charles Ogletree's Reparations Co-ordinating Committee is contemplating a suit against colleges that received money made from slavery. On its face, there is the possibility that such a suit might succeed. One supposes that a proper plaintiff might be identified: the class of people descended from slaves who worked on a particular plantation owned by a donor.[95] Using an unjust enrichment theory, the plaintiffs might successfully show that the plantation owner took profits that in justice actually belonged to the plaintiffs.[96] Although a suit against the individual plantation owner would be barred because his estate has been distributed and closed, a suit against a school that received a contribution from the donor might not be so surely foreclosed. The school would take the gift subject to all the claims against the donor, such as unjust enrichment. Now, there is still a problem of statute of limitations; however, a particularly generous court (perhaps one in the West Indies) might be willing to apply a "tolling" doctrine; that is, a doctrine that "tolls" (or suspends) the running of the statute of limitations. Or one might try a more daring theory and claim that the property was stolen from the slaves and then given to a school. Because a thief cannot pass title, it is possible that the title to the property has never passed—and maybe there is a possibility that the claim is not barred by the statute of limitations because the statute does not begin to run on the theft of personal property until a request for return of the property is made.[97] Or so one might be inclined to argue.

Potential Slave Reparations Lawsuits

One suspects that Professor Ogletree might have his sights set on the money used to endow the Royall Professorship at Harvard Law School, which was funded by Isaac Royall with money made from his plantation in Jamaica.[98] Royall donated money made on that plantation to Harvard Law School.[99] Because a donee takes a gift subject to all the claims against the donor, those descendants might assert a claim against Harvard Law School, as the stand-in for Isaac Royall. There would, of course, be serious problems with the statute of limitations. However, one might find a court—perhaps in Barbados—willing to toll the statute of limitations because the courts were unavailable to the plaintiffs at the time it was taken. Or one might apply the rule that the statute of limitations does not begin to run on stolen personal property until a claim is made for its return.[100]

But because cases like that are so rare, lawsuits look like a very difficult way of obtaining meaningful reparations. Individual lawsuits are simply not well honed to deal with claims by a group against descendants of a group of beneficiaries.[101] It may be that someday we have articles, like the ones that are written about Holocaust litigation, that celebrate the role of the federal courts in restoring justice to descendants of slaves for generations of stolen labor and physical abuse.[102] But that is unlikely, to say the least. If there are going to be reparations, they will most likely not come from the courts, because of problems with locating a substantive basis for most suits and with locating appropriate plaintiffs and defendants, and because of the statute of limitations.

There is a possibility, of course, that a creative federal court might imply a new cause of action or impose retroactive liability on corporations that profited from slave labor, much as they imposed retroactive liability in products liability cases. The calculus in those cases frequently turned on the need to spread risk across an entire industry and the foreseeability that liability would ultimately be imposed. If a twenty-first-century plaintiff could trace ancestry to people who provided labor for a corporation that currently exists, there is some possibility that a court might impose liability. Such a possibility leads to the question of whether a legislature might be able to impose liability in those cases by statute. California has already subjected insurance companies to the requirement that they search their files for evidence of insurance policies written on slaves' lives.[103] That legislation has generated an incredible document, available on the Internet, that lists the name of the slave insured, the person who purchased the insurance, and often the occupation of the slave. It is remarkable testimony to the ways that—with a diligent search—we can yet recover details of the lives of people long since forgotten. One wonders if the next step will be legislation authorizing suits against insurance companies that wrote such policies.[104]

A legislature might, indeed, pass a statute giving descendants the right to sue for past wrongs. California has taken similar action to revive claims of victims of sexual abuse.[105] That would face stiff constitutional challenges. Would it be permissible to impose retroactive liability on companies for acts that were legal when they occurred—decades ago? Perhaps, but under recent Supreme Court precedent, that would probably be legal only if the liability were small.[106]

To achieve reparations for slavery through a lawsuit will be, to put it bluntly, enormously difficult. Yet, some lawsuits for reparations for slavery have been filed in the last few years. To have a successful lawsuit, there will need to be plaintiffs who have an identifiable connection to the harm of slavery, who locate defendants who caused the harm that those plaintiffs suffered, and somehow the plaintiffs will have to get over the statute of limitations. Now we turn to a more intensive study of the bases for a lawsuit and how legal principles might be used to frame a reparations claim.

Lawsuits for Jim Crow

Given that lawsuits—to be successful—have to identify plaintiffs who have been injured and defendants who are still in existence, have to demonstrate culpability for the harm, and have to get over the hurdle of the statute of limitations, it seems much more likely that lawsuits will be most successful for (relatively) more recent crimes and for (relatively) limited groups of victims. There are some cases that seem particularly compelling for Jim Crow crimes and discrimination.[107] The Tulsa riot lawsuit, *Alexander v. Oklahoma*, sought to recover money for people whose community was destroyed during the 1921 riot. The story of the riot is complex, but a short version is that when a newspaper printed a front-page inflammatory story alluding to the rape of a young white orphan by a black teenager, a lynch mob formed at the Tulsa Courthouse. Members of the Tulsa black community, including many veterans of World War I, mobilized to stop what they feared would be a lynching. They clashed with members of the white lynch mob at the courthouse, which set off the riot. The police department chief then deputized dozens of men and used them, in conjunction with local units of the National Guard, to systematically arrest everyone in the black section of Tulsa. The hastily deputized mob and a white mob then looted and burned the black section of Tulsa. In essence, the black section was destroyed by the government.[108]

Tulsa presented one of the best cases for a lawsuit for reparations for Jim Crow, precisely because it fits into a framework that law is able to recognize. There are identifiable plaintiffs—more than 100 people still survive who were alive during the riot and were victimized by it—and there are identifiable defendants, the city and state. Moreover, there are some identifiable causes of action that are particularly strong in the case of the city, which deputized hundreds of men who subsequently participated in the riot. The city and local units of the state guard also participated in the mass arrest of everyone in the black section of Tulsa.[109]

The largest problem is the statute of limitations, and there was even a reasonable tolling argument. When we recall that statutes of limitations are based on policies of repose, that they are human creations that stop litigation at arbitrary points, we may see places where the equities suggest that we should toll them and allow lawsuits to go forward.[110] There are other specific doctrines that may allow relief as well. As was discussed earlier in this chapter, courts in recent cases have tolled the statute of limitations when relief was effectively unavailable. Thus, in *Rosner v. United States*, victims of the Holocaust overcame a statute of limitations defense in 2002.[111] They overcame a motion to dismiss when they sought to obtain gold taken from them decades after they were told incorrectly that the gold was not identifiable. The favorable opinion in *Rosner* resulted from a finding that there had been fraudulent concealment of the facts surrounding the gold in the years immediately after World War II. In *Bodner v. Banque Paribas*, the federal court based in the Eastern District of New York applied another theory, that of continuing violation. Descendants of Holocaust victims whose assets had been taken by French financial institutions during World War II—and then not returned after the war—overcame a motion to dismiss on statute of limitations grounds by successfully arguing that the failure to return property constituted a continuing violation. That is, each time there was a failure to return, the plaintiffs' rights were violated again. The continuing violation theory is often invoked by plaintiffs but is rarely successful. It usually requires a demonstration that there is some continuing action on the part of the defendant that continues to reinjure the plaintiff. A classic case of the continuing violation occurs in the context of employment. Plaintiffs who some years ago were discriminated against by their employer, and thus failed to receive promotions that they were entitled to, suffer from a continuing violation. At every pay period, they receive less pay than they would have received if they had received the promotions.[112] There are other cases that present perhaps even more promising avenues for Tulsa riot victims.

Professor Jacques deLisle has collected a series of cases from the U.S. federal courts asserting claims for human rights abuses that occurred in other countries. Those cases have tolled the statute of limitations when courts in the other countries were unavailable or when plaintiffs had well-founded fears of persecution if they sought to assert their claims.[113] Thus, when the courts are unavailable because a plaintiff cannot get access to them, federal courts have tolled the statute of limitations. As far back as the American Civil War, a plaintiff who could not file suit—because of the war—was allowed to file beyond the limitations period. The Supreme Court's rationale was that the plaintiffs were prevented from filing because of matters beyond their control.[114] Similarly, just after World War II, a victim of Japanese internment was permitted to file suit against a third party (his preinternment employer) under the Jones Act, because he was unable to file while interned.[115] In both of those cases, the suits went forward against third parties who had no culpability in causing the courts to be unavailable. The case for tolling is substantially more compelling when the defendant bears culpability for foreclosing suit, as the Northern District of California implicitly recognized in *Forti v. Suarez-Mason*, which relied on those Civil War and World War II–era precedents. *Forti* allowed a suit under the Alien Tort Claims Act to go forward in 1987 against the government of Argentina for acts in February 1977.[116] *Forti* has been extended to cases where even if the courts might be open, fears of reprisal and defendant-inspired intimidation tolled the limitations period until the officers creating that fear were removed.[117] And that doctrine applies, in turn, to cases where there is no functioning judiciary in the plaintiffs' home jurisdiction, even if a claim might *possibly* have been brought in another jurisdiction.[118]

The Tulsa case is somewhat more complex, because we are dealing with the question of when courts might have become available to Tulsa riot victims. The Southern District of Florida dealt with a similar problem in 2002 in *Barrueto v. Larios*, another Alien Tort Claims Act claim arising from human rights abuses in Chile in the early 1970s. The court tolled the statute of limitations, concluding that evidence of murder had been hidden by the Chilean government and that the pre-1990 concealment of the cause of death tolled the running of the statute of limitations until 1990. It distinguished claims where a defendant had taken no active role in concealment (known as equitable tolling) and those where the defendant had taken an active role in "preventing the plaintiff from suing in time" (equitable estoppel).[119] The court concluded that "the defendant's act of concealment postpones the accrual of the limitations period altogether."[120] *Barrueto* may be read for the proposition that when defendants take affirmative action to preclude lawsuit—by concealing evidence and by making courts unavailable—that the statute of limitations is tolled until the defendants take affirmative action to make the courts realistically available again. Tulsa presents a particularly compelling case for such a reading of *Barrueto*, because there can be relief in Tulsa without fear of extending unreasonably the statute of limitations in other cases. Fortunately, there are few if any other tragedies that present such a case for tolling the statute of limitations. There are a series of limiting factors in Tulsa that distinguish it from other cases: the culpability of the government; the efforts made to drive out plaintiffs through prosecution and destruction of their homes, again by the government; and the capitulation of the government to the Klan. A court can toll the statute of limitations in Tulsa without fear of opening up a never-ending set of lawsuits. And there are reasonable, legal arguments—recognized by other contemporary federal courts—that justify tolling. The evidence from the Klan trials in the aftermath of the Tulsa riot suggests a similar lack of effective means for justice. Even if Greenwood residents had the courage—as some did—to file claims, the courts were effectively unavailable to them.

The courts were effectively unavailable at the time. No fair-minded observer will claim that Tulsa riot victims had a decent shot at justice in the Oklahoma state courts at the time. Unavailability of relief is a key place in which courts typically toll the statute of limitations.[121] Here the argument goes that because courts were unavailable, we should not expect plaintiffs to have sought relief. Then we are into an equitable argument about whether the complete failure of the legal system to give justice should, at least in limited circumstances, be remedied. Particularly where someone asserts claims based on heinous and discrete crimes—rather than general societal discrimination—the case for tolling the statute of limitations is compelling. Then the courts are being used in ways they are designed for and in ways they work well—of providing relief in limited cases, where there are identifiable victims and defendants, where there is a well-defined cause of action, and where damages are proven with specificity and at the level of detail required in other lawsuits. When there is a claim for limited relief, not general societal discrimination, where there should have been relief through the courts at the time—and would have been relief, had the world been even minimally fair—riot victims or victims of other Jim Crow crimes have a compelling argument. When the U.S. District Court for the Northern District of Oklahoma heard the case in the spring of 2004, it dismissed on the basis that the statute of limitations had run. It accepted the plaintiffs' argument that the courts were unavailable in the 1920s but held that at some unspecified point—perhaps sometime in the 1960s—the courts became available and the statute of limitations began to run again. By the time the plaintiffs filed their suit in 2003, the two-year statute of limitations was well past. The U.S. Court of Appeals affirmed the dismissal in September 2004, thus ending the Tulsa plaintiffs' attempt to use the courts for belated justice. The dismissal of the Tulsa lawsuit seems to have taken the wind out of lawsuits for Jim Crow, although other courts might very well construe the tolling arguments differently. Another court faced with a similar lawsuit for a riot might conclude, for instance, that the statute of limitations stopped because of cases of intimidation, as happened following the Tulsa riot. It might also conclude that the statute of limitations, once stopped, should not restart.

There are other questions to ask of Jim Crow lawsuits, of course. One might ask, What remedies would Tulsa victims be entitled to? Each victim would receive compensation for deprivation of property and temporary liberty. To that extent, Tulsa is just one in another long line of civil rights lawsuits; it has identified plaintiffs who were caused harm by identified defendants. To convert Tulsa from a civil rights lawsuit—though one for harms that first occurred decades ago—into something for broader reparations, one must ask, Is other relief available, too, that might permit a more communitywide remedy? Tulsa is a strong case for reparations of some sort, through either the courts or the legislature. Indeed, four factors suggest Tulsa victims are owed reparations by the legislature: People are still alive, the incident was concentrated in time and place, government sponsored the harm, and promises were made at the time to help rebuild. Yet, Tulsa is at once both compelling and limiting. For events that go beyond Tulsa, as well move into larger reparations programs, the case becomes more difficult to fit within a typical lawsuit formulation.

There are other ways to deal with problems with the statute of limitations. There might be legislation to extend the statute of limitations. Congress passed such legislation to allow black farmers who had been discriminated against in applications for loans by the Department of Agriculture from 1981 to 1996.[122] Following the extension of the statute of limitations, the farmers sued and received a $1 billion settlement in the *Pigford v. Glickman* case.[123] In subsequent years, many farmers have been disappointed; money has been slow. Some farmers who were discriminated against have been unable to recover, because they did not participate in the lawsuit. Others were dissatisfied with the size of the payments.[124] All of that illustrates problems with lawsuits as a vehicle of reparations, in that lawsuits are poorly equipped to provide equitable treatment across a broad spectrum. They often leave deserving parties out of settlements or provide inadequate settlements. But for those looking for a successful reparations lawsuit, *Pigford* is one of the few examples.

The California legislature also attempted to extend the statute of limitations for victims of Japanese slave labor camps during World War II. That legislation was held unconstitutional.[125] However, its passage suggests that legislatures might consider such action for victims of Jim Crow crimes. Such legislation extending the statute of limitations against the government is unlikely in states where the legislature refuses to take action, as happened in Tulsa. However, state legislatures may be willing to impose the liability on companies, particularly if they do most of their business outside the state, as was the case with the California statute that required insurance companies to disclose life insurance policies written by their affiliates in Europe from 1920 to 1945.

Looking at Other Jim Crow Lawsuits

Given the difficulties for slavery reparations lawsuits, it is unlikely that significant reparations will be achieved through the courts anytime soon. There might be limited suits, such as suits to recover money earned using slave labor that is still held by the corporations. It is possible that a court might look past a defense of the statute of limitations and require disgorgement of assets still held to descendants of those enslaved. But we are a long way off, and the amount of property still held by successors to those who benefited directly from slave labor is likely to be small indeed. If one uses a slave reparations lawsuit to heighten awareness of the connections of the present to slavery, then the mere filing of a lawsuit might be considered a success. But we are a long way from a lawsuit in which money changes hands. And if symbolic relief is important, one might look to something like a lawsuit on behalf of slaves' descendants to gain access to plantations where their ancestors are buried. For there is a well-recognized right of descendants of people buried on private property to have access to the graves of their ancestors, and slaves have been buried on plantations all over the South. The image of descendants visiting the graves of their ancestors could be powerful imagery indeed. Yet, for the time being, it appears as though lawyers looking for lawsuits will spend their time more profitably (though perhaps not much more profitably) looking at more recent racial crimes.

There were a series of riots for which we can use Tulsa as a model. One might look to the East St. Louis riot of 1917, for instance, where race hatred, fed by race-baiting politicians and the use of African Americans as strikebreakers in the local iron and meatpacking industries, combined with racial violence, led the African American community to take action to protect itself. The community armed and, following an attack on the evening of July 3, some African Americans fired into an unmarked police car, believing that it contained people who had shot into some African American homes earlier that evening. That misunderstanding, which left a police officer dead, led the next day to random attacks on African Americans working in the white section of East St. Louis. Through the morning, those attacks escalated, and by the afternoon, African Americans were being attacked throughout the city. Then, the state guard, in conjunction with local police, began to invade the African American section of East St. Louis. Many guards stood by as a mob attacked the helpless community, and some guard members even joined in the attacks.

Following the riot, a Congressional investigation focused on the causes of the violence. It laid blame on local industry for using recent African American migrants from the South to keep wages low. The committee's report concluded:

> The strike in the plant of the Aluminum Ore Company was caused by a demand on the part of the organized labor for an adjustment of wages, a reduction in hours and an improvement of conditions under which the men worked. The company refused to meet any of these demands, declined to discuss the matter with the workmen's committee, and added insult to injury by importing negro strike breakers and giving them the places of the white men. . . . [T]he bringing of negroes to break a strike which was being peaceably conducted by organized labor sowed the dragon's teeth of race hatred that afterwards grew into the riot which plunged East St. Louis into blood and flame.[126]

The committee report on East St. Louis taught whites an important lesson about how to talk about the riot—as at least partially the fault of blacks who had armed to protect themselves. It also taught blacks an important lesson: Do not give up your guns, because you will be shot anyway. After East St. Louis, the riots became somewhat more violent, because the black community was better prepared to defend itself—and less likely to passively sit by as it was attacked.

The story of East St. Louis is compelling and deserves further scrutiny—perhaps even a state truth commission.[127] East St. Louis presents a somewhat different case from Tulsa, however, because riot victims received reparations through an Illinois statute that gave victims of mob violence a cause of action against the municipality where the violence occurred. It was, in essence, an attempt to provide an incentive for municipalities to protect their citizens against mob violence—for when the sheriff knew he was liable to victims, he would be more vigilant in guarding against violence. The statute was an early form of strict liability. The idea of liability without regard to fault, so novel in the early twentieth century, was tested in the U.S. Supreme Court. Justice Holmes upheld the statute.[128]

East St. Louis represents a case, then, where some people received reparations. The statute limited recovery, however, to family members of people who died. It provided nothing for those who merely lost property; it also failed to provide compensation to the entire community for its losses. As with Tulsa, there are some identifiable immediate victims, and there is a community that is currently in terrible shape. One might seek a remedy that provided something for the victims themselves. But what of the community? The important issue is finding some theory for large-scale repair of the community, rather than merely providing money to a very limited number of now elderly plaintiffs. What are the theories that one might use to repair it? Here a class action on behalf of residents of East St. Louis might make sense. The problem will be in linking relief to the harms caused by the riot. Unfortunately, the tragedy of East St. Louis is that there are so many problems that have little connection to the riot itself—problems stemming from the willful neglect born of decades of urban policy.

Other riots pose similar issues. There are well-known riots, such as Chicago and Washington in 1919. Those riots might provide a way of getting money into the hands of a relatively limited group of individuals. They may even suggest the limitations on greater harms. Yet, one does not need to move much further back in time before there are no survivors. Contrast, for example, the Atlanta riot of 1906 with that in East St. Louis. It is unlikely that people who survived the Atlanta riot are still alive today; if they are, they are very old, at least 100, even if they were infants during the riot. Yet the African American community in Atlanta suffered greatly during the riot and afterward. As Gregory Mixon demonstrated in his 2005 book *The Atlanta Riot*, there was substantial government involvement in the riot—and it reinforced the racial segregation of Atlanta.[129] But how does one repair that damage? What might reparations for that riot look like, if there are no survivors? What is the present harm that we would repair for? The problems are worthy of serious consideration, but it appears that the problems quickly become, well, almost insurmountable.

One could also work in a different direction, looking to individual cases of lynching. What do we make of lynching that often took place under the supervision of local officials? For lynching cases, one might identify factors similar to the ones in Tulsa. There are some particularly well-documented cases. In Oklahoma, for instance, the attorney general began investigating lynching in the early 1920s. Those investigations, though they did not result in successful prosecutions, provide important details about the role of government officials in the lynchings of African Americans. In those cases, as with riots, one can identify victims (the family members of the lynching victim), governmental defendants, and governmental culpability. Because there is a discrete event, the case is particularly compelling. Reparations might come in the form of payments to family members of the victim or in the more general form of a historical truth commission that reminds us of the harm that lynching—and associated Jim Crow crimes—did to the community. It is an opportunity to use a single event as a site for viewing the legacy of Jim Crow and for understanding how the whole system of racial legislation, extralegal violence, and private discrimination functioned.[130] For many of the lynching victims, however, the case is not so easily made. There is less evidence of direct governmental involvement. Instead, there is evidence—at best—of failure to protect. And the statute of limitations plagues lynching lawsuits, just as it does riot lawsuits.

That raises critical issues of legalized lynching. What do we make of criminal defendants convicted of crimes on minuscule evidence, before politically motivated judges and prosecutors and an inflamed jury? One might look to cases like *Moore v. Dempsey*, which arose out of the Elaine, Arkansas, massacre, for evidence of how those legalized lynchings worked. Fortunately for the defendants, Justice Oliver Wendell Holmes overturned the convictions of eight African American men who had been railroaded into death sentences for their "role" in a "negro uprising" in Elaine, Arkansas, in 1919.[131]

There are other instances of such laughably biased prosecutions;

one thinks of Jesse Hollins in Oklahoma[132] and the Scottsboro boys.[133] However, it begins to be more difficult to contemplate how one files a lawsuit for reparations in those cases. Is there a possibility of suing for wrongful prosecution? What is the standard? What if the defendants are no longer alive? Alternatively, as University of California–Hastings law professor David Levine has suggested, one form of reparations might be individualized review of the cases of African Americans who were convicted of crimes in the decades before modern due process protections were required. That might result in, at least, the return of voting rights. It might also result in compensation for those wrongfully convicted.[134]

Let's move a little further away from what are rather typical Civil Rights cases (though they are filed decades after the harm took place). How might lawsuits for other Jim Crow legislation be conceptualized? This legislation—some might call it crimes—affected the entire community. In some communities, virtually no African Americans were entitled to vote. How do we take account of statutes that limited voting rights? There are identifiable defendants: the state legislatures that passed discriminatory voting legislation and some state officers charged with implementing the legislation. There are also some people who are still alive who suffered the harm. However, the question becomes, What is the appropriate remedy? Remedies for voting rights violations are notoriously difficult to devise. Take the case of the grandfather clause. Just after Oklahoma statehood, for instance, the Oklahoma legislature passed a restrictive voter registration statute. It was not just the discriminatory statute, however, that kept blacks from voting. The voter registrars went beyond the statute and, in many cases, imposed a ridiculously difficult literacy test. That was challenged through a federal criminal prosecution of Oklahoma officials who denied black men the right to vote. The circuit court deciding the *Guinn v. United States* case discussed some of the outrageous denials of voting rights. In one instance, J. Halyard, the principal of the Cimarron Industrial Institute, who had graduated from Acorn A & M College in Mississippi, Lincoln University of Pennsylvania, and the Bryant and Stratton Institute in Buffalo, New York, was prevented from voting. As the U.S. Circuit Court concluded, "There is not the slightest room for doubt as to whether he could vote. . . . There seems no room for doubt that the defendants knew that fact."[135] In other instances, blacks were entitled to vote because their ancestors had been entitled to vote, but they were denied.[136] In some instances, there was no literacy test administered; they were just turned away.[137]

After the U.S. Supreme Court struck down the grandfather clause in *Guinn v. Oklahoma*, in 1915, it provided only a limited remedy: It struck down the statute. Yet, the Oklahoma legislature subsequently repassed the voter registration statute but again significantly limited the rights to register. That statute was struck down, too—in the 1930s.

What is the harm? One might have to show that voting would have made a difference—and then what type of difference it would have made.[138] The entire community suffered a harm, and that may be compensable in some way,[139] but this begins to look like a claim for general societal discrimination, which is not going to be successful.[140] But maybe an important contribution can be relearning that racially neutral statutes may be discriminatory. Reparations might be limited merely to a new judicial doctrine that retreats from the requirement of *Washington v. Davis*[141] that equal protection challenges to facially neutral statutes have to show a discriminatory motive.[142]

What of lawsuits against the counties and municipalities that limited the funding to segregated schools? There are identifiable victims—all the school-aged children in an entire community who suffered the harm. There are identifiable, governmental actors—the bodies that provided different (and very frequently inadequate) funding. Might a class action recover for the lost educational value? Even figuring what the damages were would be difficult. How much did poor schooling contribute to a student's later job prospects? The problem is that even well-educated African Americans faced poor job prospects. Might there be a more limited recovery, for negative unjust enrichment, of the value of money saved by underfunding the segregated schools? That would, of course, grossly underestimate the harm, but it might get around other proof problems of linking education to later income.

Some of these problems were worked out in the years after *Brown v. Board of Education*, when plaintiffs sought relief for segregated schools. It may be hard to now go back and ask for additional relief— even though the potential plaintiffs are different. These lawsuits merit substantial consideration, at any rate.

How about other segregation statutes—such as the ones that segregated libraries, that kept people segregated on railroads and on streetcars, or that limited where people might live? The library statute poses a particularly intriguing problem. The sadness of segregated libraries suggests precisely the insidious nature of Jim Crow: Americans decided to limit even access to knowledge. Although people like Ralph Ellison demonstrate that it is possible to overcome those barriers (his mother brought home magazines for him to read, which she collected from the white homes where she worked as a maid), it is difficult.[143] Who would sue? One supposes every African American who lived in a municipality might have a cause of action. The remedy cries out for some kind of injunctive relief, akin to desegregation of schools, with increased library facilities in the community against which the discrimination took place. Drawing upon Toby Patterson Graham's book *A Right to Read*, on segregated libraries in Alabama, which demonstrates the ways that libraries were segregated by law,[144] one might construct an argument along these lines: As a result of governmental decisions, blacks had fewer opportunities to access public libraries in the state of Alabama than did whites.[145] The harm was a decrease in educational opportunities at the time—and decades later—that is extremely hard to calculate or compensate for. However, decisions regarding library location may be continuing to the present day. The magnificent, once all-white central library in Birmingham, for instance, maybe should have been located somewhere else; similarly, decisions about collection development, which continue to have effects to this day, might be shown to have been racially motivated. Future decisions about library location and collection development may be excellent subjects for injunctive relief.[146] Moreover, the redirection of library funds to promote education has important symbolic value. Indeed, it is difficult to think of a project better designed—at least symbolically—to both repair for past Jim Crow discrimination in education and to make a symbolic statement about the future.[147]

In selecting targets for a Jim Crow lawsuit, one must ask what it is desired to accomplish through them. Partly it may be to tell a story about the past, to educate people about the role that Jim Crow played in the lives of African Americans and others, too. Partly it may be to try to repair the lives of those who suffered discrimination. That requires locating cases where statute of limitations defenses can be overcome, as well as locating substantive bases for recovery. At the same time, one should look for areas where there may be some communitywide relief, which might be forward-looking. Victories on those issues might then be tied together with legislative reparations, which are not so bounded by requirements of lawsuits.

The remedy must take account of the entire history of Jim Crow — that the entire system used extralegal violence, in conjunction with legislation that limited educational and voting opportunities, to limit opportunities for African Americans and to use their labor at below what the cost otherwise would have been. That type of remedy becomes quite difficult to contemplate, because it is difficult to show how much loss any particular harm caused. How does one measure the damage for a failure to obtain an adequate secondary school education? What if, because of the discriminatory hiring practices of firms, there would have been no jobs available? There is no question that there has been damage, but attributing it to particular individuals, businesses, or entities is difficult. This is one of the reasons that so frequently there are attempts at remedies for general societal discrimination. Yet, constructing a remedy through a lawsuit, or even using tort as a model, involves tough issues of proof. One is then left thinking about three types of recoveries: (1) disgorgement of benefits retained by the community, (2) recovery in which specific proof of loss is provable, and (3) recovery where community-based relief is appropriate. In each case, the problem with proof of loss is reduced. Each of those models can be applied to Jim Crow crimes. And still, because of the requirements that plaintiffs link their claims to specific harm caused by specific defendants, all while overcoming the statute of limitations, the likelihood of successful lawsuits is extremely limited. It is for those reasons that we must turn to the legislative reparations in the next chapter for any hope of serious reparations.

6

Legislative Reparations

As we have seen in chapter 5, lawsuits might be used to gain some limited reparations for relatively small groups of people, if lawyers can overcome the difficulty of finding a group of perpetrators to sue, if they can locate appropriate plaintiffs and demonstrate the connections between the plaintiffs and defendants, and if they can overcome statutes of limitations defenses. The people who perpetrated the crimes of slavery are gone, and their estates are distributed. A few corporations survive, and a small amount of the money made from slavery might be traceable to currently existing bank accounts. But lawsuits can grant only limited relief, to the parties before them who have proven that a limited group of defendants have harmed a limited group of plaintiffs.

Given the limitations of lawsuits, significant reparations are going to come—if at all—through legislation. Legislative bodies, such as the U.S. Congress, the California legislature, and Chicago City Council, can move with flexibility that courts do not have. Legislatures can select appropriate beneficiaries of reparations, how much they will receive, and the various modes of reparations. Chief Justice Warren Burger recognized Congress' flexibility in 1980, when the Supreme Court upheld racial set-asides in federal government building contracts: "Congress, of course, may legislate without compiling the kind of 'record' appropriate with respect to judicial or administrative proceedings."[1]

Quite simply, reparations legislation allows for the kind of flexibility and structural changes that reparations proponents seek. Legislation is flexible in fixing the beneficiaries of reparations, the payers, and the kind of relief. Yet, many of the same conceptual problems with lawsuits plague legislative reparations. A legislature will need to identify a group of people who have been harmed and who have demonstrated entitlement to relief. Just as with lawsuits, there are complex questions of fixing the amount of reparations. Should, for instance, victims receive the benefit they have conferred on others (such as the value of land taken from them) or the amount of harm they have suffered? Does it make more sense to simply establish a fixed payment to every member of a victim group? Or should reparations programs simply try to improve the lives of the group of victims, such as with funding for education and health care?

Those questions of payment are compounded by considerations of imposing liability on payers. A legislature will be concerned with imposing liability in the form of tax payments on a group of payers who may have limited or nonexistent culpability in past racial crimes. There are significant problems in imposing the liability of past generations of private actions on the current generation. One might be willing to say that we allow the benefits of past generations to descend to the present—in the form of inheritance—and we should, therefore, impose the debts of the past on the present generation. But even there, many Americans are descended from people who arrived after slavery ended, some even after Jim Crow ended, and their connection to slavery and Jim Crow is substantially limited. That is not to say that the federal and state governments are free from liability, of course.[2] It just means that the analogy may not be a class of victims against a class of perpetrators. It may be more correct to think in terms of a class of victims against the government's obligation to assist victims. Phrased in that way, reparations for slavery and Jim Crow fit comfortably into dozens of social programs, such as the Homestead Act, the New Deal, the GI Bill, and the Great Society. In each of those cases, the government used its enormous power to assist those who needed help. In each of those cases, there was the realization that with the proper cultivation, talent would benefit everyone, especially those being aided. Thus, the claim may end up being a claim of a group against an entire community. And for those claims, it seems the appropriate place to look is the legislature, which has traditionally acted as the conscience of the community and also has the ability to evaluate a particular reparations claim in the context of other claims. Whereas courts can only decide yes or no according to the case in front of them, legislatures can make a larger array of responses.

Seeking Reparations from Legislatures:
Modes of Reparations

Because of the limitations of lawsuits and the limited ability of courts to provide comprehensive relief, reparations scholarship in recent years has focused heavily on making the case to legislatures. There are four main types of reparations that legislatures could grant: truth commissions, apologies, community-based reparations, and payments to individuals. The last type can take several forms, including affirmative action plans and direct cash payments. Most reparationists support the first three and only part of the fourth. Rarely is there serious discussion of cash payments to individuals as reparations for slavery.

Truth Commissions and Apologies

Most people writing about reparations begin by talking about truth commissions that acknowledge the scope of the problem, along with an apology. United States Representative John Conyers of Michigan has introduced a bill, H.R. 40, in every Congressional term since 1989 to study slavery to understand its effects: the benefits it has conferred on and the harms it has entailed for subsequent generations, as well as the harm to society as a whole.[3]

There have been some examples of the truth commission already. Sometimes those commissions rely on disclosures by companies involved. The 2002 resolution passed by the city of Chicago, requiring companies that do business with it to disclose their connections to slavery, has yielded several news-making disclosures and apologies, first referred to in chapter 2. The first disclosure came from the investment house Lehman Brothers, which was founded before the Civil War in Montgomery, Alabama, and moved to New York City after the war. In November 2003, Lehman Brothers disclosed that while they were based in Montgomery, they owned at least one slave, Martha. The disclosure led a Chicago reporter to comment: "When she was sold as a slave at age 14, Martha could never have imagined that, nearly 150 years later, she would be at the center of a volatile debate over reparations in the Chicago City Council."[4] That Martha is now the subject of debate is further testimony, as novelist Ralph Ellison reminded an audience at Brown University in 1979, of "the unexpected outdoing itself in its power to surprise."[5] Martha's story is yet another one of those strange twists that have become so common in American history, of events of seeming inconsequence having great effects, even decades after an event. More details of Martha's life will probably come to light soon, and she will live again, even if only in apotheosis.[6]

In April 2004, as JPMorgan Chase was bidding on financing for a city project, it filed a disclosure stating that it had no connections to slavery. But Alderman Tillman uncovered evidence that Morgan's predecessors had financed the slave trade, which set off a search by historians hired by JPMorgan Chase. They rummaged through dozens of archives and learned, in the Tulane University archives, that from 1831 to 1865, two of JPMorgan Chase's predecessors, Citizens Bank and Canal Bank, both of Louisiana, accepted something like 13,000 slaves as collateral on loans. When some of those loans went into default, the banks ended up owning the slaves who had been put up as collateral. In that way, the banks became the owners of approximately 12,500 people.[7] "We apologize to the African-American community, particularly those who are descendants of slaves, and to the rest of the American public for the role that Citizens Bank and Canal Bank played," JPMorgan chief executive William Harrison and chief operating officer James Dimon wrote.[8] The bank then took the even more unusual step of pledging $5 million for college scholarships for black students from Louisiana. Bank One, a subsidiary of JPMorgan Chase, also posted on its Web site information on its predecessors' involvement in the use of slaves for financing. It lists the names of the slave owners who mortgaged their slaves, along with basic data on the slaves, when it is available. Thus, we now know the names and ages of many of the slaves.[9]

Even more recently, on June 1, 2005, Wachovia Bank likewise apologized for the actions of several of its predecessors for their involvement in the slave trade and for their use of slaves as collateral. As Wachovia CEO Ken Thompson said, "we can learn from our past, and begin a stronger dialogue about slavery and the experience of African-Americans in our country."[10] By all indications, there are more apologies on the horizon.[11]

Especially notable was the JPMorgan Chase apology and pledge of $5 million for college scholarships for black students from Louisiana. The action is important for two reasons. First, it provides money in memory of those enslaved, with the goal of building a better future. The people who were used as collateral to finance the growth of fortunes probably never dreamed that they would be remembered or that their suffering might be turned to a good cause. Their labor has taken on new meaning. Second, and perhaps more important, the bank pledged the scholarships because it learned about its history. But for the Chicago ordinance, we would never have known this history, and once we see that dark history, we are often motivated to do something about it. As the bank's executives recently stated, "We all know slavery existed in our country, but it is quite different to see how our history and the institution of slavery were intertwined."[12] The disclosure ordinance led to additional information, which then led to reparative action.

But even beyond the power of apologies and truth commissions to shape the public's understanding of history and the current effects of that history, apologies and truth commissions shape our identity. They tell us how we view ourselves and how those left "outside history"—left outside the American dream—are included (or excluded). It is an enormous project to reframe the collective memory of events, to more fully incorporate people who have been excluded and to have a history that is fair to them. As University of Hawaii law professor Eric Yamamoto has elegantly phrased it, "group members, lawyers, politicians, justice workers, and scholars possess often unacknowledged power at the very foundational stages of every redress movement. The power resides in the potential for constructing collective memories of injustice as a basis for redress."[13] Yet, even if we can change that collective conscience, it remains to be seen how that change will affect legislative and judicial policy.

At the state level, the California legislature has been trying to collect data from insurance companies. On the heels of the successful legislation that required insurance companies doing business in California to disclose policies they wrote on slaves, the legislature required insurance companies to disclose all life insurance policies they (and affiliated companies) sold in Europe from 1920 to 1945.[14] The statute, known as the Holocaust Victim Insurance Relief Act (HVIRA) was a preliminary, legislative attempt to discover the connections between insurance companies and policies that were taken by the Nazis.[15] In the summer of 2003, the U.S. Supreme Court declared the law unconstitutional, because it interfered with the president of the United

States' power to conduct foreign affairs. That decision, however, has no bearing on statutes that require U.S. companies to disclose their dealings with slavery.[16]

This form of reparations—consideration of the connections between past and present—can be undertaken by private companies and schools as well. In 2000, the Aetna Insurance Company apologized for having written policies insuring the lives of slaves and then reiterated the apology in April 2002, after Aetna was sued for reparations.[17] Aetna was soon followed by another great Connecticut institution, the *Hartford Courant*, which had helped return runaway slaves to their owners by printing ads for runaways. There are other newspapers that might consider apologies, including the *Baltimore Sun*, which ran at least some advertisements for runaways, and newspapers located in the Deep South, such as the *Mobile Register*, the *Montgomery Advertiser*, and the New Orleans *Times Picayune*. In the case of the *Mobile Register* and the *Montgomery Advertiser*, the complicity is strong. They were vehicles not just for the return of slaves but for pro-slavery advocacy.[18]

Some schools and their faculty and students have already undertaken those self-investigations. Students at Yale prepared a comprehensive investigation of the university's connections to slavery in 2001, and the University of Alabama campus had a vigorous discussion on its connections to slavery in the spring of 2004, a discussion that involved newspapers and radio throughout the state. Brown University has gone the furthest. Ruth Simmons, Brown's president, convened a Steering Committee on Slavery and Justice to investigate Brown's connections to slavery and to make recommendations about future action, including apology and reparations. President Simmons's suggestion, which appeared in the *New York Times* in March 2004, that reparations might be appropriate drew substantial opposition from Brown alumni.[19] The steering committee's several-year-long investigation of Brown University's connections to slavery, as well as abolition, is setting the standard for further university investigations. Brown University has looked broadly, including the curriculum in the years before the Civil War, the role of its faculty in slavery and antislavery work, the place of slaves on the campus and in the larger Rhode Island community, and the places where Brown's donors made their money. That introspection is spreading to other institutions. In October 2005, for instance, the University of North Carolina opened an exhibit on campus, "Slavery and the Making of the University."[20]

Institutional self-examinations and apologies when deemed appropriate are an important part of remembering the role that slavery has played in creating institutions that exist to this day. Although there are relatively few corporations that date back to the era of slavery, the list continues to grow, as companies file disclosure statements and as individuals conduct research into institutional histories. Municipal ordinances that require companies to disclose their connections to slavery and efforts by institutions—such as insurance companies and schools—to learn about their history are likely to provide a further basis for talking about the multiple ways that current institutions have benefited from and are connected to slavery. That discussion is an important, basic part of the reparations agenda.

And there is Representative Conyers's proposed national commission to study the effects of slavery, discussed in chapter 2. That national dialogue, which will remind us of the multiple connections between the past and the present, may be an important part of making the case for further reparative action. There have been local apologies for slavery, such as those given by the Southern Baptist Convention, the Presbyterian General Assembly, the *Hartford Courant*, and the University of Alabama. It is likely that truth commissions will lead to further apologies. And we are seeing continuing interest in them, such as the investigation of the 1898 Wilmington Race Riot by the North Carolina Commission, which released its report in 2006. Yet that leaves open the question—once we get past studying, talking about, and apologizing for slavery and Jim Crow—of what will be done to make the apologies more concrete. In essence, what will other legislative reparations look like?

Community-Building Programs and Payments to Individuals

Articles have established the general goals of reparations, but one of the surprising elements is that it is so difficult to define what reparations will *look like*. Most people who talk about reparations as a serious goal envision a wholesale reordering of American society. Their agenda includes redistribution of wealth and the breakdown of racism and white privilege. How the later goals will be accomplished is rarely specified. Indeed, a critical problem with the reparations debate is that reparationists have not yet specified what they want.[21] And it is exceedingly difficult to get somewhere until you know where it is you are going. As Arthur Serota has phrased the problem, "Revolutions cannot work without a realistic finance plan."[22] We have some statements, such Clarence J. Munford's in *Race and Reparations*, that reparationists should "demand it all!"[23]

Even Robert Westley, who is a leading theorist of reparations, does not provide a comprehensive plan. He does, however, offer a somewhat more detailed picture than most other reparations articles. He sees monetary payments to individuals, as well as commitment to community-building programs, as central to the reparations agenda.[24] His goal is "black economic independence from societal discrimination" and civil equality.[25] Where some talk about unjust enrichment, Westley focuses on the gaps in economic achievement and educational opportunity—and the culpability of the U.S. government for the present plight—as the predicates for reparations. Reparations are due because of a failure to repair the damage done by slavery—as well as the government's decades-long involvement with Jim Crow.[26] Westley proposes group-based reparations, which will permit institution building.

That will occur in two ways. First, the people most in need will receive cash payments. He makes no attempt to specify the amount of those payments. That must await, one expects, some assessment of the damage, which will flow from the truth commissions that will study reparations. Second, Westley proposes establishment of a trust fund, with trustees elected by African American descendants of slaves. He proposes a large (but unspecified) trust for the benefit of all black Americans, which would be funded by the federal government.[27] The trustees (elected by the beneficiaries) would use the corpus to fund projects aimed at educational and economic empowerment.[28] Westley acknowledges that his plan needs considerable refinement.[29] In fact, now is a good time to begin to explore such a plan in more detail.

Randall Robinson, who bases much of his legal argument in his book *The Debt* on Westley, also proposes a trust fund. The exact amount of the trust, Robinson believes, should be determined once "an assessment can be made of what it will cost to repair the long-term social damage."[30] Robinson proposes that the trust fund at least two generations of precollege education (with boarding schools for at-risk children), college for those who cannot afford it, additional weekend schools that teach "the diverse histories and cultures of the black world,"[31] and a study of the extent to which companies and families have been enriched by slavery, followed by recovery of that money, which would be reinvested in the trust; funding of black civil rights and political organizations; and commitments to Caribbean and African countries, including "full debt relief, fair trade terms, and significant monetary compensation."[32] But that is only the beginning, not a comprehensive plan.[33]

Roy Brooks has built the fullest model yet of what reparations might look like in his recent book, *Atonement and Forgiveness: A New Model of Black Reparations.* Brooks builds a moral case for atonement, based on the treatment of blacks in the eras of slavery and Jim Crow, and then asks what would make atonement possible and realistic. He proposes a series of programs that would repair that past harm and thus lead to atonement. Brooks's proposals include a national slavery museum and a trust fund to administer payments to individuals for two purposes: education and funding businesses. He proposes that the value of the trust fund will be computed by multiplying the average difference in income of black and white Americans by the number of black Americans.[34]

Professor Molefi Kete Asante provides a similar statement to Westley's about the range of potential reparations strategies: "Among the potential options are educational grants, health care, land or property grants, and a combination of such grants. Any reparations remedy should deal with long-term issues in the African American community rather than a onetime cash payout."[35] Other reparations plans are more outlandish. Lee Harris, who adopts the black nationalist perspective, proposes the establishment of separate states for blacks. The proposal, which would require a Constitutional amendment and a wholesale rethinking of American society, is reminiscent of Nation of Islam leader Louis Farrakhan's statement at the reparations rally in Washington, D.C., in the summer of 2002: "We cannot settle for some little jive token. We need millions of acres that black people can build."[36]

It is easier to state aspirational goals, rather than concrete plans.[37] But sometimes even the general goals are hard to articulate. Perhaps Arthur Serota has given us the best statement of what reparations promise:

> There can be no elimination of poverty in America, no rebuilding of lives for millions of Black Americans sweltering in urban chaos and isolated by rural deprivation, no chance for millions of urban black youth staring through prison bars, hiding from warrants, dropping out of school or negotiating the violence of urban battlefields, to contemplate and develop their futures without reparations. Reparations is not merely long overdue, it is a finance plan to implement a change.[38]

Considering the Morality and Constitutionality of Legislative Reparations

Factors Influencing the Morality of Legislative Reparations

Deciding whether to enact colossal reparations, who should receive them, who should pay, and the form they will take is enormously complex. Those questions are similar to ones that courts face when considering a reparations lawsuit. But legislative reparations are not bound by the limitations of lawsuits.

Just as reparations lawsuits employ two main bases for arguing for reparations—unjust enrichment and the tort model—legislative reparations build on similar bases. Legislatures might provide for a measure of "unjust enrichment"—the value of property created by slaves and unjustly retained—or, by a tort model, measure the amount of harm of slavery and compensate for it. That tort model gets into hugely complex issues of the amount of harm and of how much of the harm is attributable to slavery or to Jim Crow discrimination or to some other cause, such as black culture. A key virtue of legislative reparations is that they can provide some other measure of relief. Sometimes legislative reparations provide no specific amount for any individuals but offer community-based repair. At other times, they provide a fixed amount for each victim. Such payments avoid tough questions about exact harm and instead offer a way of fixing some mode of repair.

In deciding among those various modes of reparations, legislatures need to take account of the people who would receive payments, as well as those who would pay. Much has been made of the idea that whites owe blacks a debt for the contributions that blacks have made to the economic and social development of the United States; that is, the "unjust enrichment" argument discussed in the previous chapter. Unjust enrichment gets into complex issues of whether there is benefit retained. And there are tough arguments, raised by reparations skeptics, about whether there has already been adequate payment of those benefits. Have billions of dollars of welfare and entitlement payments paid that debt? This was addressed more fully in chapter 4. However, many reparations proponents are now turning to another argument, based on tort law: regardless of whether there is a benefit retained by white society, there is a continuing harm from the generations of slavery and Jim Crow. That argument looks to the harm, rather than the benefit.[39]

Looking to the continuing harm provides in many ways a stronger argument for reparations, but it loosens the connections between the payers and the wrongdoers. In fact, adopting a legislative model of reparations entails two moral problems: connecting the injured to beneficiaries and wrongdoers to payers. When thinking about the problems of the morality of reparations, we need to consider the fit between victims of the past crimes and people being benefited, as well as the fit between the past perpetrators and those being asked to pay now.

University of Chicago Law School professors Eric Posner and Adrian Vermuele have phrased the problem by using the term "ethical individualism."[40] For Posner and Vermuele, the problems with reparations relate to how close the people who are paying are to the people who committed the wrongs and how close the people who are receiving the reparations are to the people who were injured. The reparations schemes discussed by Posner and Vermuele, such as the payments to Japanese Americans interned during World War II, identified the victim group with specificity but allowed only a loose connection between the payers and the people who committed the harm. They found that problematic, for many people who had no culpability were asked to pay. Yet, that concern masks an important principle: The federal government frequently uses its power to repair the lives of people who have been harmed. Indeed, a significant amount of American social policy is built on precisely that premise. All of this is driving toward a single problem: how closely must payments be connected to the people harmed, and how closely must the payers be linked to the wrongdo-ers? Those relationships can be depicted graphically:

Victims	[Wrongdoers; Non-wrongdoers who benefit from wrongdoing; Non-wrongdoers who do not benefit from wrongdoing]
↓	↓
Beneficiaries	Payers of Reparations Plans

One of the most commonly invoked arguments against governmental payments for reparations for slavery is that the current taxpayers have no (or little) connection to the people who committed the harm. Adequately dealing with this argument requires one to assess whether the taxpayers *are* innocent. Surely, they had no blame for slavery, but did they benefit from slavery or Jim Crow? In this world, harm often occurs without someone else getting a benefit. Antireparationists may be correct, therefore, that the taxpayers will be paying an amount that is larger than any benefit they may have received.

Computing the value of transfer payments requires substantial attention. Here one might begin with several alternative formulas, roughly in ascending order of expense:

1. Value of slaves' services still retained
2. Money needed to bring African American poverty rate to the non-Hispanic white poverty rate
3. Difference in per capita wealth of African Americans and non-Hispanic white Americans
4. Amount needed to bring African American educational performance, health care, and wealth to that of non-Hispanic whites[41]

Selection among the competing formulas depends on what it is that one seeks to repair. If the reparations theory is based only on unjust enrichment, then the right formula is quite modest. Reparations should be only the amount of wealth that is still retained, as offset by benefits that have been conferred on slaves' descendants. If, however, one uses a tort theory of past harm, then the damage formula is the harm to the slaves themselves. If the theory is yet broader, that there is a tort of slavery that recognizes the harm to the slaves' descendants, the damages formula will need to take account of the harm as it continues for generations. It is this last formula that is most popular among reparations proponents. They conclude that slavery created generations of victims and that reparations should take account of that multigenerational harm. They argue that the failure to pay slaves for their work, coupled with the violence slaves suffered and the restrictions on their education and marriage, has led to continuing damage.[42] As Randall Robinson has stated, slavery is a crime that continues across the decades, because it leaves generations of victims in its wake:

> Like slavery, other human rights crimes have resulted in the loss of millions of lives. But only slavery, with its sadistic patience, asphyxiated memory, and smothered cultures, has hulled empty a whole race of people with inter-generational efficiency. Every artifact of the victims' past cultures, every custom, every ritual, every god, every language, every trace element of a people's whole hereditary identity, wrenched from them and ground into a sharp choking dust. It is a human rights crime without parallel in the modern world. For it produces victims *ad infinitum*, long after the active state of the crime has ended.[43]

If we adopt the view that slavery is a continuing tort, if the victims are considered to be people other than the generation of people actually enslaved, then the damage formula will need to include some calculation of harm to the present generation. Thus, the last formula will be appropriate. And it becomes more complex because we have to compute the current harm and what it will take to repair that harm.

So intergenerational reparations claims face several key problems. Those who committed the harm are no longer able to pay. Payment will have to come from their successors (the taxpayers). Those successors may not be successors to benefits extracted from the slaves or blacks during the period of Jim Crow. Quite simply, whatever benefit was conferred may no longer exist. Most frequently, great historic tragedies may not have left much in the way of benefit. But the harm may continue for generations.

In the case of slavery reparations, there are two calculations to make. First, to what extent are the benefits retained from the great wealth that slaves created for slave owners, by those who purchased and consumed the produce of slavery (such as cotton)? Second, to what extent are there still harms traceable to the institution of slavery? Those two calculations are akin to calculations of unjust enrichment and to a typical tort case: benefit retained by defendant and harm imposed on plaintiff.

In the rarer cases where a benefit is retained (even after there is an offset for benefits conferred on claimants), it is easier to see the moral claim on subsequent generations. However, even in cases of continued harm, there is a solid precedent for compensation, for many receive compensation in similar circumstances. No one, for instance, believes that the U.S. government was responsible for the terrorist attacks of 9/11. However, all U.S. taxpayers contributed to a generous compensation program[44] to victims and their families that was designed to compensate them for their lost income. The 9/11 Victims Compensation Fund led to requests by other victims of mass violence (like the 1995 Oklahoma City bombing) for compensation.[45]

When we are talking about even a modest reparations program, we will want to determine with some precision the amount of harm that continues, as well as the benefits that have been conferred.[46] Thinking about moral culpability leads us to two avenues. First, are there benefits that have been retained, which in justice belong to an oppressed group? Second, is there a connection between past injustice and current inequality? That is, has past harm descended to a group today? And is that harm in any way the "responsibility" of the community? In short, should the community seek to repair whatever harm exists to this day? When we think about the first basis for reparations—continued retention of a benefit—we are faced with difficult questions of tracing out the benefit, as well as complex issues of offset.[47] This is a hugely controversial assessment, one fraught with moral questions. Against a claim, for instance, by a descendant of someone who performed slave labor for Brown University, one must ask, what benefits has the university retained? There are likely to be few benefits still held by the university. The problem is more complex when one considers claims against a larger entity, such as the U.S. federal government. Then we may need to take into consideration the government's payments, as well as the benefits retained. Such is a common argument of reparations skeptics. We need to reexamine the bases for reparations. As long as people are talking in terms of unjust enrichment, a solely backward-looking remedy may seem appropriate.

The tort theory that computes the amount of reparations based on harm will result in a higher recovery, and it will compensate for harm more completely than will an unjust enrichment model. Therefore, it is more popular among reparations proponents. It is easier to see continued harm than continued retention of benefit. The evils of slavery— destruction of families, of hope, of desire for education, of humanity— continue across generations.

Moreover, because reparations rely on legislative grants, proponents ask us to think in legislative terms, using a public welfare perspective.[48] That perspective focuses on harm, not the substantially more limited benefits that are retained. That is, proponents ask that we think about reparations as part of a social welfare program. As Yale Law School Professor George Priest has stated, "Welfare is provided by the government to those individuals who have suffered loss—or who are in economic positions that resemble the suffering of a loss—but who have no claim in tort law against another person because of their position, and who have not adequately protected themselves through savings or private insurance."[49] Professor Priest concludes that "the internal logic of our public welfare systems is not compensation; it is basic need."[50] When the idea of reparations is reconceptualized in that way—as part of a system of justice that focuses on need as well as past injury—then it is consistent with generations of legislation. When viewed as a program that is both corrective (designed to repair past damage) and distributive (designed to provide a fair distribution of benefits), slave reparations look like other programs we see in legislatures. Much of the difficulty comes in determining the amount and identifying the beneficiaries.

Designing Reparations: Toward a Reparations Model

We can now turn to trying to figure out what factors a legislature might consider in designing a reparations plan. Who would be beneficiaries? What would they receive? The task here is to expand the reparations dialogue. The analysis must begin with a calculation of the magnitude of the harm. Then we need to figure who the appropriate beneficiaries and payers are. The moral structure of reparations claims may be diagrammed in this way:

Claimants, who are   *versus*   Payers, who have
entitled because they   responsibility because they
1. are the immediate   1. committed harm;
   victims of injustice; or   2. benefited from harm; or
2. are injured in an   3. are successors to
   identifiable and   harm-doers
   significant way

We must deal with claimants who have not suffered, as well as payers who are innocent because they have not committed a wrong or benefited from past wrongdoing. Sometimes payers may be only successors to harm. And in those cases, the claim on their checkbooks is weakened, even if not entirely eliminated. They take as successors to those earlier communities. Those members of a community may be liable for the community's debts, just as they are entitled to its benefits. Because of the loosening of connections between payers and wrongdoers, which this chapter contemplates, we must have other factors to rank-order the competing claims on limited public resources. Because those reparations claims must be judged against other claims to limited resources, such a calculus should include considerations of:

1. Magnitude of connections between victims and claimants and bad actors and payers
2. Need of claimant (magnitude of current injustice)
3. Ability to resolve claims in other ways

We could diagram this another way, as the strength of claims against payers based on the connection between wrongdoer and payer, against the connection between the people harmed and the beneficiary of reparations. As the connections on either axis weaken, the case for reparations becomes weaker (figure 6.1).

From there, let me suggest five issues to ponder when we consider reparations:

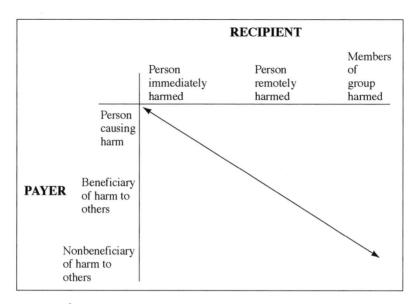

FIGURE 6.1
Diagramming Connections of Injured and Beneficiaries against Wrongdoers and Payers

1. Is the harm is so great that repair cannot be done by individuals?
2. Do the benefits that had been extracted from the group now seeking reparations (as well as the reparations now sought) go to the entire society (or to large segments of it)? For example, how much did the United States benefit from the labor extracted from slaves?
3. Will the reparations go to those with the greatest need and to places where the most repair can be effected?
4. Was the injustice perpetrated against groups? Was the injustice imposed by governmental action or neglect, which is having an identifiable impact on people currently?
5. Are there programs that repair the damage in ways that are meaningful and related to the harm that has been suffered?

As we debate legislative reparations, we should be ready to demand to see that the government's limited resources are being spent wisely. Those factors will help assure that goal.

The Constitutionality of Legislative Reparations

In addition to the question of morality and the related question of when we should use the government's extraordinary power to improve the lives of people who have been injured, there is the question of what kinds of reparations might be permitted by the Constitution. One might expect that Congress clearly has the power to provide reparations for slavery, given that the Thirteenth and Fourteenth Amendments to the Constitution were aimed at abolishing slavery and ensuring political rights for African Americans.[51] However, now that we are more than 140 years removed from slavery, it is not so clear that Congress has the power to enact race-based remedies for slavery. When Congress acts on the basis of racial group identity, it raises equal protection questions similar to those that courts face when there are requests for group relief when only some members of the group can demonstrate harm.

A critical initial question is whether a program of reparations for slavery would be subject to equal protection scrutiny as a race-based program. There is some possibility that a reparations program might not be subject to heightened scrutiny because it is tailored to people who are descended from slaves—and such a program is not race-based. Such an argument draws upon the Supreme Court's analysis in *Geduldig v. Aiello*, which upheld California's exclusion of pregnant women from coverage under its state disability insurance program against a charge that it discriminated against women.[52] The Supreme Court concluded that the discrimination was not against women: "California does not discriminate with respect to the persons or groups which are eligible for disability insurance protection under the program."[53] The fact that only women can be pregnant was not important to the Supreme Court, because California did not exclude people based on gender.[54] Using *Geduldig* to uphold reparations to descendants of slaves—all of whom are at least part African American or Native American—will be a tough sell. *Geduldig* has been heavily criticized for what David Cruz recently called "formalism run rampant."[55] Moreover, *Geduldig* involved a claim that exclusion of people with special characteristics is not an equal protection violation against those people excluded. It will be a harder sell to demonstrate that conferring special status on a large segment of the population (descendants of slaves)—which has a high correlation with race—is permissible.

Further light comes from the Civil Liberties Act of 1988, which provided compensation to Japanese Americans interned during World War II. Arthur Jacobs, an American of German ancestry who was interned during the war, challenged the act as a violation of equal protection because it did not provide him with compensation. Writing before the Supreme Court had imposed strict scrutiny on Congressional race-based set-asides, the District of Columbia Circuit Court gave great weight to Congress' conclusion that Japanese Americans were interned because of racial prejudice. There was no similar evidence that German and Italian Americans had been interned for similar reasons.[56] Therefore, the court concluded that Congress' decision to compensate Japanese Americans but not German Americans was "substantially related (as well as narrowly tailored) to the important (and compelling) governmental interest of compensating those who were interned during World War II because of racial prejudice."[57]

A reasonable interpretation of the equal protection clause—which looked to the likely effect of reparations—would almost certainly conclude that reparations would be a race-based program.[58] Still, it is worth considering the possibility that reparations for slavery would be viewed as a nonracial program.[59]

Assuming—as I suspect is likely—that reparations for slavery would be considered a race-based program, there are two other issues to address: first, the standard for judging the government's race-based action (and the issue of whether that standard applies to reparations for slavery); second, whether Congress can expand its power under Section Five of the Fourteenth Amendment (or under the Thirteenth Amendment). The U.S. Supreme Court has established that Congress may take race-based action only when it serves a compelling governmental interest and when it is narrowly tailored to further that interest.[60] The Supreme Court requires any racial classification—which is presumably what reparations would be—to meet "strict scrutiny."[61] The question then becomes, of course, what satisfies strict scrutiny?

To satisfy strict scrutiny—which the Supreme Court has emphasized is strict in theory, though not fatal in fact[62]—Congress would need to show that the program meets a compelling governmental interest and that it is narrowly tailored. To show that the program is compelling probably requires some important governmental interest—such as repairing past discrimination. As the Supreme Court has repeatedly recognized, governmental bodies may take action to respond to past discrimination.[63] The problem is defining "compelling governmental interest" and deciding what kind of evidence would show the pattern of discrimination in the past.

To show that the program is narrowly tailored requires showing that the program is aimed at remedying discrimination against African Americans in the past in the specific location and of the specific type being remedied. The *Croson* court, which struck down a program that set aside 30% of construction contracts from the city of Richmond, Virginia, for minority-owned business, identified several types of evidence that would support a limited race-based affirmative action program: systematic exclusion from the construction industry and a significant statistical disparity between the minority contractors qualified to receive contracts and those who receive them.[64] The latter test sets a high standard and suggests that the court wants a close connection between the past discrimination and the remedy being sought. Many people might have been excluded (or discouraged) long before they became contractors and were, therefore, eligible to be counted in the pool of potential bidders. Yet, the court seems unwilling—or at least reluctant—to look further out.[65] That is part of their focus on "narrowly tailoring" between the remedy and the past discrimination.

This narrow tailoring is a central point of conflict between reparations supporters and opponents. For many reparations supporters, the connection between past discrimination and present harm is easily discernible.[66] Many supporters point to evidence of discrimination in the disparate economic status of African Americans and whites.[67] Then they use group identity as a proxy for status as victim of past discrimination. However, the Supreme Court demands substantially greater evidence of discrimination by the particular entity that is taking race-based action—and of discrimination against those who are now being given preference.[68] It is a question of how one views evidence—and the amount and type of evidence that is necessary to conclude that some remedial action is permissible.

It is particularly difficult to decipher the meaning of Supreme Court precedent in that area, because the Supreme Court has said that general societal discrimination is an insufficient basis for race-based claims.[69] However, meaningful reparations programs are aimed at precisely the problem of societywide racial crimes. Here reparations advocates need to link as closely as possible the chosen remedies with specific instances of past racial crime or discrimination. Reparations advocates do not need to show that the people receiving benefits now are the exact people discriminated against—or even that they are related to the people who were discriminated against. However, it appears from *Croson* that there must be a showing of specific discrimination by the entity responsible for making the reparations now or people within its jurisdiction, anyway.[70] In deciding whether a program is narrowly tailored, the Supreme Court has also considered a program's duration and whether the same goal might be accomplished through non-race-based means in assessing whether it is narrowly tailored.[71] In short, there has to be more than a "generalized assertion that there has been past discrimination in an entire industry," for such a statement "provides no guidance for a legislative body to determine the precise scope of the injury it seeks to remedy."[72] Or, as Justice O'Connor concluded in *Croson*, we need proper findings "to define both the scope of the injury and the extent of the remedy necessary to cure its effects."[73]

To evaluate more fully the constitutionality of reparations, one would need to begin focusing on specific plans. Take, for example, Robert Westley's proposal of a federally funded trust for ten years, to be administered by trustees elected by African Americans, with the general directions to fund institution-building programs.[74] There the limited-duration program is designed to repair the discrimination and racial crimes that have constrained the ability of the African American community to fund adequate schools, financial institutions, and health care facilities. It seems unlikely that there would have to be a showing that each institution funded by the trust was necessary to remedy past discrimination in the location where it was located, for one suspects that the trustees would already have been required to show that the institutions served a significant need in the community before they were allowed to finance it. But what about the racial limitation on the people who elect the trustees? Is that narrowly tailored? The issues quickly become complex and warrant substantially more attention (and thought) than I have devoted to them.

It is much harder to see how Lee Harris's proposed political state for African Americans could pass strict scrutiny.[75] If the state were open to all African Americans (and not others), then it would be hard to see the compelling governmental interest, at least as that is currently understood. Segregation seems to have made little headway in recent years as a governmental goal, although Harris might argue that political autonomy—using an analogy to Native American sovereignty—meets important interests of those who want to migrate to the separate state. Moreover, it is difficult to see how the separate state goal—even if it serves a compelling governmental purpose—is narrowly tailored. How does the "separate state" serve to remedy past discrimination? When does the remedy end?

Vincene Verdun's proposal poses a different—but significant—set of problems. Verdun finds that "Society, through all of its consumers, producers, governments, laws, courts, and economic institutions, perpetrated and supported the institution of slavery." As a result, "all of society must pay."[76] Verdun recognizes that under mainstream approaches of linking victims to harm, "the difficulty of matching the injured party with the wrongdoer and limiting the responsibility of each wrongdoer to the scope of the wrong would be monumental."[77] One of Verdun's moderate proposals for loss of educational opportunity—what she believes fits within the "dominant perspective"—is to "distribute the compensation for all students who could have entered professions, calculated by comparative ratios with a white control group, to all African Americans who were undereducated."[78] That formula, as discussed previously, redistributes property into equal shares. It is an example of racial balancing. Without passing judgment on the appropriateness of such a proposal right now, one can observe that it is one of the problems with the Richmond ordinance invalidated in *Croson*.[79]

Take yet another commonly discussed proposal: cash payments to African Americans. Payments are arguably directed to the very problem being remedied: 250 years of uncompensated labor and another 100 of grossly undercompensated labor. To the extent that they are traced to the descendants of people whose labor was stolen or (in the era after slavery) who were underpaid, they may be narrowly tailored.[80] However, when there is no linking of payments to specific victims—and there will obviously be enormous problems in making those links—then the payments appear much more like a remedy for general societal discrimination, which is sort of where this whole debate began![81]

To stand a reasonably strong chance of survival, reparations ought to link specific discrimination by governmental entities and private actors in the location where reparations will be spent. Those findings should demonstrate the precise constitutional and statutory violations (or what would now be statutory violations if the events occurred before the contemporary Civil Rights acts) and demonstrate the current impact they are having. That linking is critical, although the Supreme Court has cast doubt on whether it will accept multistep arguments that past discrimination has limited current opportunities.[82] There should be specific remedial goals, so that the remedies have a logical, definite stopping point. There also has to be consideration of whether the goals of reparations might be accomplished through some basis other than race.[83] Are there community-building plans aimed at low-income communities, for example, that might increase educational and economic opportunities for victims of racial crimes — and others, too? This is an exceedingly complex issue, one that deserves substantial attention.

There is an additional consideration here: Congress' power under Section Five of the Fourteenth Amendment to define and repair Constitutional problems. It is possible, though unlikely, that Congress' Section Five powers permit it to legislate in a race-conscious fashion even if there is not an existing Constitutional violation. Congress might still have the power to make extensive findings, determine the scope of the problem, and then take limited race-conscious action. A series of recent cases in the Supreme Court, however, call into question Congress' Section Five power in the context of questions regarding the behavior that Congress can prohibit.[84] As the Supreme Court has recently stated, Congress has only remedial power under Section Five. It cannot expand the scope of Fourteenth Amendment rights.[85] Congress' power is limited to remedial purposes, and in those instances, there has to be a "congruence between the means used and the ends to be achieved."[86] In determining Congress' remedial power under Section Five, the court also looks to whether the means are proportional to the remedial objective.[87] In *City of Bourne v. Flores*, for instance, the Supreme Court rejected the argument that the Religious Freedom Restoration Act (RFRA), which gave a federal cause of action to people whose religious practices were burdened by state action and required the application of the test announced in *Wisconsin v. Yoder*[88] and *Sherbert v. Verner*[89] that government must establish a compelling interest to burden those practices, was a proper exercise of Congress' Section Five power.[90] The Court struck down RFRA because it was not congruent with any currently existing Constitutional violations. There was no evidence of "modern instances of generally applicable laws passed because of religious bigotry."[91] Hence, the attempted alteration of the legal standard for burdening the free exercise of religion was not remedial—and, therefore, was beyond Congress' power.[92]

What appears critical is a showing of currently existing Constitutional problems and a proportional response by Congress.[93] One might compare reparations proposals with the Voting Rights Act of 1965, for instance. The act, which was authorized under Section Two of the Fifteenth Amendment—an analogous provision to Section Five of the Fourteenth Amendment—was upheld in *Katzenbach v. Morgan*.[94] The act included race-conscious remedies, such as taking race into consideration in drawing districts. The Supreme Court upheld the limited remedies, because (at least as it was explained by the Supreme Court in 2001 in *Garrett v. University of Alabama*) there had been a marked pattern of unconstitutional action contemporaneous with the act.[95] Those principles make Section Five an unlikely candidate in supporting reparations for slavery.

Representative Conyers's reparations study commission could be critical in making findings of the scope and effect of past racial crimes that will meet the standard for Congressional action. In the process of studying slavery and its legacy, it can help to make the case for race-based action: how have past racial crimes and discrimination led to current inequalities? What goals can be set, so that a narrowly tailored program might remedy them? That leads naturally to another question, which the Supreme Court does not require be answered but which is indispensable for effective reparations: What programs are best calculated to lead to equality and to reconciliation?

There are yet other considerations in legislative reparations, such as which claims have the best case for repair. Given society's limited resources, it is impossible to come anywhere near to repairing for all past harms. Reparations writers have most frequently focused on the case for reparations in a particular instance—such as the case for reparations for slavery or particular instances of Jim Crow era violence.[96] Yet, they are beginning to address these concerns of justice across cases and payments by groups, by trying to make some assessment of how meritorious particular claims may be in relation to each other. How can we rank the claims and arrive at the most amount of repair? At the fairest amount of repair?

PART IV

Possibilities for the Future

7

Reparations Future, Realistic Reparations, and Models of Reparations

American democracy is a most dramatic form of social organization, and in that drama each of us enacts his role by asserting his own and his group's values and traditions against those of his fellow citizens. Indeed, a battle-royal conflict of interests appears to be basic to our conception of freedom, and the drama of democracy proceeds through a warfare of words and symbolic actions by which we seek to advance our private interests while resolving our political differences. Since the Civil War this form of symbolic action has served as a moral substitute for armed warfare, and we have managed to restrain ourselves to a debate which we carry on in the not always justified faith that the outcome will serve the larger interests of democracy. Unfortunately, this doesn't always work out, and when it doesn't, the winners of a given contention are likely to concern themselves with only the fruits of victory, while leaving it to the losers to grapple with the issues that are left unresolved.

Ralph Ellison, author of *Invisible Man*[1]

REPARATIONS TALK has, quite simply, advanced to the point where it needs concrete proposals. Reparations proponents know that they must gain public support for the movement to advance. And to do that, there must be concrete proposals, so that voters and legislators can understand what is at stake.[2] Once we have a set of concrete proposals, we can begin to contemplate which proposals best fit various goals, such as repairing past harm, building something positive for the future, and deciding which past tragedies have the best claim on limited public finances.

This epilogue explores in general terms four models of reparations. The models address a spectrum of options, from a limited truth commission and Civil Rights statutes, to more ambitious and costly community-based programs, to the highly controversial payments to individuals. They provide a sense of what the possibilities are and how various plans might address the goals of the reparations movement. Skeptics can use the plans to identify the moral problems with reparations.

Assessing the Goals of Reparations

To set the stage for discussion of reparations plans, we might highlight some of the key goals and conflicts of reparations. Often a primary goal of reparations is correcting past injustice. That correction can take many forms, ranging from an effort to correct the historical record and the public's understanding of past events, to compensation for past wrongs.

Proponents, thus, frequently speak about putting the current generation of victim-group members into the position they would have been in, absent the past injustice. That calculus involves computation of how a particular group would be situated, with only a limited regard to how other groups are situated. Occasionally, we are able to identify a specific group that has benefited from past injustice and ask them to give back that benefit. That is the case with people who have a specific property taken from victims, such as art stolen during the Holocaust or bank deposits never returned to Holocaust victims. However, in most instances, the tragedy of past crimes is that it is difficult or impossible to identify anyone who retains a benefit. That is, racial crimes often produce damage far exceeding any benefit that can be identified. For example, returning a group of riot victims to their rightful position involves compensating them for losses during the riot. Yet, although the riot victims suffered a loss, it is not so easy to say that someone else realized much of a gain. At an abstract level, the rioters may have gained psychologically by establishing their power over riot victims. But after a generation, even that amorphous psychological gain is likely gone. We are faced, then, with a claim by a group of victims against an amorphous group of taxpayers.

So as reparations proponents advocate correction of past injustice, the calculations must take account of imposing unfair burdens on those asked to pay reparations.[3] Reparations are not simply a question of whether to repair past damage but whether to repair past damage using the money of somewhat (or perhaps very) innocent people. We need, then, to take into account the culpability of those asked to pay. We must ask to what extent the current payers are responsible for decisions that led to injustice. To what extent are they the successors of those who were responsible? To what extent have the current payers retained some benefit of past racial crimes?

Reparations claims must also face tough questions about how the current claimants compare with others who have legitimate claims, for we must worry about repairing damage to many groups and we must, therefore, have some sense of how each victim group is situated in comparison with others. Who has the best claim on limited resources? By correcting one injustice, do we leave other, perhaps even more deserving groups, unremedied? A closely related question is how much justice can be done in any particular case and at what cost. In this cost-benefit analysis world in which we live, it is important to at least consider the amount of benefit (justice or redemption, depending on how you look at it) that can be purchased with any particular reparations plan.[4]

So let us now turn to specific reparations plans to see how likely they are to accomplish the goals we ask of reparations. This epilogue addresses four plans, in roughly ascending order of controversy, running from a truth commission through direct payments to individuals. See which ones, if any, you like—and how much you think they will accomplish.

Reparations Plans

With those concerns of correction of past injustice and fairness to those asked to contribute to the correction, we can now turn to a general look at four plans for reparations for slavery and Jim Crow crimes. The first plan is quite modest; it involves truth commissions and apologies. It is inexpensive, and its low costs are spread across a wide group. The second looks to move beyond apologies: It involves Civil Rights legislation that gives additional rights of action to victims of race discrimination. The third is substantially more controversial: community-based reparations payments for slavery. The final plan involves direct cash payments to individuals.

The Virtues and Limitations of a Truth Commission and Apologies

A modest form of reparations that has been employed in various contexts for decades is the truth commission. Often apologies follow such commissions. "Apologetic justice" has gained substantial followers, perhaps in large part because of the limited expense.[5] At the same time, by recognizing that a person or group has been harmed, it thus offers something of a halfway point (or, depending on where you stand, perhaps a quarter-way point).

Truth commissions offer a way of revisiting tragedies and apportioning guilt and innocence. They rely on the power of accurate histories to remake our understanding of events. But there are many people who do not want an accurate—whatever that means—understanding of past injustice. They may not accept a story that rejects their viewpoint. There is very little that one can do to require someone to accept a truth commission's findings. Hence, the value has to come from two key areas: first, the meaning that the truth commission has to the victim group and, second, the credibility the truth commission has for those whom it charges with culpability.

Most frequently, truth commissions are effective when they are linked with credible criminal punishment (or the offer of release from the threat of punishment). Hence, in South Africa, it was possible to obtain some semblance of truth by allowing those who testified to escape the threat of criminal punishment. In other instances, it is impossible to allow the offenders to take immunity baths—because they are no longer alive, because there is no credible threat of punishment, or because there is no desire to release criminals from liability. But even in the dark days of Jim Crow segregation, there were some "truth commissions." A Congressional investigation in the aftermath of the East St. Louis Riot of 1917 proved remarkably (for the time) insightful.[6] Then, in the aftermath of Chicago's 1919 riot, a blue ribbon committee of experts wrote a sociological study, *The Negro in Chicago*.[7]

Truth commissions offer an alternative history. That can be helpful in two ways. First, it validates a victim group's own identity as victims. Second, it offers members of the victimizer group insight into their own crimes. That insight offers the possibility of remaking the victimizers' actions—and those of the community more generally—if they have the wisdom and courage to act on that new knowledge. They also offer a form that can be provided with relatively little cost, and they can be produced by highly motivated individuals. It is a form of acknowledgment and remembrance that private individuals have engaged in since time out of mind, for often monuments are erected by private groups.[8] At other times, individual scholars have taken action to remember past racial crimes.[9]

Unfortunately, we often fail to act on that new knowledge, but there is the possibility that we could. One important avenue of further reparations research is how knowledge about historical injustice might influence judicial behavior.[10] That would link one of the richest areas of historical scholarship (how ideas influence behavior) with the goals of reparations.

There is also the opportunity for much more modest truth commissions. Individual companies, schools, and communities can undertake truth commissions. Many Southern colleges and universities have histories that include discrimination in the era of Jim Crow; some also benefited from the use of slave labor or had faculty who taught proslavery thought. Universities are prime locations for undertaking examination of past wrongdoing, for they are places where students, faculty, and staff are often concerned with knowing about their history and their community. Those groups are perfectly positioned to study their own institutions, and there is much to investigate. At the University of Alabama, for instance, an investigation of histories of the university that were readily available in the library disclosed that slaves built buildings around the campus and that the faculty were important proslavery advocates. More research in the university's archives disclosed that the faculty beat slaves when they misbehaved and that some of the slaves owned by Professor F. A. P. Barnard were (according to the diary of one of his campus rivals) visited as prostitutes by students.[11] Barnard was, after the Civil War, president of Columbia University, and Barnard College, the prestigious women's college in New York City, is named after him.

Those kinds of local studies, which led to an apology by the University of Alabama's faculty senate, could easily be replicated at schools throughout the South. To take just a few well-known examples, William and Mary's president in the 1840s, Thomas Roderick Dew, was one of the most important pro-slavery advocates in the country.[12] Two other leading pro-slavery theorists, Albert Taylor Bledsoe and George Frederick Holmes, taught at nearby University of Virginia. President William R. Smith of Randolph-Macon College in Ashland, Virginia, wrote one of the most popular college textbooks on slavery. President R. H. Rivers of Alabama Wesleyan College (now the University of North Alabama) included a segment on pro-slavery thought in his moral philosophy treatise. The Citadel, the famous Charleston, South Carolina, military school, was started to help police Charleston's slaves. How many slaves, one wonders, worked on the campuses of the Universities of Arkansas, Georgia, Mississippi, North Carolina, South Carolina, and Virginia? What was the curriculum like at Mississippi College, Howard College (now Samford University), Southern University (now Birmingham Southern College), Randolph-Macon College, Transylvania University, Washington College (now Washington and Lee University), the Virginia Military Institute, and Emory & Henry College? There is much work that can be done to investigate what universities did during the era of Jim Crow, who was excluded, and what the faculty taught about race in sociology, history, and psychology classes. Those local studies offer much promise and also the opportunity for individuals interested in the reparations movement to take concrete action.

Civil Rights Legislation as Reparations

As the previous section illustrates, sometimes reparations can come in the form of additional legal rights, which permit victims of racial crimes to use the legal system to pursue payments privately. Civil rights legislation such as the Anti–Ku Klux Klan Act of 1871,[13] the Civil Rights Act of 1964,[14] and the Voting Rights Act of 1965[15] are forms of reparations. Many acknowledge them as forms of reparations.[16] Other forms of reparations legislation are not so well known. Many states passed legislation that allowed mob victims to sue municipalities where mob violence occurred, regardless of the municipalities' fault. That legislation began in the antebellum era and continued into the early twentieth century.[17] Such legislation derives in part from the understanding that the entire community has a duty (even if rarely a legally enforceable duty) to aid other members of the community. That obligation is greater when part of the community is harmed through the government's gross failure to protect.

Such legislation has some obvious benefits: It has symbolic value and, yet, places the burden on the victims to make a case for payment. Thus, it expands rights and gives more opportunity to vindicate rights; it also assures that rights are well proven through court proceedings. It also is relatively low cost, and it ensures that those who are most directly harmed have recourse against those who harmed them (or permitted the harm to take place).

Community-Building Legislation as Reparations

As we move from the general, symbolic, and relatively inexpensive modes of reparations of truth commissions, apologies, and Civil Rights legislation, we arrive at legislation that provides for community-building programs, such as New Deal and Great Society legislation that provided assistance in community development.[18]

Such programs are probably the most popular among reparations advocates. For instance, Robert Westley speaks of a trust fund for community development.[19] Professor Charles Ogletree has recently elaborated on the idea of a trust fund:

My goal is to use the money in the same manner as the government does for veteran's benefits. This money should be available in a trust at a community level for those who have suffered the most. We will not solve these problems just by giving individuals a check. We can only solve these problems if reparations money, and substantial aspects of it, are used at the local level to address issues of health care, education, and housing.[20]

Some reparations plans aimed at entire communities will end up benefiting individuals. But in those cases, as in programs that target improving education and health care, programs are often aimed at the community in general. The beneficiaries are targeted on the basis of need. That is a problem in reparations, for those who receive the benefit may not be the people who have suffered the most. (We might, of course, define reparations on the basis of need.) Community-based reparations programs seem to be the most popular programs among reparations proponents.

The wish list of reparations proponents includes programs designed to foster educational, occupational, and health care opportunities. It is difficult to assign a price to those programs, and it is also difficult to match those programs to specific past harms. Nevertheless, one of the virtues of legislative reparations is that they can be accomplished without the close connection between demonstrated harm and benefit that lawsuits demand. That reduced connection between harm and benefit also reduces the connection between victim and victimizer. Legislatures must be aware—and satisfied—that they are granting reparations to people who are not as harmed as others who receive no compensation and that those who pay are not necessarily those who are most culpable. In essence, there are several problems with community-based reparations: The payers may not be culpable (or may not be the beneficiaries of past injustice), and the recipients may not be the most deserving.[21] However, community-based reparations promise to direct money toward programs that will help the needy. There are, as a result, many advantages of community-based reparations: They fit well with the equitable principle that the magnitude of harm determines the amount of relief.[22] They offer the hope of addressing need and of targeting expenditures where they are most needed. However, they pose the threat of weakening the links between wrongdoer and payer and between victim and recipient of reparations.

Individual Payments as Reparations

The most controversial form of reparations is direct payments to individuals. They are controversial, one supposes, because they deal so directly with redistributing wealth—and especially controversial in this instance because they deal with redistribution regardless of need. There are further serious questions regarding both payers and recipients. Are the people who receive the payments entitled to them by virtue of harm they have suffered? Are the people making those payments sufficiently culpable that they are liable for those payments, or have they received a benefit that they are now disgorging?

There are, however, strong reasons to support direct payments to individuals. If we believe, for example, that slaves were inadequately compensated for their work during slavery, then it makes sense to require those who received that benefit to disgorge it to the descendants of those who were undercompensated.[23] Slavery reparations claims do not always rest on unjust enrichment analogies, however. Direct payments might be justified on the basis of harm imposed on a claimant's ancestors.

It is difficult to find reparations proponents who seriously propose direct payments to individuals, so it is particularly hard to arrive at an estimate of what direct payments might cost. One might propose something like a payment by the U.S. government of $500,000 per enslaved person distributed to that person's descendants—the estimate one reparationist made of the present value of property taken.[24] A *New York Times* op-ed proposed a substantially more modest measure: the difference between the average for white and black wealth, which would be more like $35,000 per couple.[25] It is exceedingly difficult to obtain estimates of what the payments should be, however.[26] Some conservatives view such plans as a good idea, because they hold out the promise of ending discussion of race—a way of finally putting an end to discussions of past discrimination, by essentially paying off the claim.[27] And then there are other problems, which reparations skeptics often point to when they wish to make payments look foolish. They ask, who would get checks? Is someone who is descended from slaves and non-slaves entitled to only partial payments? We are unlikely to need to address any of those issues soon, because direct payments are such a remote possibility as to be unimaginable.

Selecting Reparations

Such, then, are the possible types of reparations: truth commissions, apologies, Civil Rights legislation, community-building programs, and individual payments. That is a wide range of options; it remains for politicians and voters to decide which of those reparations fit best with their goals. It may be that voters have very little interest in spending any money. That might suggest that little can be accomplished by way of repairing past harm. However, some inexpensive plans, involving truth commissions and apologies, might change the political atmosphere. Even those, however, have proven difficult to implement. Congressman Conyers's proposal of an investigation of reparations for slavery has never gone far, though local-level investigations—most notably, the Chicago City Council's requirement that companies that do business with the city disclose their relationship with slavery and California's investigation of insurance companies' complicity in slavery—have been successful. To the extent that there is support for doing something more expensive and meaningful than investigations, apologies, and Civil Rights statutes, there are two models: community-building programs, where the community that has been injured is rebuilt, and direct payments to individuals. The former has the virtue of targeting those most in need, and direct payments give individuals the power to decide how the payments will be used, an aspect that speaks to the American distaste for bureaucratic fiats.

Realistic Reparations

Where might there be some common ground? What if reparations proponents decide that they want reparations that are realistic? There might be a few ways to bridge the chasm between proponents and skeptics. Some of the elements that might allow us to reach a consensus include, first, a plan that quantifies the costs, for there is fear of the unknown. Second, there must be some promise of an end point. Third, there must be a consensus on the nature of the harm, how that harm is linked to past racial crimes, and how there is continuing benefit for others, if there is evidence of such benefit.

IN THE near term, look for increased focus on understanding the nature of the harms from slavery and Jim Crow. The reparations movement seems to be focusing now less on money and more on understanding history and its implications for the present. Reparations advocates have at least temporarily moved away from discussion of payment of money to individuals. In its place, they seek better understanding of the history of slavery and how the legacy of slavery and Jim Crow has left its stamp on the African American community. And maybe a focus on history is the appropriate step at this point. For if one views the legacy of slavery and Jim Crow as something that is not so bad—and if one views the history of the era of Reconstruction as one of African Americans and Yankee politicians taking advantage of a destroyed South—one is unlikely to have a favorable view of the Reconstruction amendments, or of the need to protect voting rights, or of the need for civil rights legislation, or of social welfare spending, to say nothing of reparations.

Perhaps what will emerge from this discussion are local, state, and national truth commissions and some apologies, followed by social welfare spending aimed at helping raise those people left furthest behind. And, perhaps, given the prevailing public opinion poll numbers, that social welfare spending will be aimed at providing opportunities and the bounties of our country for those who are left behind, regardless of race. One might predict that reparations will be the entry point for serious discussion of the causes of poverty and what to do about them. Maybe there will be the will to do something about poverty and perhaps that action will be aimed at everyone who is suffering, though programs may be particularly targeted at those with a legacy of slavery and Jim Crow.

WE SHOULD now look back again on some of the key questions that appeared in the introduction. Those questions are not susceptible of ready answers, but they do permit lots of discussion, and they also suggest areas that need further research:

1. How much has the legacy of slavery led to the current chasm between black and white wealth? How much have other fac-

tors affected that chasm? What is the effect of the legacy of slavery and Jim Crow crimes on the current opportunities of African Americans?

2. What is the amount of benefit that slave labor contributed to the growth of American economy and society? How much of that benefit is retained still? How much have legacies of slavery been forgotten, whipped out from historical memory?[28]

3. How much have the federal and state governments contributed to slavery and Jim Crow?

4. Should we compute what is owed by the wealth slaves created or by the harm that slavery imposed on slaves and their descendants?

5. How much of what is owed has been paid by welfare programs? By the North's expenditures during the Civil War?

There are yet other questions that bear on reparations and also need further research. Answers to these questions will help define where reparations will go next:

1. Should we suspend the statute of limitations for Jim Crow or even slavery lawsuits? Which cases present the most compelling cases for tolling?

2. How important is it to remember the history of slavery and Jim Crow—or any other historical periods? What are the advantages (and costs) of doing so—for blacks and whites?

We need to consider how closely we need to link evidence of past injustice with current victims, as well as evidence of past culpability with current payers. Then we can settle on the amount of redemption and justice that legislatures will purchase. We need to consider the costs as well as the benefits in choosing models of reparations, as we struggle to find a way, as novelist Ralph Ellison asked, for the future to overcome the past.[29]

The near future of reparations talk is likely to involve discussion of the moral case for repairing generations of violence, of slavery, and of the state-sponsored discrimination of Jim Crow. The moral case may very well be just, but it looks from this vantage to be hopeless politically. Reparations may prove to be yet another instance in which black

Americans will have to be content with the knowledge that they have contributed more than their share of blood to the development of America. Such, one suspects, is the history of slavery at universities, at any rate. The endowments filled with money made by the slave trade and by money made off slave labor have enriched generations of students and, through their education, many of the rest of us. Perhaps we will conclude that this is a typically American story, of people laboring for the community, so that people whose names they do not know will have a better life. And the end result of the talk, truth commissions, and apologies may be a wider public knowledge about the ways that blacks have contributed to our country.

The costs of a meaningful program of reparations—and racial justice—will be colossal, though so will the benefits. Much of our work now requires dealing not with overt racism (though some of it remains) but with the relics of centuries of state-sponsored racism. This is not the easy moral case of rooting out overt racism. It will not be accomplished by a single act of Congress or executive order. It is now a battle against apathy. It is important that we care for the 30% of black children who live in poverty and make sure that there are opportunities for advancement. Reparations, if carefully crafted, thus hold out the hope of accomplishing two important, elusive goals: correcting an injustice and building something more positive for the future. Maybe those goals are still attainable.

APPENDICES

Documents Related to Reparations

APPENDIX 1

Special Field Orders, No. 15 (1865)

I. The islands from Charleston, south, the abandoned rice fields along the rivers for thirty miles back from the sea, and the country bordering the St. Johns river, Florida, are reserved and set apart for the settlement of the negroes now made free by the acts of war and the proclamation of the President of the United States.

II. At Beaufort, Hilton Head, Savannah, Fernandina, St. Augustine and Jacksonville, the blacks may remain in their chosen or accustomed vocations—but on the islands, and in the settlements hereafter to be established, no white person whatever, unless military officers and soldiers detailed for duty, will be permitted to reside; and the sole and exclusive management of affairs will be left to the freed people themselves, subject only to the United States military authority and the acts of Congress. By the laws of war, and orders of the President of the United States, the negro is free and must be dealt with as such. He cannot be subjected to conscription or forced military service, save by the written orders of the highest military authority of the Department, under such regulations as the President or Congress may prescribe. Domestic servants, blacksmiths, carpenters and other mechanics, will be free to select their own work and residence, but the young and able-bodied negroes must be encouraged to enlist as soldiers in the service of the United States, to contribute their share towards maintaining their own freedom, and securing their rights as citizens of the United States.

Negroes so enlisted will be organized into companies, battalions and regiments, under the orders of the United States military authorities, and will be paid, fed and clothed according to law. The bounties paid on enlistment may, with the consent of the recruit, go to assist his family and settlement in procuring agricultural implements, seed, tools, boots, clothing, and other articles necessary for their livelihood.

III. Whenever three respectable negroes, heads of families, shall desire to settle on land, and shall have selected for that purpose an island or a locality clearly defined, within the limits above designated, the Inspector of Settlements and Plantations will himself, or by such subordinate officer as he may appoint, give them a license to settle such island or district, and afford them such assistance as he can to enable them to establish a peaceable agricultural settlement. The three parties named will subdivide the land, under the supervision of the Inspector, among themselves and such others as may choose to settle near them, so that each family shall have a plot of not more than (40) forty acres of tillable ground, and when it borders on some water channel, with not more than 800 feet water front, in the possession of which land the military authorities will afford them protection, until such time as they can protect themselves, or until Congress shall regulate their title. The Quartermaster may, on the requisition of the Inspector of Settlements and Plantations, place at the disposal of the Inspector, one or more of the captured steamers, to ply between the settlements and one or more of the commercial points heretofore named in orders, to afford the settlers the opportunity to supply their necessary wants, and to sell the products of their land and labor.

IV. Whenever a negro has enlisted in the military service of the United States, he may locate his family in any one of the settlements at pleasure, and acquire a homestead, and all other rights and privileges of a settler, as though present in person. In like manner, negroes may settle their families and engage on board the gunboats, or in fishing, or in the navigation of the inland waters, without losing any claim to land or other advantages derived from this system. But no one, unless an actual settler as above defined, or unless absent on Government service, will be entitled to claim any right to land or property in any settlement by virtue of these orders.

V. In order to carry out this system of settlement, a general officer will be detailed as Inspector of Settlements and Plantations, whose duty it shall be to visit the settlements, to regulate their police and general management, and who will furnish personally to each head of a family, subject to the approval of the President of the United States, a possessory title in writing, giving as near as possible the description of boundaries; and who shall adjust all claims or conflicts that may arise under the same, subject to the like approval, treating such titles altogether as possessory. The same general officer will also be charged with the enlistment and organization of the negro recruits, and protecting their interests while absent from their settlements; and will be governed by the rules and regulations prescribed by the War Department for such purposes.

VI. Brigadier General R. SAXTON is hereby appointed Inspector of Settlements and Plantations, and will at once enter on the performance of his duties. No change is intended or desired in the settlement now on Beaufort [Port Royal] Island, nor will any rights to property heretofore acquired be affected thereby.

BY ORDER OF MAJOR GENERAL W. T. SHERMAN:

Special Field Orders, No. 15, Headquarters Military Division of the Mississippi, 16 Jan. 1865, Orders & Circulars, ser. 44, Adjutant General's Office, Record Group 94, National Archives.

Published in *The Wartime Genesis of Free Labor: The Lower South*, pp. 338–40.

APPENDIX 2

A Bill (H.R. 29) Relative to Damages Done to Loyal Men, and for Other Purposes [Confiscation] (1867)

Whereas it is due to justice, as an example to future times, that some proper punishment should be inflicted on the people who constitute the "confederate States of America," both because they, declaring an unjust war against the United States for the purpose of destroying republican liberty and permanently establishing slavery, as well as for the cruel and barbarous manner in which they conducted said war, in violation of all the laws of civilized warfare, and also to compel them to make some compensation for the damages and expenditures caused by said war: Therefore,

Be it enacted by the Senate and House of Representatives of the United States of America in Congress assembled, That all the public lands belonging to the ten States that formed the government of the so-called "confederate States of America" shall be forfeited by said States and become forthwith vested in the United States.

SEC. 2. *And be it further enacted,* That the President shall forthwith proceed to cause the seizure of such of the property belonging to the belligerent enemy as is deemed forfeited by the act of July 17, A.D. 1862, and hold and appropriate the same as enemy's property, and to proceed to condemnation with that already seized.

SEC. 3. *And be it further enacted,* That in lieu of the proceeding to condemn the property thus seized as enemy's property, as is provided by the act of July 17, A.D. 1862, two commissions or more, as by him may be deemed necessary, shall be appointed by the President for each of the said "confederate States," to consist of three persons each, one of whom shall be an officer of the late or present Army, and two shall be civilians, neither of whom shall be citizens of the States for which he shall be appointed; and that the said commissions shall proceed to adjudicate and condemn the property aforesaid, under such forms and proceedings as shall be prescribed by the Attorney General of the United States, whereupon the title to said property shall become vested in the United States.

SEC. 4. *And be it further enacted*, That out of the lands thus seized and confiscated the slaves who have been liberated by the operations of the war and the amendment to the Constitution or otherwise, who resided in said "confederate States" on the 4th day of March, A.D. 1861, or since, shall have distributed to them as follows, namely; to each male person who is the head of a family, forty acres; to each adult male, whether the head of a family or not, forty acres; to each widow who is the head of a family, forty acres—be held by them in fee-simple, but to be inalienable for the next ten years after they become seized thereof. For the purpose of distributing and allotting said land the Secretary of War shall appoint as many commissions in each State as he shall deem necessary, to consist of three members each, two of whom at least shall not be citizens of the State for which he is appointed. Each of said commissioners shall receive a salary of $3,000 annually and all his necessary expenses. Each commission shall be allowed one clerk, whose salary shall be $2,000 per annum. The title to the homestead aforesaid shall be vested in trustees for the use of the liberated persons aforesaid. Trustees shall be appointed by the Secretary of War, and shall receive such salary as he shall direct, not exceeding $3,000 per annum. At the end of ten years the absolute title to said homesteads shall be conveyed to said owners or to the heirs of such as are then dead.

SEC. 5. *And be it further enacted*, That out of the balance of the property thus seized and confiscated there shall be raised, in the manner hereinafter provided, a sum equal to fifty dollars, for each homestead, to be applied by the trustees hereinafter mentioned toward the erection of buildings on the said homesteads for the use of said slaves; and the further sum of $500,000,000, which shall be appropriated as follows, to wit: $200,000,000 shall be invested in United States six per cent. Securities: and the interest thereof shall be semi-annually added to the pensions allowed by law to pensioners who have become so by reason of the late war: $300,000,000, or so much thereof as may be needed, shall be appropriated to pay damages done to loyal citizens by the civil or military operations of the government lately called the "confederate States of America."

SEC. 6. *And be it further enacted*, That in order that just discrimination may be made, the property of the no one shall be seized whose whole estate on the 4th day of March, A.D. 1865, was not worth more than $5,000, to be valued by the said commission, unless he shall have voluntarily become an officer or employé in the military or civil service of the "confederate States of America," or in the civil or military service of someone of said States, and in enforcing all confiscations the sum or value of $5,000 in real or personal property shall be left or assigned to the delinquent.

SEC. 7. *And be it further enacted*, That the commission shall put a just and impartial valuation on all the property thus seized and forfeited, and when such valuation shall be completed in the several States all the said commissioners shall meet in the city of Washington and assess the $300,000,000 aforesaid, as well as the allowances for homestead buildings, *pro rata*, on each of the properties or estates thus seized, and shall give notice of such assessment and apportionment by publication for sixty days in two daily newspapers in the capitals of each of the said "confederate States."

SEC. 8. *And be it further enacted*, That if the owners of said seized and forfeited estates shall, within ninety days after the first of said publications, pay into the Treasury of the United States the sum assessed on their estates respectively, all of their estates and lands not actually appropriated to the liberated slaves shall be released and restored to their owners.

SEC. 9. *And be it further enacted*, That all the land, estates and property, of whatever kind, which shall not be redeemed as aforesaid within ninety days, shall be sold and converted into money, in such time and manner as may be deemed by the said commissioners most advantageous to the United States: *Provided*, That no arable land shall be sold in larger tracts than five hundred acres: *And provided further*, That no longer credit shall be given than three years.

Congressional Globe, 40th Congress, 1st Session, 203 (March 19, 1867).

APPENDIX 3

Slavery Study Bill, H.R. 40, 106th Congress, 1st Session (1999)

To acknowledge the fundamental injustice, cruelty, brutality, and inhumanity of slavery in the United States and the 13 American colonies between 1619 and 1865 and to establish a commission to examine the institution of slavery, subsequently de jure and de facto racial and economic discrimination against African-Americans, and the impact of these forces on living African-Americans, to make recommendations to the Congress on appropriate remedies, and for other purposes.

IN THE HOUSE OF REPRESENTATIVES, JANUARY 6, 1999

Mr. CONYERS (for himself, Mr. FATTAH, Mr. HASTINGS of Florida, Mr. HILLIARD, Mr. JEFFERSON, Ms. EDDIE BERNICE JOHNSON of Texas, Mrs. MEEK of Florida, Mr. OWENS, Mr. RUSH, and Mr. TOWNS) introduced the following bill; which was referred to the Committee on the Judiciary

---

A BILL

To acknowledge the fundamental injustice, cruelty, brutality, and inhumanity of slavery in the United States and the 13 American colonies between 1619 and 1865 and to establish a commission to examine the institution of slavery, subsequently de jure and de facto racial and economic discrimination against African-Americans, and the impact of these forces on living African-Americans, to make recommendations to the Congress on appropriate remedies, and for other purposes.

Be it enacted by the Senate and House of Representatives of the United States of America in Congress assembled,

SECTION 1. SHORT TITLE.

This Act may be cited as the 'Commission to Study Reparation Proposals for African-Americans Act.'

SEC. 2. FINDINGS AND PURPOSE.

(a) FINDINGS- The Congress finds that—

    (1) approximately 4,000,000 Africans and their descendants were enslaved in the United States and the colonies that became the United States from 1619 to 1865;

    (2) the institution of slavery was constitutionally and statutorily sanctioned by the Government of the United States from 1789 through 1865;

    (3) the slavery that flourished in the United States constituted an immoral and inhumane deprivation of Africans' life, liberty, African citizenship rights, and cultural heritage, and denied them the fruits of their own labor; and

    (4) sufficient inquiry has not been made into the effects of the institution of slavery on living African-Americans and society in the United States.

(b) PURPOSE- The purpose of this Act is to establish a commission to—

    (1) examine the institution of slavery which existed from 1619 through 1865 within the United States and the colonies that became the United States, including the extent to which the Federal and State Governments constitutionally and statutorily supported the institution of slavery;

    (2) examine de jure and de facto discrimination against freed slaves and their descendants from the end of the Civil War to the present, including economic, political, and social discrimination;

    (3) examine the lingering negative effects of the institution of slavery and the discrimination described in paragraph (2) on living African-Americans and on society in the United States;

    (4) recommend appropriate ways to educate the American public of the Commission's findings;

    (5) recommend appropriate remedies in consideration of the Com-

mission's findings on the matters described in paragraphs (1) and (2); and

(6) submit to the Congress the results of such examination, together with such recommendations.

SEC. 3. ESTABLISHMENT AND DUTIES.

(a) ESTABLISHMENT- There is established the Commission to Study Reparation Proposals for African-Americans (hereinafter in this Act referred to as the 'Commission').

(b) DUTIES- The Commission shall perform the following duties:

(1) Examine the institution of slavery which existed within the United States and the colonies that became the United States from 1619 through 1865. The Commission's examination shall include an examination of—

(A) the capture and procurement of Africans;

(B) the transport of Africans to the United States and the colonies that became the United States for the purpose of enslavement, including their treatment during transport;

(C) the sale and acquisition of Africans as chattel property in interstate and intrastate commerce; and

(D) the treatment of African slaves in the colonies and the United States, including the deprivation of their freedom, exploitation of their labor, and destruction of their culture, language, religion, and families.

(2) Examine the extent to which the Federal and State governments of the United States supported the institution of slavery in constitutional and statutory provisions, including the extent to which such governments prevented, opposed, or restricted efforts of freed African slaves to repatriate to their home land.

(3) Examine Federal and State laws that discriminated against freed African slaves and their descendants during the period between the end of the Civil War and the present.

(4) Examine other forms of discrimination in the public and private sectors against freed African slaves and their descendants during the period between the end of the Civil War and the present.

(5) Examine the lingering negative effects of the institution of slavery and the matters described in paragraphs (1), (2), (3), and (4)

on living African-Americans and on society in the United States.

(6) Recommend appropriate ways to educate the American public of the Commission's findings.

(7) Recommend appropriate remedies in consideration of the Commission's findings on the matters described in paragraphs (1), (2), (3), and (4). In making such recommendations, the Commission shall address, among other issues, the following questions:

(A) Whether the Government of the United States should offer a formal apology on behalf of the people of the United States for the perpetration of gross human rights violations on African slaves and their descendants.

(B) Whether African-Americans still suffer from the lingering effects of the matters described in paragraphs (1), (2), (3), and (4).

(C) Whether, in consideration of the Commission's findings, any form of compensation to the descendants of African slaves is warranted.

(D) If the Commission finds that such compensation is warranted, what should be the amount of compensation, what form of compensation should be awarded, and who should be eligible for such compensation.

(c) REPORT TO CONGRESS- The Commission shall submit a written report of its findings and recommendations to the Congress not later than the date which is one year after the date of the first meeting of the Commission held pursuant to section 4(c).

SEC. 4. MEMBERSHIP.

(a) NUMBER AND APPOINTMENT-

(1) The Commission shall be composed of 7 members, who shall be appointed, within 90 days after the date of enactment of this Act, as follows:

(A) Three members shall be appointed by the President.

(B) Three members shall be appointed by the Speaker of the House of Representatives.

(C) One member shall be appointed by the President pro tempore of the Senate.

(2) All members of the Commission shall be persons who are espe-

cially qualified to serve on the Commission by virtue of their education, training, or experience, particularly in the field of African-American studies.

(b) TERMS- The term of office for members shall be for the life of the Commission. A vacancy in the Commission shall not affect the powers of the Commission, and shall be filled in the same manner in which the original appointment was made.

(c) FIRST MEETING- The President shall call the first meeting of the Commission within 120 days after the date of the enactment of this Act, or within 30 days after the date on which legislation is enacted making appropriations to carry out this Act, whichever date is later.

(d) QUORUM- Four members of the Commission shall constitute a quorum, but a lesser number may hold hearings.

(e) CHAIR AND VICE CHAIR- The Commission shall elect a Chair and Vice Chair from among its members. The term of office of each shall be for the life of the Commission.

(f) COMPENSATION-

(1) Except as provided in paragraph (2), each member of the Commission shall receive compensation at the daily equivalent of the annual rate of basic pay payable for GS-18 of the General Schedule under section 5332 of title 5, United States Code, for each day, including travel time, during which he or she is engaged in the actual performance of duties vested in the Commission.

(2) A member of the Commission who is a full-time officer or employee of the United States or a Member of Congress shall receive no additional pay, allowances, or benefits by reason of his or her service on the Commission.

(3) All members of the Commission shall be reimbursed for travel, subsistence, and other necessary expenses incurred by them in the performance of their duties to the extent authorized by chapter 57 of title 5, United States Code.

SEC. 5. POWERS OF THE COMMISSION.

(a) HEARINGS AND SESSIONS- The Commission may, for the purpose of carrying out the provisions of this Act, hold such hearings and sit and act at such times and at such places in the United States, and request the attendance and testimony of such witnesses and the production of such books, records, correspondence, memoranda, papers, and documents, as the Commission considers appropriate. The Commission may request the Attorney General to invoke the aid of an appropriate United States district court to require, by subpoena or otherwise, such attendance, testimony, or production.

(b) POWERS OF SUBCOMMITTEES AND MEMBERS- Any subcommittee or member of the Commission may, if authorized by the Commission, take any action which the Commission is authorized to take by this section.

(c) OBTAINING OFFICIAL DATA- The Commission may acquire directly from the head of any department, agency, or instrumentality of the executive branch of the Government, available information which the Commission considers useful in the discharge of its duties. All departments, agencies, and instrumentalities of the executive branch of the Government shall cooperate with the Commission with respect to such information and shall furnish all information requested by the Commission to the extent permitted by law.

SEC. 6. ADMINISTRATIVE PROVISIONS.

(a) STAFF- The Commission may, without regard to section 5311(b) of title 5, United States Code, appoint and fix the compensation of such personnel as the Commission considers appropriate.

(b) APPLICABILITY OF CERTAIN CIVIL SERVICE LAWS- The staff of the Commission may be appointed without regard to the provisions of title 5, United States Code, governing appointments in the competitive service, and without regard to the provisions of chapter 51 and subchapter III of chapter 53 of such title relating to classification and General Schedule pay rates, except that the compensation of any employee of the Commission may not exceed a rate equal to the annual rate of basic pay payable for GS-18 of the General Schedule under section 5332 of title 5, United States Code.

(c) EXPERTS AND CONSULTANTS- The Commission may procure the services of experts and consultants in accordance with the provisions of section 3109(b) of title 5, United States Code, but at rates for individuals not to exceed the daily equivalent of the highest rate payable under section 5332 of such title.

(d) ADMINISTRATIVE SUPPORT SERVICES- The Commission may enter into agreements with the Administrator of General Services for procurement of financial and administrative services necessary for the discharge of the duties of the Commission. Payment for such services shall be made by reimbursement from funds of the Commission in such amounts as may be agreed upon by the Chairman of the Commission and the Administrator.

(e) CONTRACTS- The Commission may—

(1) procure supplies, services, and property by contract in accordance with applicable laws and regulations and to the extent or in such amounts as are provided in appropriations Acts; and

(2) enter into contracts with departments, agencies, and instrumentalities of the Federal Government, State agencies, and private firms, institutions, and agencies, for the conduct of research or surveys, the preparation of reports, and other activities necessary for the discharge of the duties of the Commission, to the extent or in such amounts as are provided in appropriations Acts.

SEC. 7. TERMINATION.

The Commission shall terminate 90 days after the date on which the Commission submits its report to the Congress under section 3(c).

SEC. 8. AUTHORIZATION OF APPROPRIATIONS.

To carry out the provisions of this Act, there are authorized to be appropriated $8,000,000.

APPENDIX 4

California Slavery Era Insurance Registry (2000)

SECTION 1. The Legislature finds and declares all of the following:

(a) Insurance policies from the slavery era have been discovered in the archives of several insurance companies, documenting insurance coverage for slaveholders for damage to or death of their slaves, issued by a predecessor insurance firm. These documents provide the first evidence of ill-gotten profits from slavery, which profits in part capitalized insurers whose successors remain in existence today.

(b) Legislation has been introduced in Congress for the past 10 years demanding an inquiry into slavery and its continuing legacies.

(c) The Insurance Commissioner and the Department of Insurance are entitled to seek information from the files of insurers licensed and doing business in this state, including licensed California subsidiaries of international insurance corporations, regarding insurance policies issued to slaveholders by predecessor corporations. The people of California are entitled to significant historical information of this nature.

SEC. 2. Chapter 5 (commencing with Section 13810) is added to Division 3 of the Insurance Code, to read:

CHAPTER 5. SLAVERY ERA INSURANCE POLICIES

13810. The commissioner shall request and obtain information from insurers licensed and doing business in this state regarding any records of slaveholder insurance policies issued by any predecessor corporation during the slavery era.

13811. The commissioner shall obtain the names of any slaveholders or slaves described in those insurance records, and shall make the information available to the public and the Legislature.

13812. Each insurer licensed and doing business in this state shall research and report to the commissioner with respect to any records within the insurer's possession or knowledge relating to insurance policies issued to slaveholders that provided coverage for damage to or death of their slaves.

13813. Descendants of slaves, whose ancestors were defined as private property, dehumanized, divided from their families, forced to perform labor without appropriate compensation or benefits, and whose ancestors' owners were compensated for damages by insurers, are entitled to full disclosure.

APPENDIX 5

Chicago Slavery Era Insurance Disclosure Ordinance, 2-92-585 (2003)

This section shall be known and cited as the "Slavery Era Insurance Ordinance." The purpose of this section is to promote full and accurate disclosure to the public about any slavery policies sold by any companies (or their predecessors) who are doing business with the City.

Each contractor with whom the City enters into a contract, whether subject to competitive bid or not, must complete an affidavit verifying that the contractor has searched any and all records of the company or any predecessor company regarding records of slaveholder insurance policies during the slavery era. The names of any slaves or slaveholders described in those records must be disclosed in the affidavit. The chief procurement officer shall make the information available to the public and provide an annual report to the City Council.

Failure to comply with this section shall deem the contract voidable on behalf of the City.

APPENDIX 6

President Bush Speaks at Goree Island in Senegal (2003)

Mr. President and Madam First Lady, distinguished guests and residents of Goree Island, citizens of Senegal, I'm honored to begin my visit to Africa in your beautiful country.

For hundreds of years on this island peoples of different continents met in fear and cruelty. Today we gather in respect and friendship, mindful of past wrongs and dedicated to the advance of human liberty.

At this place, liberty and life were stolen and sold. Human beings were delivered and sorted, and weighed, and branded with the marks of commercial enterprises, and loaded as cargo on a voyage without return. One of the largest migrations of history was also one of the greatest crimes of history.

Below the decks, the middle passage was a hot, narrow, sunless nightmare; weeks and months of confinement and abuse and confusion on a strange and lonely sea. Some refused to eat, preferring death to any future their captors might prepare for them. Some who were sick were thrown over the side. Some rose up in violent rebellion, delivering the closest thing to justice on a slave ship. Many acts of defiance and bravery are recorded. Countless others, we will never know.

Those who lived to see land again were displayed, examined, and sold at auctions across nations in the Western Hemisphere. They entered societies indifferent to their anguish and made prosperous by their unpaid labor. There was a time in my country's history when one in every seven human beings was the property of another. In law, they were regarded only as articles of commerce, having no right to travel, or to marry, or to own possessions. Because families were often separated, many were denied even the comfort of suffering together.

For 250 years the captives endured an assault on their culture and their dignity. The spirit of Africans in America did not break. Yet the spirit of their captors was corrupted. Small men took on the powers and airs of tyrants and masters. Years of unpunished brutality and bullying and rape produced a dullness and hardness of conscience. Christian men and women became blind to the clearest commands of their faith and added hypocrisy to injustice. A republic founded on equality for all became a prison for millions. And yet in the words of the African proverb, "no fist is big enough to hide the sky." All the generations of oppression under the laws of man could not crush the hope of freedom and defeat the purposes of God.

In America, enslaved Africans learned the story of the exodus from Egypt and set their own hearts on a promised land of freedom. Enslaved Africans discovered a suffering Savior and found he was more like themselves than their masters. Enslaved Africans heard the ringing promises of the Declaration of Independence and asked the self-evident question, then why not me?

In the year of America's founding, a man named Olaudah Equiano was taken in bondage to the New World. He witnessed all of slavery's cruelties, the ruthless and the petty. He also saw beyond the slave-holding piety of the time to a higher standard of humanity. "God tells us," wrote Equiano, "that the oppressor and the oppressed are both in His hands. And if these are not the poor, the broken-hearted, the blind, the captive, the bruised which our Savior speaks of, who are they?"

Down through the years, African Americans have upheld the ideals of America by exposing laws and habits contradicting those ideals. The rights of African Americans were not the gift of those in authority. Those rights were granted by the Author of Life, and regained by the persistence and courage of African Americans, themselves.

Among those Americans was Phillis Wheatley, who was dragged from her home here in West Africa in 1761, at the age of seven. In my country, she became a poet, and the first noted black author in our nation's history. Phillis Wheatley said, "In every human breast, God has implanted a principle which we call love of freedom. It is impatient of oppression and pants for deliverance."

That deliverance was demanded by escaped slaves named Frederick Douglass and Sojourner Truth, educators named Booker T. Washington and W. E. B. DuBois, and ministers of the Gospel named Leon Sullivan and Martin Luther King, Jr. At every turn, the struggle for equality was resisted by many of the powerful. And some have said we should not judge their failures by the standards of a later time. Yet, in every time, there were men and women who clearly saw this sin and called it by name.

We can fairly judge the past by the standards of President John Adams, who called slavery "an evil of colossal magnitude." We can discern eternal standards in the deeds of William Wilberforce and John Quincy Adams, and Harriet Beecher Stowe, and Abraham Lincoln. These men and women, black and white, burned with a zeal for freedom, and they left behind a different and better nation. Their moral vision caused Americans to examine our hearts, to correct our Constitution, and to teach our children the dignity and equality of every person of every race. By a plan known only to Providence, the stolen sons and daughters of Africa helped to awaken the conscience of America. The very people traded into slavery helped to set America free.

My nation's journey toward justice has not been easy and it is not over. The racial bigotry fed by slavery did not end with slavery or with segregation. And many of the issues that still trouble America have roots in the bitter experience of other times. But however long the journey, our destination is set: liberty and justice for all.

In the struggle of the centuries, America learned that freedom is not the possession of one race. We know with equal certainty that freedom is not the possession of one nation. This belief in the natural rights of man, this conviction that justice should reach wherever the sun passes leads America into the world.

With the power and resources given to us, the United States seeks to bring peace where there is conflict, hope where there is suffering, and liberty where there is tyranny. And these commitments bring me and other distinguished leaders of my government across the Atlantic to Africa.

African peoples are now writing your own story of liberty. Africans have overcome the arrogance of colonial powers, overturned the cruelties of apartheid, and made it clear that dictatorship is not the future of any nation on this continent. In the process, Africa has produced heroes of liberation—leaders like Mandela, Senghor, Nkrumah, Kenyatta, Selassie and Sadat. And many visionary African leaders, such as my friend, have grasped the power of economic and political freedom to lift whole nations and put forth bold plans for Africa's development.

Because Africans and Americans share a belief in the values of liberty and dignity, we must share in the labor of advancing those values. In a time of growing commerce across the globe, we will ensure that the nations of Africa are full partners in the trade and prosperity of the world. Against the waste and violence of civil war, we will stand together for peace. Against the merciless terrorists who threaten every nation, we will wage an unrelenting campaign of justice. Confronted with desperate hunger, we will answer with human compassion and the tools of human technology. In the face of spreading disease, we will join with you in turning the tide against AIDS in Africa.

We know that these challenges can be overcome, because history moves in the direction of justice. The evils of slavery were accepted and unchanged for centuries. Yet, eventually, the human heart would not abide them. There is a voice of conscience and hope in every man and woman that will not be silenced—what Martin Luther King called a certain kind of fire that no water could put out. That flame could not be extinguished at the Birmingham jail. It could not be stamped out at Robben Island Prison. It was seen in the darkness here at Goree Island, where no chain could bind the soul. This untamed fire of justice continues to burn in the affairs of man, and it lights the way before us.

May God bless you all.

APPENDIX 7

108th Congress, 2d Session, Senate Joint Resolution 37 (2004)

To acknowledge a long history of official depredations and ill-conceived policies by the United States Government regarding Indian tribes and offer an apology to all Native Peoples on behalf of the United States.

IN THE SENATE OF THE UNITED STATES, MAY 6, 2004

Mr. BROWNBACK (for himself, Mr. CAMPBELL, and Mr. INOUYE) introduced the following bill; which was read twice and referred to the Committee on Indian Affairs

JOINT RESOLUTION

To acknowledge a long history of official depredations and ill-conceived policies by the United States Government regarding Indian tribes and offer an apology to all Native Peoples on behalf of the United States.

Whereas the ancestors of today's Native Peoples inhabited the land of the present-day United States since time immemorial and for thousands of years before the arrival of peoples of European descent;

Whereas the Native Peoples have for millennia honored, protected, and stewarded this land we cherish;

Whereas the Native Peoples are spiritual peoples with a deep and abiding belief in the Creator, and for millennia their peoples have maintained a powerful spiritual connection to this land, as is evidenced by their customs and legends;

Whereas the arrival of Europeans in North America opened a new chapter in the histories of the Native Peoples;

Whereas, while establishment of permanent European settlements in North America did stir conflict with nearby Indian tribes, peaceful and mutually beneficial interactions also took place;

Whereas the foundational English settlements in Jamestown, Virginia, and Plymouth, Massachusetts, owed their survival in large measure to the compassion and aid of the Native Peoples in their vicinities;

Whereas in the infancy of the United States, the founders of the Republic expressed their desire for a just relationship with the Indian tribes, as evidenced by the Northwest Ordinance enacted by Congress in 1787, which begins with the phrase, 'The utmost good faith shall always be observed toward the Indians';

Whereas Indian tribes provided great assistance to the fledgling Republic as it strengthened and grew, including invaluable help to Meriwether Lewis and William Clark on their epic journey from St. Louis, Missouri, to the Pacific Coast;

Whereas Native Peoples and non-Native settlers engaged in numerous armed conflicts;

Whereas the United States Government violated many of the treaties ratified by Congress and other diplomatic agreements with Indian tribes;

Whereas this Nation should address the broken treaties and many of the more ill-conceived Federal policies that followed, such as extermination, termination, forced removal and relocation, the outlawing of traditional religions, and the destruction of sacred places;

Whereas the United States forced Indian tribes and their citizens to move away from their traditional homelands and onto federally established and controlled reservations, in accordance with such Acts as the Indian Removal Act of 1830;

Whereas many Native Peoples suffered and perished—

(1) during the execution of the official United States Government policy of forced removal, including the infamous Trail of Tears and Long Walk;

(2) during bloody armed confrontations and massacres, such as the Sand Creek Massacre in 1864 and the Wounded Knee Massacre in 1890; and

(3) on numerous Indian reservations;

Whereas the United States Government condemned the traditions, beliefs, and customs of the Native Peoples and endeavored to assimilate them by such policies as the redistribution of land under the General Allotment Act of 1887 and the forcible removal of Native children from their families to faraway boarding schools where their Native practices and languages were degraded and forbidden;

Whereas officials of the United States Government and private United States citizens harmed Native Peoples by the unlawful acquisition of recognized tribal land, the theft of resources from such territories, and the mismanagement of tribal trust funds;

Whereas the policies of the United States Government toward Indian tribes and the breaking of covenants with Indian tribes have contributed to the severe social ills and economic troubles in many Native communities today;

Whereas, despite continuing maltreatment of Native Peoples by the United States , the Native Peoples have remained committed to the protection of this great land, as evidenced by the fact that, on a per capita basis, more Native people have served in the United States Armed Forces and placed themselves in harm's way in defense of the United States in every major military conflict than any other ethnic group;

Whereas Indian tribes have actively influenced the public life of the United States by continued cooperation with Congress and the Department of the Interior, through the involvement of Native individuals in official United States Government positions, and by leadership of their own sovereign Indian tribes;

Whereas Indian tribes are resilient and determined to preserve, develop, and transmit to future generations their unique cultural identities;

Whereas the National Museum of the American Indian was established within the Smithsonian Institution as a living memorial to the Native Peoples and their traditions; and

Whereas Native Peoples are endowed by their Creator with certain unalienable rights, and that among those are life, liberty, and the pursuit of happiness: Now, therefore, be it

Resolved by the Senate and House of Representatives of the United States of America in Congress assembled,

SECTION 1. ACKNOWLEDGMENT AND APOLOGY.

The United States, acting through Congress—

(1) recognizes the special legal and political relationship the Indian tribes have with the United States and the solemn covenant with the land we share;

(2) commends and honors the Native Peoples for the thousands of years that they have stewarded and protected this land;

(3) acknowledges years of official depredations, ill-conceived policies, and the breaking of covenants by the United States Government regarding Indian tribes;

(4) apologizes on behalf of the people of the United States to all Native Peoples for the many instances of violence, maltreatment, and neglect inflicted on Native Peoples by citizens of the United States;

(5) expresses its regret for the ramifications of former offenses and its commitment to build on the positive relationships of the past and present to move toward a brighter future where all the people of this land live reconciled as brothers and sisters, and harmoniously steward and protect this land together;

(6) urges the President to acknowledge the offenses of the United States against Indian tribes in the history of the United States in order to bring healing to this land by providing a proper foundation for reconciliation between the United States and Indian tribes; and

(7) commends the State governments that have begun reconciliation efforts with recognized Indian tribes located in their boundaries and encourages all State governments similarly to work toward reconciling relationships with Indian tribes within their boundaries.

SECTION 2. DISCLAIMER.

Nothing in this Joint Resolution authorizes any claim against the United States or serves as a settlement of any claim against the United States.

APPENDIX 8

United States Senate Apology for Failure to Pass Anti-Lynching Legislation, 109th Congress, 1st Session

S. RES. 39

Apologizing to the victims of lynching and the descendants of those victims for the failure of the Senate to enact anti-lynching legislation.

IN THE SENATE OF THE UNITED STATES RESOLUTION

Apologizing to the victims of lynching and the descendants of those victims for the failure of the Senate to enact anti-lynching legislation.

Whereas the crime of lynching succeeded slavery as the ultimate expression of racism in the United States following Reconstruction;

Whereas lynching was a widely acknowledged practice in the United States until the middle of the 20th century;

Whereas lynching was a crime that occurred throughout the United States, with documented incidents in all but 4 States;

Whereas at least 4,742 people, predominantly African-Americans, were reported lynched in the United States between 1882 and 1968;

Whereas 99 percent of all perpetrators of lynching escaped from punishment by State or local officials;

Whereas lynching prompted African-Americans to form the National Association for the Advancement of Colored People (NAACP) and prompted members of B'nai B'rith to found the Anti-Defamation League;

Whereas nearly 200 anti-lynching bills were introduced in Congress during the first half of the 20th century;

Whereas, between 1890 and 1952, 7 Presidents petitioned Congress to end lynching;

Whereas, between 1920 and 1940, the House of Representatives passed 3 strong anti-lynching measures;

Whereas protection against lynching was the minimum and most basic of Federal responsibilities, and the Senate considered but failed to enact anti-lynching legislation despite repeated requests by civil rights groups, Presidents, and the House of Representatives to do so;

Whereas the recent publication of 'Without Sanctuary: Lynching Photography in America' helped bring greater awareness and proper recognition of the victims of lynching;

Whereas only by coming to terms with history can the United States effectively champion human rights abroad; and

Whereas an apology offered in the spirit of true repentance moves the United States toward reconciliation and may become central to a new understanding, on which improved racial relations can be forged: Now, therefore, be it

Resolved, That the Senate —

  (1) apologizes to the victims of lynching for the failure of the Senate to enact anti-lynching legislation;

  (2) expresses the deepest sympathies and most solemn regrets of the Senate to the descendants of victims of lynching, the ancestors of whom were deprived of life, human dignity, and the constitutional protections accorded all citizens of the United States; and

  (3) remembers the history of lynching, to ensure that these tragedies will be neither forgotten nor repeated.

NOTES

1. Richard W. Stevenson, *Bush, in Africa, Promises Aid but Offers No Troops for Liberia*, N.Y. Times, July 8, 2003 ("Years of unpunished brutality and bullying and rape produced a dullness and hardness of conscience. Christian men and women became blind to the clearest commands of their faith and added hypocrisy to injustice. A republic founded on equality for all became a prison for millions") (quoting President Bush).

2. *See* An Act for the Release of Certain Persons Held to Labor in the District of Columbia, 12 Stat. 376–78 (1862).

3. Cal. Ins. Code Ann. 13812 (2000). Information on the registry is *available at* http://www.insurance.ca.gov/0100-consumers/0300-public-programs/0200-slavery-era-insur/. The slaves' names are *available at* http://www.insurance.ca.gov/0100-consumers/0300-public-programs/0200-slavery-era-insur/slave-names.cfm.

CHAPTER 1

1. *Compare* Mary Ann Glendon, *Rights Talk* (1991). The growth in the public debate can be roughly gauged by searching for articles mentioning slavery and reparations in the major papers file of Nexis. There were 83 stories before 1991; 81 stories in 1995; 103 in 1999; 382 in 2000; 1107 stories in 2001. One suspects that the effect of September 11 is seen in a decline to 699 stories in 2002. The decline has continued. In 2003, there were 266 stories; there were 233 in 2004, 175 in 2005. In the legal academy, the story has been of continued—indeed, largely growing interest—as measured by publications in law journals. A search of the Westlaw *Journals & Law Reviews* database for articles that mention slavery and reparations in the same sentence discloses that there were 56 articles before 2000, 15 in 2000, 27 in 2001, 60 in 2002, 78 in 2003, 98 in 2004, and 47 in 2005. Given the recent talk of apologies at Brown University, the University of Virginia, and the University of Alabama and Chicago's requirement of disclosure of corporate connections to slavery, there may be a resurgence again.

Another indication of the importance within the legal academy is that the nation's finest law journals have begun to publish on the topic. In recent years, the *Harvard Law Review*, *Columbia Law Review*, *Texas Law Review*, and the *Georgetown Law Journal* have all published articles, essays, or comments devoted to reparations for slavery. *See* Note, *Bridging the Color Line: The Power of African-American Reparations to Redirect America's Future*, 115 Harv. L. Rev. 1689 (2002); Saul Levmore, *Changes, Anticipations, and Reparations*, 99 Colum. L. Rev. 1657 (1999); Alfred L. Brophy, *Losing the [Understanding of the Importance of] Race: Evaluating the Significance of Race and the Utility of Reparations*, 80 Texas L. Rev. 911 (2002); Kevin Hopkins, *Forgive U.S. Our Debts? Righting the Wrongs of Slavery*, 89 Georgetown L. J. 2531 (2001).

Moreover, there are frequent, thoughtful discussions of reparations on radio, public television, and web broadcasts. *See, e.g.,* Hugh LaFollett and Andrew Valls, "Ideas Issues," WETS-FM, *available at* http://www.etsu.edu/philos/radio/valls.htm; "Leading Scholars Discuss 'Forty Acres and a Mule: The Case for Black Reparations,'" Columbia University Forum (March 10, 2003), *available at* http://www.columbia.edu/cu/news/vforum/03/struggle_black_reparations/.

2. The new scholarship is best represented by Eric Yamamoto's humane work, particularly *Interracial Justice: Conflict and Reconciliation in Post–Civil Rights America* (1998). *See also* Eric K. Yamamoto, *Racial Reparations: Japanese American Redress and African American Claims*, 40 B.C. L. Rev. 477 (1998); Eric K. Yamamoto, *Critical Race Praxis: Race Theory and Political Lawyering Practice in Post–Civil Rights America*, 95 Mich. L. Rev. 821 (1997); Eric K. Yamamoto, *Rethinking Alliances: Agency, Responsibility and Interracial Justice*, 3 Asian Pac. Am. L.J. 33 (1995); Eric K. Yamamoto, *Conflict and Complicity: Justice among Communities of Color*, 2 Harv. Latino L. Rev. 495 (1997); Julie A. Su & Eric K. Yamamoto, *Critical Coalitions: Theory and Praxis*, *in* Crossroads, Directions and a New Critical Race Theory 379 (Francisco Valdes, Jerome McCristal Culp & Angela P. Harris eds., 2002). Professor Yamamoto's unceasing efforts to emphasize racial healing through reparations are critical, I believe, to advancing the cause of reparations.

3. The most ambitious of the state investigations was the commission that investigated the 1921 Tulsa race riot. The commission was remarkably successful in recovering an understanding of the riot's origins in the racial violence of the United States after World War I. However, despite that history, there were no reparations paid. *See generally* Alfred L. Brophy, *Reconstructing the Dreamland: The Tulsa Riot of 1921 — Race, Reparations, Reconciliation* (2002).

The fountainhead of serious reparations talk within the legal academy is Mari Matsuda, *Looking to the Bottom: Critical Legal Studies and Reparations*, 22 Harv. C.R.-C.L. L. Rev. 323 (1987).

Building on Matsuda, three other articles advanced the cause in significant ways. Two were student notes: Rhonda V. Magee, *The Master's Tools from the Bottom Up: Responses to African-American Reparations Theory in Mainstream and Outsider Remedies Discourse*, 79 Va. L. Rev. 863 (1993); Tureen E. Chisholm, *Sweep around Your Own Front Door: Examining the Argument for Legislative African American Reparations*, 147 U. Pa. L. Rev. 677 (1999). Magee has recently expanded significantly upon her earlier work. *See* Magee-Andrews, *The Third Reconstruction*, 54 Ala. L. Rev. 599 (2002). The third was Robert Westley's brilliant statement of the case for reparations from a moral standpoint. *See* Robert Westley, *Many Billions Gone: Is It Time to Reconsider the Case for African American Reparations?*, 19 B.C. Third World L. Rev. 429 (1998).

4. *See, e.g.*, Elazar Barkan, *The Guilt of Nations: Restitution and Negotiating Historical Injustices* (2000).

5. Nontombi Tutu, *Afterword, in Should America Pay? Slavery and the Raging Debate over Reparations* 311, 312 (Raymond A. Winbush ed. 2003).

6. *See* Cato v. United States, 70 F.3d 1103 (9th Cir. 1995). More recently, the United States Court of Claims has dismissed a suit seeking reparations for slavery based on an equal protection argument, claiming that victims of slavery are entitled to share in the Civil Liberties Act of 1988, which provided compensation to Japanese Americans interned during World War II. *See* Obadele v. United States, 52 Fed.Cl. 432 (2002). Other recent cases seeking reparations for slavery have been dismissed. *See* Abdullah v. U.S., 2003 West law 1741922 (D.Conn.); cf. United States v. Bridges, 217 F.3d 841 (4th Cir. 2000) (unpublished opinion) (tax fraud to rely upon reparations tax credit); Wilkins v. C.I.R. 120 T.C. No. 7, U.S. Tax Ct. 2003 (denying tax credit for reparations for slavery). *See also* Jackson v. United States, 1994 U.S. Dist. LEXIS 7872 (N.D. Calif.); Lewis v. United States, 1994 U.S. Dist. LEXIS 7868 (N.D. Calif.); Powell v. United States, 1994 U.S. Dist. LEXIS 8628 (N.D. Calif.); Bell v. United States, 2001 U.S. Dist. Lexis 14,812 (N.D. Tex.) (dismissing suit for reparations for slavery and observing that "without a concrete, personal injury that is not abstract and that is fairly traceable to the government conduct that plaintiff challenges as unconstitutional, Bell lacks standing").

7. *See* Farmer-Paellmann v. FleetBoston. The complaint is conveniently reprinted in *Should America Pay?*, *supra* note 5, at 344–55. Farmer-Paellmann then filed suit in California. *See* Hurdle v. FleetBoston, CGC -02–412,388 (Sup. Ct., San Francisco Calf. 2003), discussed in John S. Friedman, *Corporate Bill for Slavery*, The Nation (February 20, 2003), *available at* http://www.thenation.com/doc.mhtml?i=20030310&s=friedman.

The cases were consolidated. *See* In re. African American Litig. No. 02-CV-7764 (N.D. Ill., 2003) and dismissed in January 2004, then refiled, and then redismissed again in 2005. The two opinions and much of the other pleadings are available on the Aetna Web site: http://www.aetna.com/legal_issues/suits/reparations.html. In particular, readers may be interested in the second opinion, of July 6, 2005, which quoted from several articles that are incorporated, in revised form, into this book. The second opinion is *available at* http://www.aetna.com/legal_issues/suits/data/Judges_July6_Opinion_Order DismissingSlaveryLitigation.pdf.

8. *See* Brent Staples, *Coming to Grips with the Unthinkable in Tulsa*, N.Y. Times (March 16, 2003) (discussing lawsuit and concluding: "The courts will have to decide whether or not the riot survivors have a plausible case. But in the moral sense at least, Tulsa and Oklahoma have already lost. They did so by failing to accept responsibility for one of the most blood-curdling events in American history."). The complaint is *available at* http://www.tulsareparations .org/Complaint2ndAmend.pdf.

The dismissal was affirmed by the U.S. Court of Appeals in September 2004. *See* Alexander v. Oklahoma, 382 F.3d 1206 (10th Cir 2004).

9. Sam Hodges, *Slavery Payments a Divisive Question*, Mobile Register (June 23, 2002). *See also* USA Today (Feb. 22, 2002) (summarizing similar results in CNN/USA TODAY poll); Lee A. Harris, *"Reparations" as a Dirty Word: The Norm against Slavery Reparations*, 33 U. Mem. L. Rev. 409 (2003); Sasha Polakow-Suransky, *Sins of Our Fathers*, Brown Univ. Alumni Mag. (July/August 2003) (discussing division over support for reparations).

10. http://www.wewontpay.com/about.html. There are many similar expressions, such as Bruno VanderVelde's essay "Reparations for What?" which concluded: "Get over it. And stop living in the past, waiting for someone else to give you money for something you'd better be happy you'll never have to endure." *Available at* http://www.liberator.net/articles/VanderVeldeBruno/ reparations.html.

11 James Davison Hunter, *Culture Wars* (1992); Danny Goldberg, *Dispatches from the Culture Wars: How the Left Lost Teen Spirit* (2003). A central feature of the culture war is how we view American history. *See, e.g.,* Mona Charen, *Useful Idiots: How Liberals Got It Wrong in the Cold War and Still Blame America First* (2003).

12. Allison Benedikt and David Mendell, *Keyes Has Plan for Reparations: He Would Exempt Blacks from Taxes*, Chicago Tribune (Aug. 17, 2004):

> Prompted by a reporter's question, Keyes gave a brief tutorial on Roman history and said that in regard to reparations for slavery, the U.S. should do what the Romans did: "When a city had been devastated [in the Roman empire], for a certain length of time—a generation or two—they exempted the damaged city from taxation."

Keyes proposed that for a generation or two, African-Americans of slave heritage should be exempted from federal taxes—federal because slavery "was an egregious failure on the part of the federal establishment." In calling for the tax relief, Keyes appeared to be reaching out to capture the black vote, something that may prove difficult to do, particularly after his unwelcome reception at the Bud Billiken Day Parade Saturday.

13. Two professors at the University of Chicago Law School, Eric Posner and Adrian Vermeule, offer a series of defining criteria in an article in the *Columbia Law Review*: reparations schemes typically relax the connection between wrongdoer and victim; they are justified "on the basis of backward-looking reasons, such as remediation of, or compensation for, past injustices, rather than on the basis of forward-looking reasons"; finally, cases where money is paid because of a legal claim are not reparations. *See* Posner & Vermeule, *Reparations for Slavery and Other Historical Injustices*, 103 Colum. L. Rev. 689, 691–92 (2003). But their classification scheme excludes too many cases from the definition of reparations. As discussed more fully in chapter 3, the Posner and Vermeule definition leaves out many programs that have been seen as reparations. Moreover, few proponents of reparations limit reparations so narrowly as to exclude forward-looking programs.

14. *See* Kyle Logue, *Reparations and Redistribution*, 84 B.U. L. Rev. 1319 (2004); Westley, *Many Billions Gone, supra* note 3, at 467; *see* Tuneen E. Chisholm, *Sweep around Your Own Front Door: Examining the Argument for Legislative African American Reparations*, 147 U. Pa. L. Rev. 677 (1999).

15. Given the broad range of programs claimed by both reparations and skeptics, reparations should be defined broadly. They are programs, often provided by a legislature, but sometimes by courts or private bodies, to repair past injustice. They are designed in part to make up for past injustice, but they may not address exactly the past harm. That is, reparations may not measure exactly the harm; they may provide only symbolic repair. And they are often focused not so much on measuring the past harm as in improving life into the future. That is, the case for reparations is built on backward-looking principles, like repairing past harm; reparations are almost always forward-looking. They seek to improve life into the future; the form and measure of reparations are almost always computed by what will be best for the future. A favorite argument against reparations is that they are too focused on the past; yet, reparations proponents almost always see reparations as justified on the past and designed to improve the future.

16. Charles J. Ogletree, *The Current Reparations Debate*, 36 U.C. Davis L. Rev. 1051, 1055 (2003).

17. *Id.* at 1056.

18. *Id.* at 1071.

19. Westley, *supra* note 3, at 432, 437. He continues:

In arguing for Black reparations, this article supports the idea of compensation through money transfers and group entitlements because I
believe that reparations present an opportunity for institution-building
that is badly needed, and should not be squandered in the consumer
market. Nevertheless, I also believe that the poorest among us should
be compensated first and through meaningful (not symbolic) monetary transfers.

20. *See, e.g.*, Albert Mosley, *Affirmative Action as a Form of Reparations*,
33 U. Mem. L. Rev. 353 (2003); Swann v. Charlotte-Mecklenburg Bd. Ed., 402
U.S. 1 (1971) (desegregation). Few people speak about prisons in regard to repa-
rations, but that is a subject badly in need of attention. *See generally* Larry W.
Yackle, *Reform and Regret: The Story of Federal Judicial Involvement in the
Alabama Prison System* (1989).

21. *See, e.g.*, John McWhorter, *Against Reparations*, New Republic 32
(June 17, 2001).

22. Some scholars exclude apologies and truth commissions from their
definition of reparations. *See* Roy L. Brooks, *Atonement and Forgiveness: A
New Model for Black Reparations* (2004).

23. Eric Yamamoto, *Interracial Justice, supra* note 2, at 174–91. Yamamoto
also discusses this as redress, reparations, and reconciliation. *Id.* at 213. *See also*
Eric K. Yamamoto, *Racial Reparations: Japanese American Redress and
African American Claims*, 40 B.C. L. Rev. 477 (1998). Yamamoto focuses on
what reparations mean to the people receiving them in their attitudes toward
the government. That focus may be somewhat more possible with Japanese
Americans than African Americans, because the former actually have received
reparations. Hence, it may be easier to ask that community to accept the payments and move forward. There may be a greater possibility for what Yamamoto calls "contributing to institutional and attitudinal restructuring." *Id.*
at 479.

24. *See* Sherrilyn A. Ifill, *Creating a Truth and Reconciliation Commission
for Lynching*, 21 Law & Ineq. 263 (2003); Emma Coleman Jordan, *A History
Lesson: Reparations for What?* 58 NYU Annual Survey American Law 557
(2003); Alfred L. Brophy, *Reparations Talk: The Tort Law Analogy and Reparations for Slavery*, 24 B.C. Third World L.J. 81 (2004) (discussing reparations in
the context of Jim Crow, for such diverse crimes as segregated libraries, lynchings, and exploitation of convict labor).

25. *See* Ifill, *supra* note 24; Jordan, *supra* note 24 (suggesting lynching as centerpiece of Jim Crow reparations strategy).

26. Ann Scales, *Clinton, in Senegal, Revisits Slavery's Horrors Emotional End to Historic Trip*, Boston Globe A2, April 3, 1998 (discussing Clinton's condemnation of slavery during visit to Goree Island); John F. Harris, *Coming out of Africa with a Double Boost; White House Elated by Trip, Ruling*, Washington Post A1, April 3, 1998 (quoting Clinton in Uganda).

27. Roger Simon, *Clinton Ends Visit by Touring Slave Port Africans Praised for Their Role in Building the U.S.*, Chicago Tribune 1, April 3, 1998. Many people have interpreted his remarks as an apology. *See, e.g.*, William F. Buckley, *No on Liberia* (July 9, 2003) ("We are not beholden to Liberia in the sense that the British, French and Belgians can be thought to be beholden to Rhodesia, Sierra Leone, the Ivory Coast and Congo. To talk about responsibilities traceable to events a century and a half past gets you into the kind of historical sandpit Clinton got into when he decided to apologize, in Africa, for slavery."); Walter Williams, *Reparations for Slavery* (January 12, 2001) ("Incidentally, President Clinton apologizing for slavery in Africa, of all places, is stupid—apologizing to descendants of slave traders for slavery in America."), *available at* http://capmag.com/article.asp?ID=89.

28. Richard W. Stevenson, *Bush, in Africa, Promises Aid but Offers No Troops for Liberia*, N.Y. Times, July 8, 2003 ("Years of unpunished brutality and bullying and rape produced a dullness and hardness of conscience. Christian men and women became blind to the clearest commands of their faith and added hypocrisy to injustice. A republic founded on equality for all became a prison for millions.") (quoting President Bush).

29. John Donnelly, *Bush Condemns Slavery as One of 'Greatest Crimes' Speech at Source of African Trade Gives No Apology*, Boston Globe, July 9, 2003.

30. *See, e.g.*, Cheryl I. Harris, *Mining in Hard Ground*, 116 Harv. L. Rev. 2487, 2489–92 (2003) (discussing Supreme Court's color-blind jurisprudence and its implications for remedying racial inequality).

31. *See, e.g.*, Barkan, *supra* note 4.

32. *See* Martha Minnow, *Between Vengeance and Forgiveness: Facing History after Genocide and Mass Violence* 42–90 (1998).

33. Lisa Cardyn, *Sexualized Racism/Gendered Violence*, 100 Mich. L. Rev. 675 (2002).

34. 115 Harv. L. Rev. 1689 (2002).

35. *Id.* at 1693.

36. *Id.* at 1704 ("Politicians and community leaders, not just lawyers, should frame the public debate over reparations").

37. *Id.* at 1706 ("Incrementalism that focuses first on the creation of a

commission to investigate the wrong will provide politicians and reparations proponents with the opportunity to lay the evidentiary groundwork necessary to educate the public regarding the effects, past and present, of slavery and Jim Crow—creating a strong moral and economic claim for reparations in the second place").

38. *Id.* at 1708. That is certainly an important goal—and study must, obviously, precede action. One is concerned, however, that the author of "Bridging the Color Line" is placing too much hope in the ability of a study to transform American thought. One thinks of similar episodes in history, like the Kerner Commission Report on racial violence, and their inability to fundamentally transform values. The politics of historical commissions is itself an important topic, deserving substantial attention.

39. *See J.P. Morgan Says Two Precursor Banks Held Slaves,* Los Angeles Times, January 21, 2005; Jeff Jacoby, *The Slavery Shakedown,* Boston Globe, June 9, 2005. The JPMorgan Chase and Wachovia cases are discussed in more depth in chapter 6.

40. *See* United Daughters of the Confederacy v. Vanderbilt University, 173 S.W.3d. 98 (Tenn. Ct. App. 2005). The case is *available at* http://www.tsc .state.tn.us/OPINIONS/TCA/PDF/o52/UDCOPN.pdf.

There is also a concurring opinion *available at* http://www.tsc.state.tn.us/ opinions/tca/PDF/o52/UDC2CON.pdf.

41. Joshua Lawrence Chamberlain, *The Passing of the Armies* 260–62 (Stan Clark Military Books 1994) (1915). For more on Chamberlain, see Jeremiah Goulka, ed., *The Grand Old Man of Maine: Selected Letters of Joshua Lawrence Chamberlain* (2005).

42. 174 S.W.3d at 122–24.

43. See John Branston, *In a City on the Move, A Civil War Issue Refuses to Die,* N.Y. Times, August 5, 2005.

44. *See* N.Y. Times, November 30, 2005.

45. *See, e.g.,* Yamamoto, *Interracial Justice, supra* note 2, at 213; Brooks, *Atonement and Forgiveness, supra* note 23, at 141–79.

46. Richard Newman spoke on the National Public Radio program *The Connection* on June 1, 2001, on a show about the Tulsa race riot and reparations. Newman's comments on the Marshall Plan appeared at 32 minutes into the show. The show is *available at* http://archives.theconnection.org/archive/ 2001/06/o601a.shtml.

47. *Id.* Newman's comments on the cost appear at 32:54 into the show.

48. Charles Krauthammer, *Reparations for Black Americans,* Time 18, December 31, 1990. *See also* Dalton Conley, *The Cost of Slavery,* N.Y. Times A25, February 15, 2003 (suggesting the average difference in white and black wealth as a measure and suggesting that the average black, two-parent family would

receive approximately $35,000). *See also* Dalton Conley, *Calculating Slavery Reparations: Theory, Numbers, and Implications* in Politics and the Past: On Repairing Historical Injustices 117 (John Torpey ed. 2003).

CHAPTER 2

1. David Brion Davis, *The Problem of Slavery in the Age of Emancipation* 226 (1975) (discussing Quaker ideas about freedom and compensation in the late eighteenth century); Gary B. Nash & Jean Soderlund, *Freedom by Degrees: Emancipation in Pennsylvania and Its Aftermath* (1991).

2. Eric Foner, *Reconstruction: America's Unfinished Revolution* 232–34 (1988) (discussing proposals for providing land to former slaves and the limitations on the idea of compensation to them).

3. See David Walker, *Walker's Appeal in Four Articles; Together with a Preamble, To the Coloured Citizens of the World, but in Particular, and Very Expressly, to Those of the United States of America* 80 (Third ed. Boston, 1830). The Appeal is discussed in Adjoa A. Aiyetoro, *Formulating Reparations Litigation through the Eyes of the Movement,* 58 N.Y.U. Ann. Surv. Am. L. 457 (2003). It is conveniently *available at* http://docsouth.unc.edu/nc/walker/menu.html.

4. *See generally* David Menschel, *Abolition without Deliverance: The Law of Connecticut Slavery 1784–1848,* 111 Yale L.J. 183, 184 (2001); Paul Finkelman, *Thomas R.R. Cobb and the Law of Negro Slavery,* 5 Roger Williams U. L. Rev. 75, 82 n. 30 (1999); Charles H. Baron, *The Supreme Judicial Court in Its Fourth Century: Meeting the Challenge Of the "New Constitutional Revolution,"* 77 Mass. L. Rev. 35 n. 89 (1992); Emily Blanck, *Seventeen Eighty-Three: The Turning Point in the Law of Slavery and Freedom in Massachusetts,* 75 New England Quarterly 24 (March 2002).

5. Negro Peter v. Steel, 3 Yeates 250 (Pa. 1801). I am indebted to Andrew Kull's outstanding article, *Restitution in Favor of Former Slaves,* 82 B.U. L. Rev. 1277 (2004), which alerted me to the cases discussed in this paragraph.

6. Thompson v. Wilmost, 4 Ky. (1 Bibb) 422 (1809).

7. *See* Leon Litwack, *Been in the Storm So Long: The Aftermath of Slavery* 333–34 (1979). The letter is conveniently *available at* http://www.sewanee.edu/faculty/Willis/Civil_War/documents/Oldmaster.html.

8. Gordon v. Duncan, 3 Mo. 385 (1834). In many other cases, slave owners who "rented" their slaves to others recovered when the slaves were used in ways inconsistent with the "rental" agreement. It is obvious that the idea that slaves are property and their labor is a commodity was central to the institution of slavery.

9. *The Ideology of Slavery: Proslavery Thought in the Antebellum South, 1830–1860* 21, 24 (Drew Faust ed. 1981). For more on Thomas R. Dew's thought, see Eugene Genovese and Elizabeth Fox-Genovese, *The Mind of the Master Class: History and Faith in the Southern Slaveholders' Worldview* esp. 307–8 (2005).

10. Atkinson, quoted in Foner, *supra* note 2, at 237.

11. *See* Foner, *supra* note 2, at 74 (discussing Lincoln's consideration of compensation to slaveowners).

12. Foner, *supra* note 2, at 50–60.

13. Foner, *supra* note 2, at 142; Yusuf Nuruddin, *Promises and Pitfalls of Reparations*, Socialism and Democracy 88, 93–95 (2002).

14. Foner, *supra* note 2, at 142; *An Act to Establish a Bureau for Relief of Freedmen and Refugees*, 13 Statutes at Large 507–09 (March 3, 1865); Donald G. Nieman, *To Set the Law in Motion: The Freedman's Bureau and the Legal Rights of Blacks, 1865–1868* (1979).

15. *An Act to Establish a Bureau for Relief of Freedmen and Refugees*, 13 Statutes at Large 507–09 (March 3, 1865).

16. Katherine M. Franke, *Becoming a Citizen: Reconstruction Era Regulation of African American Marriages*, 11 Yale J.L. & Human. 251 (1999).

17. Foner, *supra* note 2, at 158–60.

18. Stevens quoted in Foner, *supra* note 2, at 236.

19. Speech of the Hon. Thaddeus Stevens of Pennsylvania, Delivered in the House of Representatives, March 19, 1867, on the Bill (H.R. No. 20) Relative to Damages to Loyal Men, and for Other Purposes [Washington, D.C.]: Republican Congressional Executive Committee, 1867]. Stevens's speech is also available in the *Congressional Globe*, 40th Congress, 1st Sess App. 203–08 (March 19, 1867). The quotation appears at page 204.

20. H.R. 29 (March 11, 1867) (Thaddeus Stevens); Eric Foner, *Thaddeus Stevens, Confiscation, and Reconstruction, in* Politics and Ideology in the Age of Civil War 128–49 (1980); Foner, *supra* note 2, at 234–36.

21. *See, e.g.*, Foner, *supra* note 2, at 158–60 (discussing entrance of former slaves into Southern legislatures).

22. Foner, *supra* note 2, at 199–201.

23. *See* United States v. Cruickshank, 92 U.S. 542 (1876).

24. W. E. B. Dubois, *Black Reconstruction in America, 1860–1880*, at 167 (1935) (rev. ed. 1992) (discussing black codes).

25. *See generally* C. Vann Woodward, *The Strange Career of Jim Crow* (Commemorative Edition, 2002). In more recent years, historians have emphasized the complex society that existed in the years between Civil War and the Progressive era and have focused on the ways that African Americans operated

within the system of Jim Crow. In some instances, African Americans created their own communities to negotiate around the constraints of Jim Crow. *See, e.g.,* Glenda Gilmore, *Gender and Jim Crow: Women and the Politics of White Supremacy in North Carolina, 1896–1920* (1996). However, in our rush to recover that complex world and the ways that the human spirit resisted legal subordination, we should not underestimate the limitations Southern society placed on African Americans. *See, e.g.,* Randall Kennedy, *Reconstruction and the Politics of Scholarship,* 98 Yale L.J. 521 (1989) (reviewing Foner, *supra* note 2).

26. *See generally* Randall Kennedy, *Race Relations Law and the Tradition of Celebration: The Case of Professor Schmidt,* 86 Colum. L. Rev. 1622 (1986) (emphasizing the harshness of Progressive-era jurisprudence on race).

27. *Lynchings by State and Race, 1882–1968* (1979).

28. *See* H.R. 1119, 51st Cong., 1st Sess. (1890).

29. See Mary F. Berry, *My Face Is Black Is True: Callie House and the Struggle for Ex-Slave Reparations* (2005); Mary F. Berry, *Reparations for Freedman, 1890–1916: Fraudulent Practices or Justice Deferred?* 57 J. Negro History 219 (1972); Vincene Verdun, *If the Shoe Fits, Wear It: An Analysis of Reparations for African Americans,* 67 Tul. L. Rev. 597, 600 (1993).

30. Johnson v. McAdoo, 45 U.S. App. D.C. 440, 441 (1916), aff'd 244 U.S. 643 (1917). *See also* Calvin J. Allen, *The Continuing Quest of African Americans to Obtain Reparation for Slavery,* 9 National Bar Assoc. Mag. 33 (May/June 1995); Randall Robinson, *The Debt: What America Owes to Blacks* 206–07 (2000). In a strange twist of fate, Jones was subsequently prosecuted for soliciting clients for the lawsuit. *See* Allen, *supra,* at 33.

31. Jeremy Levitt, *Black African Reparations: Making a Claim for Enslavement and Systematic de Jure Segregation and Racial Discrimination under American and International Law,* 25 S.U. L. Rev. 1 (1997).

32. Aiyotoro, *supra* note 3, at 457, 462.

33. *See, e.g.,* Kennedy, *Race Relations Law and the Tradition of Celebration, supra* note 26 (discussing burdens of NAACP's work at seeking basic fairness).

34. Roscoe Dunjee, *Segregation and Discrimination,* Oklahoma City Black Dispatch (July 29, 1926).

35. *See, e.g.,* Mary L. Dudziak, *Brown as a Cold War Case,* 91 J. Am. Hist. 32 (2004).

36. Danielle Allen, *Law's Necessary Forcefulness: Ralph Ellison vs. Hannah Arendt on the Battle of Little Rock,* 26 Okla. City U. L. Rev. 857–900 (2001) (discussing the conflict over integration in the black and white communities).

37. *See generally* Alan J. Matusow, *The Unraveling of America: A History of Liberalism in the 1960s* (1984); Maurice Isserman, *The Not-So-Dark and Bloody Ground: New Works on the 1960s,* 94 Am. Historical Rev. 990 (1989);

Michael Kazin, *America Divided: The Civil War of the 1960s* (2000); David Chalmers, *And the Crooked Places Made Straight: The Struggle for Social Change in the 1960s* (1991).

38. Harold Hyman, *American Singularity: The 1787 Northwest Ordinance, the 1862 Homestead and Morrill Acts, and the 1944 G.I. Bill* (1986).

39. Reparations proponents have often focused on King's call for payments. Professor Anthony Cook uses King's call for reparations as a starting point:

> No amount of gold could provide an adequate compensation for the exploitation and humiliation of the Negro in America down through the centuries. Not all the wealth of this affluent society could meet the bill. Yet a price can be placed on unpaid wages. The ancient common law has always provided a remedy for the appropriation of the labor of one human being by another. This law should be made to apply for American Negroes. The payment should be in the form of a massive program by the government of special, compensatory measures which could be regarded as a settlement in accordance with the accepted practice of common law. Such measures would certainly be less expensive than any computation based on two centuries of unpaid wages and accumulated interest. I am proposing, therefore, that, just as we granted a GI Bill of Rights to war veterans, America launch a broad-based and gigantic Bill of Rights for the Disadvantaged, our veterans of the long siege of denial.

Martin Luther King Jr., *Why We Can't Wait* 150–51 (1964) (quoted by Anthony Cook, *King and the Beloved Community: A Communitarian Defense of Black Reparations*, 68 Geo. Wash. L. Rev. 959, 962 (2000); James Forman Jr., *A Little Rebellion Now and Then Is a Good Thing*, 100 Mich. L. Rev. 1408, 1415 (2002). King's relationship to reparations is discussed by, among others, Charles J. Ogletree Jr., *Repairing the Past: New Efforts in the Reparations Debate in America*, 38 Harv. C.R.-C.L. L. Rev. 279 (2003); Eric J. Miller, *Reconceiving Reparations: Multiple Strategies in the Reparations*, 24 B.C. Third World L.J. 45 (2004). For King's importance for legal thought more generally, *see* Randall Kennedy, *Martin Luther King's Constitution: A Legal History of the Montgomery Bus Boycott*, 98 Yale L.J. 999 (1989). Lee Harris's article correctly observes that "while Martin Luther King and several civil rights leaders of the time did believe in reparations, that issue to them was never central." Lee A. Harris, *Political Autonomy as a Form of Reparations to African-Americans*, 29 S.U. L. Rev. 25, 37 (2001).

Cook sees reparations as part of a "new paradigm" that arrives as reconciliation through atonement, which includes confession and restitution-based repentance. Cook, *supra*, at 963.

40. Boris Bittker, *The Case for Black Reparations* 8–9 & 141 n. 8 (citing Martin L. King Jr., *Why We Can't Wait* 152 (1964)) (1973). *See also* David Boyle, *Unsavory White Omissions? A Review of Uncivil Wars*, 105 W. Va. L. Rev. 655, 689 (2003) (discussing King and reparations).

41. *See* James Forman, *The Black Manifesto*, in Black Manifesto: Religion, Racism, and Reparations 114–26 (Robert S. Lecky & H. Elliot Wright eds. 1969).

42. Arnold Schuchter, *Reparations: The Black Manifesto and Its Challenge to White America* 5 (1970), quoted in Rhonda V. Magee, *The Master's Tools, from the Bottom Up: Responses to African-American Reparations Theory in Mainstream and Outsider Remedies Discourse*, 79 Va. L. Rev. 863 (1993). The Black Manifesto is also conveniently available in *Black Manifesto: Religion, Racism, and Reparations* 114–26 (Robert S. Lecky & H. Elliott Wright eds. 1969).

43. *Black Manifesto, supra* note 42, at 1.

44. *Id.*

45. *See* Mark Tushnet, *The Utopian Technician*, 93 Yale L.J. 208, 209 (1983) (discussing Bittker's thesis).

46. *See* Bittker, *supra* note 40. *See also* Bernard Boxhill, *The Morality of Reparations*, in Reverse Discrimination 270 (Barry R. Grass, 1977).

47. Derrick Bell, *Dissection of a Dream*, 9 Harv. C.R.-C.L. L. Rev. 156, 162 (1974) (reviewing Bittker, *supra* note 40).

48. 25 U.S.C. § 70; Sandra C. Danforth, *Repaying Historical Debts: The Indian Claims Commission*, N.D. L. Rev. 359 (1973).

49. Michael Leder & Jack Page, *Wild Justice* 59 (1997) (summarizing Collier's argument in favor of the commission). *See also* Stephen McSloy, *Revisiting the "Courts of the Conqueror": American Indian Claims against the United States*, 44 Am. U. L. Rev. 537 (1994); Nell Jessup Newton, *Compensation, Reparations, & Restitution: Indian Property Claims in the United States*, 28 Ga. L. Rev. 453 (1994).

50. Alaska Native Claims Settlement Act of 1971, 43 U.S.C. § 1601 (1998); John F. Walsh, *Settling the Alaska Claims Settlement Act*, 38 Stan. L. Rev. 227 (1985).

51. Newton, *supra* note 49, at 476.

52. 50 U.S.C. app. § 1989b (1994). In 1992, the funding for the act was increased from $1.25 billion to $1.65 billion. 50 U.S.C. app. §1989b- 3(e) (1994). *See also* Comm'n on Wartime Relocation and Internment of Civilians, Comm. on Internal and Insular Affairs, 102nd Cong., Personal Justice Denied (Comm. Print 1992) (describing the history of exclusion that was being compensated).

53. Japanese-American Evacuation Claims Act of 1948, Pub. L. No. 80–886, 62 Stat. 1231 (1948). *See also* Keith Aoki, *No Right to Own? The Early Twentieth-Century "Alien Land Laws" as a Prelude to Internment*, 40 B.C. L. Rev. 37 (1998).

54. *See* Hohri v. United States, 586 F.Supp. 769 (D.D.C. 1984), *aff'd in part*, 782 F.2d 227 (D.C. Cir. 1986), vacated, 482 U.S. 64 (1987), on remand, 847 F.2d 779 (D.C. Cir. 1988); Eric K. Yamamoto, *Racial Reparations: Japanese American Redress and African American Claims*, 40 B.C. L. Rev. 477, 490 (1998); Michelle E. Lyons, *World Conference against Racism: New Avenues for Slavery Reparations?* 35 V and. J. Transnat'l Law 1235, 1242–43 (2002).

55. *See* Global Alliance for Preserving the History of WWII in Asia, *at* http://www.global-alliance.net/SFPT/ApplicationOf1988CivilLibertiesAct.htm.

56. *See generally* Burt Neuborne, *Holocaust Reparations Litigation: Lessons for the Slavery Reparations Movement*, 58 N.Y.U. Annual Survey Am. L. 615 (2003); Svetlana Shirinova, *Challenges to Establishing Jurisdiction over Holocaust Era Claims in Federal Court*, 34 Golden Gate U. L. Rev. 159 (2004). For earlier efforts at compensation, see Menachem Z. Rosensaft & Joana D. Rosensaft, *The Early History of German-Jewish Reparations*, 25 Fordham Int'l L.J. 1 (2001); Kurt Schwerin, *German Compensation for Victims of Nazi Persecution*, 67 Nw. U. L. Rev. 479 (1972).

57. *See, e.g.*, Elazar Barkan, *The Guilt of Nations* at 88–111 (2000). *See* In re Holocaust Victims Asset Litig., 225 F.3d 191, 193 (2d Cir. 2000) (upholding limitation of settlement to Jews, Jehovah's Witnesses, Romani, and gays); In re Holocaust Victims Assets Litig., 105 F. Supp.2d 139 (E.D.N.Y. 2000) (approving settlement). For more recent aspects of the litigation, see In re Holocaust Victim Assets Litig., 282 F.3d 103, 109–11 (2d Cir. 2002). There is some dispute about the value of the settlement. Some place the value closer to $1.25 billion.

58. Neuborne, *supra* note 56, at 617. *See also* Burt Neuborne, *Preliminary Reflections on Aspects of Holocaust-Era Litigation in American Courts*, 80 Wash. U. L.Q. 795 (2002).

59. *See* Rosner v. United States, 231 F. Supp.2d 1202, 1208 (S.D. Fla. 2002).

60. *See* Michael J. Bazyler, *Holocaust Justice: The Battle for Restitution in America's Courts* 202–68 (2003).

61. *See, e.g.*, Alex Boraine, *A Country Unmasked: Inside South Africa's Truth and Reconciliation Commission* (2001); Richard A. Wilson, *The Politics of Truth and Reconciliation in South Africa: Legitimizing the Post-Apartheid State* (2001); Truth v. Justice (Robert I. Rotberg & Dennis Thompson eds. 2000); Antjie Krog, *Country of My Skull: Guilt, Sorrow, and the Limits of Forgiveness in the New South Africa* (2000).

62. *See* Martha Minow, *Between Vengeance and Forgiveness: Facing History After Genocide and Mass Violence* (1998).

63. *See, e.g.,* Barkan, *supra* note 57, at 262–82.

64. *See id.* at 46–64.

65. *See id.* at 54–55.

66. *See Sierra Leone Truth and Reconciliation Commission Calls for Reparations*, UN News Center, *available at* http://www.un.org/apps/news/story.asp?NewsID=12370&Cr=sierra&Cr1=leone.

67. The International Center for Transitional Justice tracks the many truth and reconciliation commissions in operation around the world: http://www.ictj.net/default.asp. The United States Institute for Peace also has a comprehensive listing, along with links to the reports: http://www.usip.org/library/truth.html.Further information is also available for Sierra Leone at http://www.trcsierraleone.org/drwebsite/publish/index.shtml; for East Timor at http://www.easttimor-reconciliation.org/; and for Ghana at http://www.ictj.net/downloads/Ghana.NRC.release.pdf.

68. Deborah Orin, *W. Pledges Liberia's Dictator Is Outta There*, N.Y. Post, July 6, 2003 ("Former President Bill Clinton made headlines by apologizing for U.S. inaction on Rwanda genocide, U.S. support for African dictators and nearly apologizing for slavery when he said America was 'wrong' to profit from it."). There are some reports that Clinton worried about the legal implications of an apology. Paige A. Fogarty, *Speculating a Strategy: Suing Insurance Companies to Obtain Legislative Reparations for Slavery*, 9 Conn. Ins. L.J. 211, 216 (2002) (citing Douglas Stanglin, *Clinton Opposes Slavery Apology*, U.S. News and World Report, 7, April 6, 1998).

69. Elizabeth Sullivan, *World Tunes Out Bloody Congo*, Cleveland Plain Dealer, May 29, 2003; Philip C. Aka, *The "Dividend of Democracy": Analyzing U.S. Support for Nigerian Democratization*, 22 B.C. Third World L.J. 225, 276 (2002) (discussing Clinton's high-profile apologies).

70. Richard Pyle, *U.S. Commanders Told Troops to Shoot Korean Civilians*, Milwaukee Sentinel, November 25, 2001 (Clinton rejected calls for formal apology, but issued statement of regret instead); Martha Mendoza, *No Gun Ri: A Coverup Exposed a Commentary*, 38 Stan. J. Int'l L. 153 (2002).

71. John M. Broder, *Clinton Offers His Apologies to Guatemala*, N.Y. Times, March 11, 1999, at A1.

72. Matthew Kaufman, *The Debt; The Cost of Slavery Was High. But Who Will Pay for It?* Hartford Courant, September 29, 2002 (discussing Clinton's apology for Tuskegee experiments).

73. *Human Guinea Pigs Another Example of "Scientific" Abuse*, Pittsburgh Post-Gazette, June 10, 2002.

74. See Public Law 103–150, 107 Stat. 1510 (1993); Jean Marbella, *A Mellow Revolution Stirs among Hawaiians; Sovereignty: Some Envision the Islands Not as the 50th State — But as an Independent Country*, Baltimore Sun, May

10, 2003 (discussing joint resolution of Congress, signed by Clinton, apologizing for deprivation of land); Ediberto Roman, *Reparations and the Colonial Dilemma: The Insurmountable Hurdles and Yet Transformative Benefits*, 13 Berkeley La Raza L.J. 369, 379 (2002).

For more on reparations to Native Hawaiians, see Eric Yamamoto, *Race Apologies*, 1 J. Gender, Race & Justice 47, 74 (1997); Eric Yamamoto, *Race Theory and Political Lawyering in Post–Civil Rights America*, 95 Mich. L. Rev. 821 (1997); Eric Yamamoto, *Rethinking Alliances: Agency, Responsibility and Interracial Justice*, 3 UCLA Asian Pacific L.J. 33 (1995); Robert S. Chang, *Facing History, Facing Ourselves: Eric Yamamoto and the Quest for Justice*, 5 Mich. J. Race & Law 111 (1999) (reviewing Yamamoto, *Interracial Justice, supra* note 2); Joint Resolution 19 (103d Congress), P. Law 103-150 (Nov. 23, 1993), *available at* http://www.hawaii-nation.org/publawall.html.

75. In 2001, the 213th General Assembly of the Presbyterian Church received the following resolution:

Apology to Americans of African Descent for the Institution of Slavery. That the 213th General Assembly (2001):

1. Confesses the corporate guilt the Presbyterian Church (U.S.A.) shares for the evils of slavery and requests forgiveness from God and from all God's children whose lives have been damaged by these sins.
2. Pledges and promises to seek, through words and deeds, as individuals and as a denomination, to demonstrate our sorrow by committing ourselves to work with our African American brothers and sisters to overcome the vestiges of slavery that manifest themselves today in church and society as racism.

Available at http://www.pcusa.org/ga213/business/cro103.htm.

The Presbyterian Church in America passed a similar resolution in 2002 at its annual meeting in Birmingham, Alabama. It declared:

The heinous sins attendant with unbiblical forms of servitude–including oppression, racism, exploitation, manstealing, and chattel slavery-stand in opposition to the Gospel. The effects of these sins have created and continue to create barriers between brothers and sisters of different races and/or economic spheres.

Therefore we confess our involvement in these sins. As a people, both we and our fathers, have failed to keep the commandments, the statutes, and the laws God has commanded. We therefore publicly repent of our pride, our complacency, and our complicity. Furthermore, we seek the forgiveness of our brothers and sisters for the reticence of our hearts that have constrained us from acting swiftly in this matter. We will strive, in a manner consistent with the Gospel imperatives, for the encouragement of racial reconciliation, the establishment of urban and minority congregations, and the enhancement of existing ministries of mercy in our cities, among the poor, and across all social, racial, and economic boundaries, to the glory of God.

Available at http://www.crosswalk.com/1143724.html.

76. Helen T. Gray, *Church Calls for Government Apology for Slavery*, Kansas City Star, July 16, 2001.

77. President Simmons's charge to the committee and much other information on the committee is *available at* http://www.brown.edu/Research/Slavery_Justice/.

78. Detailed information on Brown's history and the Brown family is *available at* http://www.brown.edu/Administration/News_Bureau/Info/Slavery.html.

79. For further information on Wayland, Fuller, and Brown in the antebellum era, see Alfred L. Brophy, *Considering Universities' Culpability in Slavery*, paper delivered at Conference of the Brown University Steering Committee on Slavery and Justice Committee, March 17, 2005.

80. *See* Senate Joint Resolution 37 108th Congress, 2d Session (May 6, 2004) ("To acknowledge a long history of official depredations and ill-conceived policies by the United States Government regarding Indian tribes and offer an apology to all Native Peoples on behalf of the United States"). The draft joint resolution is reprinted in appendix 7.

81. The Senate apology is reprinted in appendix 8.

82. *See, e.g.*, Andrew Meier, *Burnt Offerings*, Financial Times, February 18, 2005 ("Perhaps no issue in America polls as poorly among white respondents as reparations").

83. *See, e.g.*, Lauren Markoe, *Senate Votes an Apology on Lynching*, Philadelphia Inquirer, June 14, 2005; Pratik Shah, *Supreme Court Noticeably Absent from Anti-Lynching Apology*, Birmingham News, June 26, 2005 (noting that under current Supreme Court precedent, the Senate does not even now have the power to pass key parts of the antilynching legislation and suggesting that perhaps it is the U.S. Supreme Court that should be apologizing).

84. The California Insurance Commissioner's Slavery Era Insurance Registry Web site is *available at* http://www.insurance.ca.gov/0100-consumers/0300-public-programs/0200-slavery-era-insur/.

85. *See* Business, Corporate, and Slavery Era Insurance Ordinance, Municipal Code of Chicago, § 2–92–585 (2002).

86. Nicholas Stein, *How Slavery Still Haunts Some Firms*, Fortune, December 22, 2003. *See also* Laura Washington, *Tillman Isn't Helping Debate over Slave Reparations; A Good Thing about the Reparations Discussion Is That It Forces Us to Confront Our Legacy of Slavery*, Chicago Sun-Times 45, December 8, 2003 (editorial).

87. Ellen Barry, *Killen Gets 60 Years in '64 Killings*, Los Angeles Times, June 24, 2005.

88. *See, e.g.,* Jon M. Van Dyke *The Fundamental Human Right to Prosecution and Compensation*, 29 Denver Int'l L. & Policy 77, 87 (2001) (listing Clinton-era apologies); Joe Hermer, *Gift Encounters: Conceptualizing the Elements of Begging Conduct*, 56 U. Miami L. Rev. 77 (2001) ("Some commentators, in the wake of the recent conduct of former President Clinton, have suggested that the apology has become a central trope of political discourse in the late twentieth century"); Elizabeth Latif, *Apologetic Justice: Evaluating Apologies Tailored toward Legal Solutions*, 81 B.U. L. Rev. 289 (2001); Alfred L. Brophy, *Grave Matters: The Ancient Rights of the Graveyard*, forthcoming B. Y. U. L. Rev. (2006).

CHAPTER 3

1. Many see affirmative action as a form of reparations—and reparations talk as a continuance of the affirmative action debate. *See, e.g.,* Albert Mosley, *Affirmative Action as a Form of Reparations*, 33 U. Mem. L. Rev. 353 (2003).

2. *See* U.S. Census Bureau, *Current Population Reports, Income, Poverty, and Health Insurance Coverage in the United States: 2004*, 10 (2005), *available at* http://www.census.gov/prod/2005pubs/p60-229.pdf. A quick summary of the U.S. Census Bureau 2004 data is *available at* http://www.census.gov/hhes/www/poverty/poverty04/table3.pdf.

3. U.S. Census Bureau, *supra* note 2, at 53, 54. It is bold, then, to argue that African Americans today "have never even remotely known the world that spawned Victimology." McWhorter, *supra* note, at 37. A significant percentage of children—nearly one in three—knows a world of poverty, limited educational opportunities, and limited hope.

4. U.S. Census Bureau, *supra* note 2, at 53 (reporting 8.6% of non-Hispanic whites in poverty); *id.* at 54 (reporting that 10.5% of white non-Hispanic children live in poverty).

5. *See* U.S. Census Bureau, *supra* note 2, at 33, 34 (reporting median income of families by race).

6. *See* U.S. Census Bureau, *Median Income by Selected Characteristics, Race, and Hispanic Origin: 2000, 1999, and 1998, Households,* at 5 (black families), 9 (non-Hispanic white families) *available at* http://www.census.gov/hhes/income/income00/inctab1.html.

7. *See also* Joe Feagin, *Racist America: Roots, Current Realities, and Future Reparations* (2000).

8. *See* Melvin L. Oliver & Thomas M. Shapiro, *Black Wealth/White Wealth: A New Perspective on Racial Inequality* 102 (1997).

9. U.S. Census Bureau, Educational Attainment in the United States: March 2002 Detailed Tables (PPL-169), Percent of High School and College Graduates of the Population 15 Years and Over, by Age, Sex, Race, and Hispanic Origin, Table 1A, at 4, 7, *available at* http://www.census.gov/population/socdemo/education/ppl-169/tab01a.pdf.

One might also observe that among people of Hispanic origin, only 57% have high school diplomas, and only 9.4% have college degrees. *See id.* at 13.

10. *See* Jewel Crawford and Wade W. Nobles, *Reparations and Health Care for African Americans: Repairing the Damage from the Legacy of Slavery* in Should America Pay? Slavery and the Raging Debate Over Reparations 251, 268 (Raymond A. Winbush ed. 2003).

11. For, as Tulane Law School Professor Robert Westley has said,

> there is no need to recount here the horrors of slavery. Suffice to say
> that, if the land redistribution program pursued by Congress during
> Reconstruction had not been undermined by President Johnson, if
> Congress' enactments on behalf of political and social equality for
> Blacks had not been undermined by the courts, if the Republicans had
> not sacrificed the goal of social justice on the altar of political compro-
> mise, and Southern whites had not drowned Black hope in
> a sea of desire for racial superiority, then talk of reparations—or
> genocide—at this point in history might be obtuse, if not perverse.
> (Robert Westley, *Many Billions Gone: Is It Time to Reconsider the Case
> for Black Reparations?* 19 B.C. Third World L. Rev. 429, 464 (1998).)

Westley sees the discrimination as a systemwide problem:

> The pervasiveness of white supremacist structures . . . inhabit our
> literature and the canons of literary interpretation; they inhabit our
> speech; they inhabit popular culture, from films and television, to
> music, dance and fashion; they determine classroom curricula
> throughout the educational system; they influence the friends we
> make, the restaurants we choose to eat in, the places we shop; they es-
> tablish national priorities and the means employed to resolve social

problems; often, they define what it means to be a problem. White supremacist structures insinuate their presence into the most intimate encounters among people, especially sexual ones; they inform critical standards in art and philosophy, legal standards in politics, educational standards in school and professional standards in employment. (*Id.* at 448)

12. *See, e.g.*, Richard W. Stevenson, *Bush, in Africa, Promises Aid but Offers No Troops for Liberia*, N.Y. Times, July 8, 2003 ("Years of unpunished brutality and bullying and rape produced a dullness and hardness of conscience. Christian men and women became blind to the clearest commands of their faith and added hypocrisy to injustice. A republic founded on equality for all became a prison for millions") (quoting President Bush).

13. *See, e.g.*, Kim Forde-Mazrui, *Taking Conservatives Seriously: A Moral Justification for Affirmative Action and Reparations*, 92 Cal. L. Rev. 683 (2004). An earlier version of the article is available on the Internet. *See* Kim Forde-Mazrui, *Taking the Right Seriously: America's Moral Responsibility for Effects of Past Racial Discrimination* (2002), *available at* http://papers.ssrn.com/sol3/delivery.cfm/SSRN_ID311860_code020613630.pdf?abstractid=311860.

14. Fullilove v. Klutznick, 481 U.S. 472 (1980).

15. 467 U.S. 561, 575 (1984). *See also* Peter Schuck, *Affirmative Action: Past, Present, and Future*, 20 Yale L. & Pol'y Rev. 1 (2002).

16. 478 U.S. 1014 (1986).

17. Adarand v. Pena, 515 U.S. 200, 235 (1995).

18. *Id.* at 226.

19. *Id.* at 237.

20. *See, e.g., id.* at 237 ("The unhappy persistence of both the practice and the lingering effects of racial discrimination against minority groups in this country is an unfortunate reality, and government is not disqualified from acting in response to it"); Richmond v. J. A. Croson, 488 U.S. 469, 509 (1988).

21. *Id.*

22. Justice O'Connor acknowledged the shameful history of racism—and its likely effect on the number of African-American contractors. However, that history was insufficiently tied to the quota that Richmond established. *Id.* at 499 ("The 30% quota cannot in any realistic sense be tied to any injury suffered by anyone").

23. Adarand v. Pena, 515 U.S. 200, 235 (1995).

24. Writing in 1998, Tulane University law professor Robert Westley saw reparations as an alternative way of thinking about both black entitlement and racial justice. Westley, *Many Billions Gone, supra* note 11, at 471. There is some tension, it seems, in a reparations program that argues that it is necessary

because African Americans have not been able to succeed economically—and then still asks for compensation for those who have succeeded. Of course, Westley would likely point out that even those who succeeded did so in the face of—and in spite of—government discrimination.

25. Perhaps we will see a departure from the requirements of desegregation cases, like *Missouri v. Jenkins*, which struck down a creative solution to the Kansas City School District's racist past. The federal trial court had ordered the city to spend hundreds of millions of dollars to make the city's schools so desirable that students would voluntarily choose to go there. Yet, Chief Justice Rehnquist wrote for the Supreme Court in 1995 that the remedy must be designed to repair the constitutional harm. Of course, *Jenkins* places limits on what courts can do, and *Grutter* is dealing with what are essentially legislative and executive decisions.

26. *See, e.g., infra* chapter 6 (discussing the likely constitutional problems with reparations for slavery and suggesting what findings would be necessary to support them); Eric Posner and Adrian Vermeule, *Reparations for Slavery and Other Historical Injustices*, 103 Colum. L. Rev. 689 (2003) (discussing constitutional problems with reparations for slavery).

27. Stuart Eizenstat, *Racial Preferences as Slavery Reparation; Michigan Case Opens Broader Questions*, Los Angeles Times, March 31, 2003.

28. Mari Matsuda, *Looking to the Bottom: Critical Legal Studies and Reparations*, 22 Harv. C.R.-C.L. L. Rev. 323, 374 (1987).

29. *Id.* at 374.

30. *See, e.g.*, Randall Kennedy, *Racial Critiques of Legal Academy*, 102 Harv. L. Rev. 1741, 1791 n. 205 (1989) (discussing Richard Delgado and the various meanings of affirmative action, as reparations, because of their utility, or as distributive justice). Professor Kennedy challenges Professor Matsuda's point that minority scholars bring a unique understanding to the debate. He suggests that all people possess the potential for the humanity to suggest ideas that might challenge and remake the law.

31. Vincene Verdun, *If the Shoe Fits, Wear It: An Analysis of Reparations to African Americans*, 67 Tul. L. Rev. 597 (1993).

32. *Id.* at 621.

33. *See infra* section IV (on constitutionality of reparations).

34. Verdun, *supra* note 31, at 628. Verdun's work aims less at courts and more at legislatures than Matsuda's. It is also part of a much larger debate over the nature of African American culture. It therefore touches on issues of Afrocentrism, along with citations to suspect scholarship on the biological determinants of personality differences between African Americans and European Americans. *See id.* at 668 nn. 90–91.

35. *Id.* at 630.

36. *Id.* at 638. She continues: "Society, unlike individuals, does not have a natural life. The society that committed the wrong is still thriving. In a sense, reparationists would analogize society to a trustee who holds the corpus of the trust—the benefit society derived from slave labor during slavery and since emancipation—and would view African Americans as the beneficiaries of the trust who are entitled to trace the assets of the trust in whatever form they can be found."

37. *See* Rhonda V. Magee, *The Master's Tools from the Bottom Up: Responses to African-American Reparations Theory in Mainstream and Outsider Remedies Discourse,* 79 Va. L. Rev. 863 (1993).

38. *Id.* at 874, 875.

39. *Id.* at 876.

40. *Id.* at 914.

41. *Id.* at 910.

42. *See, e.g., id.* at 910:

> The central point is that "the system" of American law and politics merely consists of the aggregate actions of racially hyperconscious individual participants. As long as whites continue to predominate in positions of power over Blacks within the system, they bring their subconscious beliefs in white supremacy to bear on the processes at hand. This done by tens of thousands of individuals every minute of every day creates a system by which racism continues to operate in institutions—so-called institutionalized racism, or rather, institutionalized white supremacy. Institutionalized white supremacy is driven by the internalized white-over-Black world views of millions of individual participants acting daily in their individual offices and ranges of responsibility. There simply is no public-private distinction when it comes to the white supremacist world view. One believes it, more or less.

43. Magee, *supra* note 37, at 899. *See also* T. Alexander Alienkoff, *A Case for Race-Consciousness,* 91 Colum. L. Rev. 1060 (1991); Kimberle Williams Crenshaw, *Colorblindess, History, and the Law,* in The House that Race Built: Black Americans, U.S. Terrain 280–87 (Wahneema Lubiano ed. 1997).

44. *See* Tuneen E. Chisholm, *Sweep around Your Own Front Door: Examining the Argument for Legislative African American Reparations,* 147 U. Pa. L. Rev. 677 (1999).

45. *See* Westley, *supra* note 11.

46. *See* James Baldwin, *Many Thousands Gone,* in Notes of a Native Son 27 (1963), cited in *id.* at 466 n. 154. More recently, Ira Berlin has adopted that

phrase as well. *See* Ira Berlin, *Many Thousands Gone: The First Two Centuries of Slavery in North America* (2000).

47. Kenneth T. Jackson, *Crabgrass Frontier: The Suburbanization of the United States* 197–217 (1985). Jackson discusses the multiple ways that redlining, which made it impossible to obtain FHA financing and hence difficult to sell a home in a redlined area, kept minorities and poorer whites from building equity in their homes.

48. Westley, *supra* note 11, at 441–43.

49. Westley, *supra* note 11, at 432 (citing Mari Matsuda, *Looking to the Bottom*, *supra* note 28, at 326) (defining "critical legalism").

50. Westley, *supra* note 11, at 438. *See also id.*, at 468 ("because it is my belief that Blacks have been and are harmed as a group, that racism is a group practice, I am opposed to individual reparations as a primary policy objective").

51. *Id.* at 436.

52. *Id.*

53. *Id.* at 470. Others see money as central to reparations, even though they do not propose payments to individuals. As Molefi Kete Asante has phrased the issue, "one way to approach the issue of reparations is to speak about money, but not necessarily about *cash*. Reparations will cost, but it will not have to be the giving out of billions of dollars of cash to individuals, although it will cost billions of dollars." Molefi Kete Asante, *The African American Warrant for Reparations: The Crime of European Enslavement of Africans and Its Consequences*, in Should America Pay?, *supra* note 10.

54. Westley, *supra* note 11, at 476.

55. *See* Randall Robinson, *The Debt: What America Owes to Blacks* ix (2000) (crediting Ibrahim Gassama and Robert Westley with providing legal precedent for the argument). Moreover, many of Robinson's specific proposals, such as a trust fund, come directly from Westley. *See id.* at 242–43.

56. *See* Robinson, *supra* note 55, at 8.

57. *Id.* at 247.

58. Richard F. America, *Paying the Social Debt: What White America Owes Black America* (1993) (assessing the amount of money saved by systematic undercompensation of African Americans); *The Wealth of Races: The Present Value of Benefits from Past Injustices* (Richard F. America ed. 1990).

59. *See, e.g.*, George Schedler, *Racist Symbols and Reparations: Philosophical Reflections on Vestiges of the American Civil War* (1998); Albert Mosley, *supra* note 1; Joseph Jenkins, *Inheritance Law as Constellation in Lieu of Redress: A Detour Through Exceptional Terrain*, 24 Cardozo L. Rev. 1043 (2003); George Schedler, *Responsibility for and Estimation of the Damages of American Slavery*, 33 U. Mem. L. Rev. 307 (2003).

60. *See* chapter 1, note 1.

61. Manning Marable, *In Defense of Black Reparations*, in Along the Color Line (October 2002), *available at* http://www.manningmarable.net/works/pdf/octo2a.pdf.

62. *Id.*

63. Manning Marable, *In Defense of Black Reparations, Part II*, in Along the Color Line (October 2002) ("First, and perhaps foremost, is the fact that white racism is structural in character, and is largely grounded in institutional processes rather than by individuals' behavior. Racial prejudice is reproduced by America's basic institutions—economic educational, social, and political—of our society. The racial myths of white history are used to rationalize, explain away, and justify white supremacy and black inequality"). *Available at* http://www.manningmarable.net/works/pdf/octo2b.pdf.

That Marable is seeking to reform the entire society is apparent from his 1983 book, *How Capitalism Underdeveloped Black America*. For him, reparations talk is a vehicle for advocating those changes. Jeffery M. Brown has recently put Marable's call for structural reparations into a legal context. *See Deconstructing Babel: Toward a Theory of Structural Reparations*, 56 Rutgers L. Rev. 463 (2004).

64. Marable's talk, the 2003 Paul Robeson Lecture, "Forty Acres and a Mule: The Case for Black Reparations," is *available at* http://www.law.columbia.edu/law_school/education_tech/streaming/video_1.

The quotes appear at 1:38 and he repeats those themes around 1:58.

65. William Bradford, *"With a Very Great Blame on Our Hearts": Reparations, Reconciliation, and an American Indian Plea for Peace with Justice*, 27 Am. Indian L. Rev. 1, 99–100 (2002–03).

66. One might begin the investigation with Stephan Thernstrom & Abigail Thernstrom, *America in Black and White: One Nation, Indivisible* (1997); Kirby Moss, *Color of Class: Poor Whites and the Paradox of Privilege* (2003).

67. *See, e.g.,* David Lyons, *Reparations and Equal Opportunity*, 24 B.C. L. Rev. 177 (2003).

68. Lee A. Harris, *Political Autonomy as a Form of Reparations to African-Americans*, 29 S.U. L. Rev. 25 (2001). Harris locates the reparations debate in concerns about corrective and distributive justice—that is, claims for correcting past injustices and claims for assuring equal (or fairer) distributions of wealth now. His solution, though, is a radical one.

69. *See* Roy L. Brooks, *Integration or Separation? A Strategy of Racial Equality* (1996).

70. *See* Eric Yamamoto, *Interracial Justice: Conflict and Reconciliation in Post–Civil Rights America* (1998). *See also Breaking the Cycles of Hatred: Memory, Law, and Repair* (Martha Minow & Nancy L. Rosenblum eds. 2003).

71. Adjoa A. Aiyetoro, *The National Coalition of Blacks for Reparations in America (N'COBRA): Its Creation and Contribution to the Reparations Movement*, in Should America Pay? *supra* note 10, at 209, 225. In some of her more academic writings, Aiyetoro explores strategies for lawsuits. *See, e.g.*, Adjoa A. Aiyetoro, *Formulating Reparations through the Eyes of the Movement*, 58 N.Y.U. Annual Survey Am. L. 457, 464 (2003) (discussing ways to fit reparations claims into categories required for a lawsuit).

72. Roy Brooks, *Atonement and Forgiveness: A New Model for Black Reparations* xii (2004).

73. *See id.* at 2–3.

74. *See* Kenneth Cooper-Stevenson, *Theoretical Underpinnings for Reparations: A Constitutional Tort Perspective*, 22 Windsor Yearbook of Access to Justice 3–40 (2003). Cooper-Stevenson's paper and other important ones delivered at the University of Windsor's June 2003 reparations symposium are *available at* http://cronus.uwindsor.ca/users/j/jberrym/main.nsf.

Recently, Christian Sundquist has criticized reparations for aiming too narrowly and failing to attack white privilege. Christian Sundquist, *Critical Praxis, Spirit Healing, and Community Activism: Preserving a Subversive Dialogue on Reparations*, 58 N.Y.U. Annual Survey Am. L. 659, 661 (2003) ("current models of reparations present a narrow understanding of the 'debt' owed, limit the potential of spirit-healing within the Black community, do not seek to undermine privilege, and promote white backlash and intra-community divisiveness").

75. One might contrast Eric Yamomoto's book *Interracial Justice*, *supra* note 70; Matsuda, *supra* note 28 (corrective justice); Anthony Cook, *King and the Beloved Community: A Communitarian Defense of Black Reparations*, 68 Geo. Wash. L. Rev. 959 (2000) (redistribution of privilege); Jerome Culp, *To The Bone: Race and White Privilege*, 83 Minn. L. Rev. 1637 (1999) (redistribution of privilege); and Lee A. Harris, *Political Autonomy as a Form of Reparations to African-Americans*, 29 S.U. L. Rev. 25 (2001).

CHAPTER 4

1. The op-ed, David Horowitz, "Ten Reasons Why Reparations for Slavery Is a Bad Idea—and Racist Too" is *available at* http://www.frontpagemag.com/Articles/ReadArticle.asp?ID=1153. It is also conveniently reprinted in David Horowitz, *Uncivil Wars: The Controversy over Reparations for Slavery* 12–16 (2001). *See also* http://www.wewontpay.com.

2. Eric A. Posner and Adrian Vermeule, *Reparations for Slavery and Other Historical Injustices*, 103 Colum. L. Rev. 689, 703 (2003).

3. Horowitz, *supra* note 1, at 13. Journalist Walter Williams has a similar argument: "If we acknowledge that government has no resources of its very own, and that to give one American a dollar government must first confiscate it from some other American, we might ask what moral principle justifies forcing a white of today to pay a black of today for what a white of yesteryear did to a black of yesteryear?" *See* Walter Williams, *Reparations for Slavery* (January 12, 2001), *available at* http://capmag.com/article.asp?ID=89.

4. *See* Williams, *supra* note 3 ("In Africa, Moslems dominated the slave trade in the 18th and 19th centuries. Africans also engaged in slave trade with Europeans. In fact, there was plantation slavery in some parts of Africa, such as the Sudan, Zanzibar, and Egypt"); Horowitz, *supra* note 1, at 13 ("Black Africans and Arabs were responsible for enslaving the ancestors of African-Americans. There were 3,000 black slave-owners in the ante-bellum United States. Are reparations to be paid by their descendants too?").

5. *See, e.g,* Charles J. Ogletree, *The Current Reparations Debate*, 36 U.C. Davis L. Rev. 1051, 1069 (2003) ("I believe that suing a corporation is much different than suing a person. Legally, corporations are immortal; they do not die except by their own hand. So a company that is around in 2002 can be the same company that was around in 1602. And where that company owes its present profitability to its slave trading, that company should acknowledge that fact and make some form of restitution. Now, this principle of corporate responsibility is neither new, nor controversial. Holocaust victims have successfully sued corporations to recover the property stolen from them during the Second World War").

6. *Id.* (crediting Cornel West with the analogy).

7. All of which leads to the question whether the federal and state governments were liable for the harms of slavery—or whether those harms were created by private citizens who purchased slaves.

8. *See* Walter Williams, *The Legacy of the Slavery Hustle* (July 16, 2001) (quoting Aiyetoro), *available at* http://capmag.com/article.asp?ID=968.

9. *Id.*

10. *Id.*

11. *Id.*

12. *See generally* Charles Murray, *Losing Ground: American Social Policy, 1950–1980* (1992).

13. *See, e.g.*, Keith Hylton, *Slavery and Tort Law*, 84 Boston University Law Review 1209 (2004).

14. William Julius Williams, *The Truly Disadvantaged: The Inner City, the Underclass and Public Policy* (1990). Two excellent introductions to these issues come from Michael Fumento, *Is the Great Society to Blame? If Not, Why Have Problems Worsened since '60s?* Investor's Business Daily (June 19, 1992), and James

Q. Wilson, *Slavery and the Black Family*, Public Interest (Spring 2002), *available at* http://www.thepublicinterest.com/archives/2002spring/article1.html.

15. Anti-reparationists frequently invoke President Lyndon Johnson's Great Society and war on poverty as a form of reparations—and claim that those programs have paid off the debt. *See* Williams, *supra* note 3 ("Would reparations payments accomplish what the 6 trillion dollars spent since 1965 on the War on Poverty didn't?"). Horowitz phrases the argument in this way:

> Since the passage of the Civil Rights Acts and the advent of the Great
> Society in 1965, trillions of dollars in transfer payments have been
> made to African-Americans in the form of welfare benefits and
> racial preferences (in contracts, job placements and educational
> admissions)—all under the rationale of redressing historic racial griev-
> ances. It is said that reparations are necessary to achieve a healing be-
> tween African-Americans and other Americans. If trillion dollar resti-
> tutions and a wholesale rewriting of American law (in order to
> accommodate racial preferences) for African-Americans is not enough
> to achieve a "healing," what will?

Horowitz, *Uncivil Wars, supra* note 1, at 14.

16. Williams, *supra* note 3.

17. Michael Levin, *Why Race Matters* 259 (1997). Stephen Kershnar's arti-cle alerted me to Levin's argument. *See* Stephen Kershnar, *Reparations for Slavery and Justice*, 33 U. Memphis L. Rev. 277, 292–93 (2003). He rebuts Levin by pointing out that welfare payments are not meant as compensatory programs—that is, they are designed to sustain recipients, not to repair past harm. I tend to think that the distinction is not terribly helpful—and I think that reparations should be focused on those in greatest need, so that I am sym-pathetic to the argument that welfare payments are part reparations. But I also see them as needed because of the harm of slavery and Jim Crow. They are, in my mind, a partial payment of reparations, not sufficient.

18. *See, e.g.*, Kershnar, *supra* note 17, at 295–98; Keith N. Hylton, *Slavery and Tort Law*, 38–42.

19. *See* Jeremy Waldron, *Superseding Historic Injustice*, 103 Ethics 4, 18–19 (1992); Kershnar, *supra* note 17, at 298.

20. *See* Allen Guelzo, *Reason in Disrepair*, Wall Street Journal (Novem-ber 22, 2002); Allen Guelzo, *Reparations Then and Now*, 124 First Things 32–36 (June/July 2002) *at* http://print.firstthings.com/ftissues/ft0206/articles/guelzo.html.

21. *Second Inaugural Address*, in Abraham Lincoln: Speeches and Writ-ings, 1859–1865 686, 687 (Don E. Fehrenbacher ed. 1989).

22. *Id.*

23. Roscoe Dunjee, *Segregation and Discrimination*, Oklahoma City Black Dispatch, July 29, 1926.

24. Horowitz phrases it as:

Slavery existed for thousands of years before the Atlantic slave trade was born, and in all societies. But in the thousand years of its existence, there never was an anti-slavery movement until white Christians—Englishmen and Americans—created one. If not for the anti-slavery attitudes and military power of white Englishmen and Americans, the slave trade would not have been brought to an end. If not for the sacrifices of white soldiers and a white American president who gave his life to sign the Emancipation Proclamation, blacks in America would still be slaves. If not for the dedication of Americans of all ethnicities and colors to a society based on the principle that all men are created equal, blacks in America would not enjoy the highest standard of living of blacks anywhere in the world, and indeed one of the highest standards of living of any people in the world. They would not enjoy the greatest freedoms and the most thoroughly protected individual rights anywhere. Where is the gratitude of black America and its leaders for those gifts?

See Horowitz, *supra* note 1, at 15; Horowitz, *Ten Reasons, supra* note 1 (reason nine).

25. *Bush Calls Slavery One of History's "Greatest Crimes,"* Houston Chronicle, July 8, 2003.

26. *See* Keith N. Hylton, *A Framework for Reparations Claims*, 24 B.C. Third World L.J. 31, 34–35 (2004).

27. *See id.* at 34.

28. *Id.* at 35.

29. Armstrong Williams, *Presumed Victims*, in Should America Pay? Slavery and the Raging Debate over Reparations at 165 (Raymond A. Winbush ed. 2003).

30. *See* Carol Swain, *The New White Nationalism in America: Its Challenges to Integration* 181 (2002).

31. At least that is the suggestion of Wendy Kaminer. *See* Wendy Kaminer, *Up from Reparations*, American Prospect, May 22, 2000 ("The Calvinism of seventeenth century colonials proved less quintessentially American than did the notion that you can choose to be born again in Christ. This is not a culture inclined to embrace ideas of predestination, spiritual or financial. In the mythic, utterly egalitarian America—the democratic America Tocqueville

described—we create our own futures, unburdened by our familial pasts"). Whether early American religious and political ideals continue to motivate us is a subject a little beyond the scope of this chapter. One might on this issue compare Robert Ferguson's *The American Enlightenment, 1750–1820* (1994), which establishes the boundaries of those ideas, with Andrew Delbanco's *The Real American Dream: A Meditation on Hope* (1999), which speculates about Americans' declension from certain founding principles.

32. Morton J. Horwitz, *Republicanism and Liberalism in American Constitutional Thought*, 29 Wm. & Mary L. Rev. 57 (1987) (emphasizing liberalism in American law); Mari Matsuda, *Looking to the Bottom: Critical Legal Studies and Reparations*, 22 Harv. C.R.-C.L. L. Rev. 323, 373–88 (1987).

33. *Cf.* Ralph Waldo Emerson, *American Scholar*, in Ralph Waldo Emerson: Essays and Lectures 53, 56–57 (Joel Porte ed. 1983) ("Each age, it is found, must write its own books; or rather, each generation for the next succeeding. The books of an older period will not fit this").

34. *See* Jim Sidanius *et al.*, *It's Not Affirmative Action, It's the Blacks: The Continuing Relevance of Race in American Politics*, in Racialized Politics: The Debate about Racism in America 191–235 (David O. Sears *et al.*, eds. 1999) (evaluating the significance of racism versus "political ideology and values such as self-reliance, individual responsibility, fairness, and equity" in opposing affirmative action). *See also* Lawrence Bobo, *Race and Beliefs about Affirmative Action*, in *id.* at 137–64 (focusing on role that racism plays in opposing affirmative action).

35. *See, e.g.*, Ala. Code § 43-2-350 (prescribing time for filing claims against estate); Reed v. Campbell, 476 U.S. 852, 855–56 (1986). In the context of reparations for slavery, however, Helen Jenkins has recently made a provocative argument in favor of reopening some estates that have now been closed for decades. *See* Helen Bishop Jenkins, *A Study of the Intersection of DNA Technology, Exhumation, and Heirship Determination as It Relates to Modern-Day Descendants of Slaves in America*, 50 Ala. L. Rev. 39 (1998).

36. *See, e.g.*, Kaminer, *supra* note 31.

37. Ralph Waldo Emerson, *Emerson in His Journals* 358 (Joel Porte ed. 1983).

38. *See, e.g.*, Alfred L. Brophy, The Intersection of Slavery and Property in Southern Legal Thought: From Missouri Compromise through Civil War (Ph.D. diss., Harvard University, 2001) (discussing centrality of property in Southerners' thinking).

39. *See, e.g.*, Gregory Alexander, *Propriety and Commodity: Competing Visions of Property in American Legal Thought, 1776–1970* (1997) (exploring the competing considerations—of protection of individual and community rights—throughout American legal history); Morton J. Horwitz, *The Transfor-*

mation of American Law, 1780–1860 31–62 (1977) (identifying changes in property interests that are protected).

40. *See, e.g.,* West River Bridge v. Dix, 47 U.S. (6 How.) 507, 521 (1848) (Unless cabined, the eminent domain power threatens to advance the "most leveling ultraisms of Anti-rentism or Agrarianism or Abolitionism") (argument of Daniel Webster). James Fenimore Cooper's Littlepage trilogy revolves around the Antirent movement and supports the arguments of the property owners. *See* James Fenimore Cooper, *The Redskins; Or Indian and Injin* . . . (New York, Stringer & Townsend 1852); James Fenimore Cooper, *The Chainbearer; or, The Littlepage Manuscripts* (New York, Burgess, Stringer & Co. 1845); James Fenimore Cooper, *Satanstoe; or, The Littlepage Manuscripts* (New York, Burgess, Stringer & Co. 1845).

41. *See, e.g.,* Joseph Singer, *Property Law: Rules, Policies, Practices* 1226 (3rd ed. 2002) (discussing the Worker Adjustment and Retraining Notification Act, 29 U.S.C. §§ 2101–2102). *See also* Joseph Singer, *Entitlement: The Paradoxes of Property* (2000) (discussing accommodation of property rights with social considerations).

42. Ralph Waldo Emerson, *The Conservative,* in Emerson: Essays and Lectures, *supra* note 33, at 173, 179.

43. Timothy Walker, *The Reform Spirit of the Day* (Cambridge, 1850).

44. George Bancroft, *An Oration Delivered before the Democracy of Springfield* . . . *July 4, 1836,* at 6–7 (Springfield, George and Charles Merriam 1836).

45. *See* Ralph Ellison, *Juneteenth* 286–309 (1999).

46. *Id.* at 19. The question of "how can the future deny the past" is susceptible of several interpretations. It seems from the context that Sunraider is asking how can the future overcome the past? Some of Sunraider's speech is Bliss speaking through the mask of the Senator; other parts of it are pure, racist Sunraider. *See id.* at 17 (Senator asking himself, *"Am I drunk, going insane?"*).

47. *Id.* at 15–16.

48. *See id.* at 23.

49. Ralph Ellison, *Going to the Territory,* in The Collected Essays of Ralph Ellison 591, 595 (John F. Callahan ed. 1995).

50. Watson Branch has summarized the goals of many reparations proponents as trying to find a new approach to racial inequality that is not based on integration: "Because integrationist policies and affirmative action based on civil rights statutes have failed to solve the problems of racial discrimination and subordination of blacks, it is time to undertake a new program of race reform — namely reparations." Watson Branch, *Reparations for Slavery: A Dream Deferred,* 3 San Diego Int'l L.J. 177, 194 (2002).

51. *See* Eric Yamamoto, *Interracial Justice: Conflict and Reconciliation in Post–Civil Rights America* (1998).

52. Rhonda V. Magee Andrews, *The Third Reconstruction: An Alternative to Race Consciousness and Color-Blindness in Post-Slavery America*, 54 Ala. L. Rev. 483 (2002).

CHAPTER 5

1. Commentators have begun to explore in some depth the problems with the lawsuit against Aetna and CSX. *See, e.g.*, Paige A. Fogarty, *Speculating a Strategy: Suing Insurance Companies to Obtain Legislative Reparations for Slavery*, 9 Conn. Ins. L.J. 211 (2002); Anthony Sebok, *Prosaic Justice: In America, Legal Advocates for Slavery Reparations Are Relying on the Cold Logic of Property Law, Not the Moral Force of Human Rights. It Might Well Work, but at What Cost?* Legal Affairs 51 (September/October 2002). Of course, as one could easily have predicted, the commentators were correct that the lawsuit had little chance for success.

2. Mari Matsuda, *Looking to the Bottom: Critical Legal Studies and Reparations*, 22 Harv. C.R.-C.L. L. Rev. 323, 374 (1987).

3. *Id.* at 375.

4. Perhaps the article that has advanced the cause the most is Rhonda V. Magee, *The Master's Tools, from the Bottom Up: Responses to African-American Reparations Theory in Mainstream and Outsider Remedies Discourse*, 79 Va. L. Rev. 863 (1993). For earlier examples, see Boris Bittker, *The Case for Black Reparations* (1973); Graham Hughes, *Reparations for Blacks*, 43 N.Y.U. L. Rev. 1063 (1968). Recently, Adrienne Davis has provided a suggestive case for reparations based on the Thirteenth Amendment. *See* Adrienne D. Davis, *The Case for United States Reparations to African Americans*, 7 Human Rights Brief 3 (2000).

5. The connection does not need to be perfect, as the Supreme Court has explained in affirmative action cases and busing cases. *See, e.g.*, Swann v. Charlotte-Mecklenburg Board of Education, 402 U.S. 1, 15–16 (1971) (providing for race-conscious remedy for school desegregation); United States v. Paradise, 480 U.S. 149, 167 (1980) (permitting race-conscious hiring, given extreme evidence of discrimination against African-Americans in the past by the employer, even though beneficiaries may not have been the same people previously excluded). The Supreme Court has recently reemphasized that there can be race-conscious government action, if there is a history of discrimination in the location (and perhaps by the government entity taking action). *See* Richmond v. J. A. Croson, 488 U.S. 469, 499–509 (1988). Of course, the pro-

gram must be "narrowly tailored" to the discrimination—that is, it must seek to rectify specific discrimination and have a logical stopping point. There are a number of specific instances of racial crimes, such as the riots used to terrorize and destroy African American communities throughout the South and Southwest, and lynchings. *See, e.g.*, Alberto Lopez, *Focusing the Reparations Debate beyond 1865*, 69 Tenn. L. Rev. 653–76 (2002) (discussing reparations for Jim Crow); Lisa Cardyn, *Sexualized Racism/Gendered Violence: Outraging the Body Politic in the Reconstruction South*, 100 Mich. L. Rev. 675, 851–52 (2002) (discussing intergenerational effects of racial violence of Jim Crow era and its implications for reparations).

6. Matsuda, *supra* note 2, at 376.

7. *Id.* at 380 ("Victims and perpetrators belong to groups that, as a matter of history, are logically treated in the collective sense of reparations rather than the individual sense of the typical legal claim").

8. *See, e.g., id.* at 376 ("Victims think of themselves as a group, because they are treated and survive as a group"); *id.* at 379 ("In short, the experience of the Hawaiians and Japanese-Americans as members of a victim group is raw, close, and real").

9. *Id.* at 377 ("Indigenous Hawaiians . . . are on the bottom of every demographic indicator of social survival; they have lower birth weights, higher infant mortality, and, if they survive, higher rates of disease, illiteracy, imprisonment, alcoholism, suicide and homelessness. Hawaiians realize their forgotten status in their own land. Poor and rich, Democrat and Republican, commoner and royalty—native Hawaiians largely agree that they have been robbed").

10. *See, e.g.*, Wygant v. Jackson Board Educ., 476 U.S. 267, 280–81 (1986).

11. This is part of what has been called "liberalism." (Here there may be confusion, because we often think of the word *liberal* today as a label for someone is on the left wing of politics, like Senator Edward Kennedy of Massachusetts or Reverend Jesse Jackson. But "liberalism" refers in legal thought to the idea of "classical liberalism," which is the idea that each individual is responsible for his or her own actions only.) *See* Louis Hartz, *The Liberal Tradition in America* (1955); Robert J. Cottrol, *The Long, Lingering Shadow: Law, Liberalism, and Cultures of Racial Hierarchy and Identity in the Americas*, 76 Tul. L. Rev. 11, 40–49 (2001).

12. Matsuda, *supra* note 2, at 374.

13. Andrew R. Klein, *Hazardous Waste Cleanup and Intermediate Landowners: Reexamining the Liability-Based Approach*, 21 Harv. Envlt. L. Rev. 337 (1997) (discussing liability of subsequent owners for predecessors' torts).

14. The Supreme Court has recently called into question the imposition of liability on successors in Eastern Enterprises v. Apfel, 118 S.Ct. 2131 (1998).

15. Matsuda, *supra* note 2, at 385.

16. Matsuda, *supra* note 2, at 374, 385–88.

17. *See, e.g.*, Story Parchment Co. v. Paterson Parchment Paper Co., 282 U.S. 555 (1931).

18. The state-of-the art on this topic is Suzette Malveaux, *Statutes of Limitations: A Policy Analysis in the Context of Reparations Litigation*, 74 George Washington L. Rev. 68 (2005). There may, of course, be other claimants to the property, who—if we are willing to toll the statute of limitations—may have a superior claim to those seeking to use it for reparations purposes. *See* Ernest Weinrib, *Restitutionary Damages as Corrective Justice*, 1 Theoretical Inquiries in Law 1 (2000).

19. Keith N. Hylton, *Slavery and Tort Law*, 84 Boston University Law Review 1209 (2004).

20. Harriet Beecher Stowe, *A Key to Uncle Tom's Cabin* (1853) (summarizing statute law of slave states).

21. Typically, in cases of loss of consortium, those who may make a claim are limited to close family members, and sometimes even to those who are dependent on the decedent for support. *See, e.g.*, Mitchell v. United States, 141 F.3d 8 (1st Cir. 1998) (adult nondependent children may recover); Masunage v. Gapasin, 790 P.2d 171 (Wash. Ct. App. 1990) (nondependent parents unable to recover).

22. *See, e.g.*, Prosser & Keeton, Torts § 55, at 369; Julie A. Greenberg, *Reconceptualizing Preconception Torts*, 64 Tenn. L. Rev. 315 (1997); Albala v. New York, 429 N.E.2d 786 (N.Y. 1981) (limiting, based on belief that it would "require the extension of traditional tort concepts beyond manageable bounds").

23. *See, e.g.*, Pruitt v. Allied Chemical Corp., 523 F.Supp. 975 (E.D. Va. 1981) (drawing limits around liability for damage caused by dumping chemicals in the James River and Chesapeake Bay).

24. Hylton, *supra* note 19. It is unnecessary to enter the Fogel-Engerman world in order to contemplate reparations. However, it is important to recall that their work is largely discredited. Many of the findings of *Time on the Cross* were called into disrepute in the years afterward. *See, e.g., Reckoning with Slavery* (1976); *Slavery and the Numbers Game: A Critique of Time on the Cross* (Herbert George Gutman ed. 1975). It is similarly significant that legal scholars cite *Time on the Cross* far more frequently than they cite either of the two books responding to it—and largely demolishing it. A recent Westlaw search in the "journals and law review" file turned up 48 articles citing *Time on the Cross*, 9 citing *Reckoning with Slavery*, and 11 citing *Slavery and the Numbers Game*.

25. *See, e.g.*, John McWhorter, *Losing the Race: Self-Sabotage and Black Culture* (2000).

26. Stephan Thernstrom & Abigail Thernstrom, *America in Black and White: One Nation, Indivisible* (1997). *See also* Stephan Thernstrom & Abigail Thernstrom, *Reflections on the Shape of the River*, 46 UCLA L. Rev. 1583 (1999).

27. Douglas Massey & Nancy A. Denton, *American Apartheid: Segregation and the Making of the Underclass* 9 (1993).

28. After reading *Ryan*, one might ask Professor Schwartz to remind us why he thinks nineteenth-century tort law was so plaintiff-friendly.

29. Of course, some tort cases in the nineteenth century were premised on precisely that idea. *See, e.g.,* Snee v. Trice, 2 S.C.L. (2 Bay) 345 (S.C. 1802) (limiting liability for field burned by slaves' negligence). *See also* William W. Fisher, *Ideology and Imagery in the Law of Slavery*, 69 Chi.-Kent L. Rev. 1051, 1060 & n. 49 (1993) (discussing *Snee*). *Snee* is a remarkable case, a strong parallel to *Ryan*. And it is one that (I think) ought to be included in casebooks along with *Ryan*, for it illustrates the economic and social bases underlying decisions regarding proximate cause in tort.

30. *See, e.g.,* Doedt v. Wiswall 15 How.Pr. 128 (N.Y.Sup. 1857) (imposing liability, relying upon New York wrongful death statute); Langlois v. Buffalo & R.R. Co. 19 Barb. 364 (N.Y.Sup. 1854) (imposing liability in absence of statute); Dunhene's Adm'x v. Ohio Life Insurance & Trust Co. 12 Ohio Dec.Rep. 608 (Ohio Super. 1856) (Ohio wrongful death statute); Knightstown & S.R. Co. v. Lindsay 8 Ind. 278 (1856) (Indiana statute). The common law's reasons for refusing compensation for wrongful death are surveyed in *Connecticut Mut. Life Ins. Co. v. New York & N.H.R. Co.* 25 Conn. 265 (1856). Justice Storrs discloses the bases for limiting liability and suggests how cold-hearted the common law was in this area. *See also* Carey v. Berkshire R. Co. 55 Mass. 475 (1848) (noting the Massachusetts lack of a wrongful death statute).

31. Many cases provided owners with compensation by those who caused their loss of slaves. Gray v. Crocheron, 8 Port. 191 (Ala. 1838); Delery v. Mornet, 11 Mart. (O.S.) 4 (Louisiana 1822); Hedgepeth v. Robertson, 18 Tex. 858 (1857); Harvey v. Epes 53 Va. 153 (1855) (employing language of moral philosophy, held person who sold liquor liable for slave's death); Harrison v. Berkley 32 S.C.L. 525 (S.C.App. 1847). One might inquire how courts' desire to impose liability on those who interfered with the slave system leads to innovation in tort law?

32. Again, there is a growing debate on this subject. I favor the side that focuses on the ways that the cold common law rules neglected the injured. *See* Alfred L. Brophy, *The Moral Worlds and Modes of Reasoning of Antebellum Jurists*, 79 B.U. L. Rev. 1161 (1999) (interpreting common law in the antebellum era as driven by respect for middle-class values, which generally supported only limited liability but also protected interests of morality). However, there is

an emerging body of scholarship that claims that tort law in the nineteenth century protected the weak and injured. *See, e.g.,* Gary Schwartz, *The Character of Early American Tort Law,* 36 UCLA L. Rev. 641 (1989). This is not the place for an extended review of that debate. However, I think proponents of the later position focus undue attention on unrepresentative cases. One must look to the overall thrust of the law, not just what is being done at the margins.

33. Sometimes we consider unjust enrichment under the heading of tort and other times under a separate heading of "unjust enrichment." Although I think most of the following discussion derives from consideration of unjust enrichment as an independent action—not as a tort—I think it is important to discuss here, for the sake of completeness. *See* Douglas Laycock, *The Scope and Significance of Unjust Enrichment,* 69 Tex. L. Rev. (1989).

34. *See, e.g.,* Randall Robinson, *The Debt: What America Owes to Blacks* 207 (2000). *See also* Richard F. America, *Paying the Social Debt: What White America Owes Black America* (1993) (assessing the amount of money saved by systematic undercompensation of African Americans).

35. Robinson, *supra* note 34, at 207.

36. *See* Joe R. Feagin, *Racist America: Roots, Current Realities, and Future Reparations* 261 (2001).

37. *See id.* at 262 ("Africans and African Americans created much wealth and capital that to a significant degree spurred not only the economic development of the South but also the industrial revolution in the United States and Europe. . . . The current prosperity, relatively long life expectancies, and relatively high living standards of whites as a group in the United States, as well as in the West generally, are ultimately rooted in the agony, exploitation, and impoverishment of those who were colonized and enslaved, as well as in the oppression and misery of their descendants").

38. *Id.* at 263.

39. *See* David Horowitz, *Uncivil Wars: The Controversy over Reparations for Slavery* (2002).

40. *See also* George Schedler, *Racist Symbols & Reparations* 103–07 (1998) (discussing reparations theory and its limitations, such as offset of benefits). Schedler proposes an alternative measure, not based on unjust enrichment, but on lost opportunity. *Id.* at 108 ("I measure the loss by what the individuals could have had but for enslavement; . . . The damage done by slavery is not the work performed under it, but the freedom of which individuals were deprived. I measure the value of that by what they would have been able to do, not by the value of what they did as slaves").

41. The cases on this are legion. In addition to the cases that permitted an owner to recover for the loss of slaves' services that are mentioned in the next note, one can look to cases that allowed owners to recover for those who en-

ticed slaves away, who facilitated escape of fugitive slaves, and those who injured slaves. *See, e.g.*, Northern Central Railway v. Scholl, 16 Md. 331 (1860) (allowing recovery against railroad company that sold ticket to a known fugitive and thus facilitate his escape); Oliver v. Kauffman 1 Am. Law Reg. 142 (C.C.Pa. 1850) (Justice Grier's charges to jury regarding standards for claim that defendants interfered with plaintiff's recovery of his fugitive slaves); Tyson v. Ewing, 26 Ky. (3 J.J.Marsh.) 185 (Ky.App. 1830) (allowing recovery against riverboat captain who enticed a slave away from his owner).

42. Moseley v. Wilkinson, 24 Ala. 411 (1854); *see also* Fail v. McArthur, 31 Ala. 26 (1857).

43. It also makes sense that traceable descendants of those people are entitled to assert the unjust enrichment claim for their ancestors. There are some legal—if not moral—problems, of course, since slavery was legal at the time. Statutes of limitations and the transfer of the property to others add additional hurdles. Even if the transfers are gratuitous, there are limitations on opening estates. Finally, anyone who has ever tried to trace money understands the difficulty of demonstrating with any kind of certainty the origins of money.

44. Some might add that there was an intangible benefit to whiteness, though I think it is impossible to quantify the benefits of "whiteness."

45. On that difficult issue, one might contrast Thernstrom & Thernstrom, *America in Black and White, supra* note 26 (finding roughly equal opportunity) with Andrew Hacker, *Two Nations: Black and White, Separate, Hostile, Unequal* (1992) (emphasizing both unequal achievement and lack of opportunity). For a middle approach, see Orlando Patterson, *The Moral and Intellectual Crisis of Liberal Advocacy,* in Orlando Patterson, *The Ordeal of Integration* 83–107 (1998).

46. I address the incoherence of this argument elsewhere in the book; here, my only point is that offsetting the benefits is a doctrine one must consider when talking about a *debt.*

47. Horowitz, *Uncivil Wars, supra* note 39, at 125–27. *See also id.* at 127–28 ("Given the dramatic trends of black upward mobility in the last sixty years, it is far more reasonable to assume that if there *are* lingering legacies of slavery, segregation and discrimination they are rapidly vanishing, than to conclude that their accelerating damage is so great that reparations are required to overcome them. It is certainly not clear that all or even a majority of blacks alive today suffer economic injuries from past injustice requiring reparative measures, and it is an unanswered question as to whether those blacks who are still poor are suffering from the legacies of oppression or from personal dysfunctions which have little to do with 'social injustice' or race").

48. Restatement of the Law: Restitution and Unjust Enrichment (Discussion Draft, March 31, 2000) § 1.

49. *Id.*

50. *Id.* at 8.

51. *Id.* at § 14(3) ("If a wrongful threat is tantamount to physical compulsion, a transfer induced thereby is void, and the purported transferee obtains no title").

52. There is not yet a section exploring the nature of those breaches, but they are scheduled to appear as § 37. *Id.* at xxi.

53. 317 F.3d 954 (9th Cir. 2002).

54. There are a series of cases that recognized the owner's property interest in slaves and protected that interest. *See, e.g.,* Seay v. Marks, 23 Ala. 532 (1853) (permitting owner to recover value of slave who was employed by subcontractor in a way inconsistent with contract for employment between owner and subcontractor); Wilkinson v. Moseley, 30 Ala. 562 (1857) (limiting subcontractor's rights to employ slave in trade specified in contract). When other people injured slaves, those people were liable to the owners. *See, e.g.,* Lacoste v. Pipkin, 21 Miss. (13 Smedes & M.) 589 (1850); Carter v. Streator, 49 N.C. 62 (1856); Harrison v. Lloyd, 9 Rich. Law 161 (S.C. 1851) (providing owner—or subcontractor—may recover value of slave wrongfully killed).

Moreover, courts recognized the owner's property rights in slaves when others injured them. *See, e.g.,* Knox v. North Carolina R. Co., 51 N.C. 415 (1859) (placing burden of proof of cause of death on hirer and otherwise permitting suit for wrongful death); Helton v. Caston, 2 Bailey 95 (S.C. 1831) (permitting suit by owner against contractor who beat slave). Such cases illustrate the well-developed rules around slave labor as property and the liability that whites who abused slaves had to be slave owners. Those rules establish a complex network of duties among whites and illustrate the relationship of white owners, white nonowners, and slaves. That world of property relationships established that, while owners might have virtual license to treat their slaves however they would like, whites who "rented" slaves from their owners were responsible to the owners for harm to the slave.

55. See Douglas Laycock, *The Scope and Significance of Restitution,* 67 Tex. L. Rev. 1277, 1279 (1989) (observing that restitution is both a recovery for unjust enrichment and a measurement of enrichment). There are several times that one will invoke restitution. When it provides a *substantive basis* for recovery. That is the case for people who claim based on their ancestors' work with pay. Alternatively, there may already be a basis for recovery—such as tort—but the measure of damages is inadequate or difficult to prove, such as it may be impossible to show amount of harm. Restitution provides a concrete, though often rather limited, measure of harm. *See, e.g.,* Olewell v. Nye & Nisson Co., 173 P. 2d 652 (Wash. 1946).

56. I have suggested how this claim might work against a charitable organ-

ization that is the beneficiary of a gift by a slaveholder. There is still a problem with the statute of limitations. *See* Alfred L. Brophy, *Some Conceptual and Legal Problems in Reparations*, 58 N.Y.U. Annual Survey of Am. L. 498, 514–15 (2003).

57. *See* US for Use of Palmer v. Cal. State Elec., 940 F.2d 1260, 1262 (the Cir. 1991).

58. *See* Hohri v. United States, 782 F.2d 227 (D.C. Cir. 1986).

59. United States v. Hohri, 482 U.S. 64 (1987).

60. Hohri v. United States, 847 F.2d 779, 779 (Fed. Cir. 1988) (citing 586 F.Supp. 769 (D.D.C. 1984)).

61. Hohri v. United States, 793 F.2d 304, 313 (D.C. Cir. 1986).

62. *See* Kaneko v. United States, 122 F.3d 1048 (Fed. Cir. 1997) (denying recovery to surviving spouse of person who lost his federal government job before the internments began); Jacobs v. Barr, 959 F.2d 313 (D.C. Cir. 1992) (denying compensation to German American interned during World War II).

63. *See* Michael Bayzler, *Holocaust Justice: The Battle for Restitution in America's Courts* (2003); Elazar Barkan, *The Guilt of Nations: Restitution and Negotiating Historical Injustices* (2000). *See also* In re Holocaust Victims Assets Litig., 105 F. Supp. 2d 139 (E.D.N.Y. 2000) (approving settlement).

64. *See* Bodner v. Banque Paribis, 114 F.Supp. 2d. 117 (E.D.N.Y. 2000).

65. *See* Bayzler, *supra* note 63, at 198.

66. *See* Bayzler, *supra* note 63, at 202–68.

67. California Insurance Code 13800–807.

68. *See* American Insurance Ass'n v. Garamendi, 539 U.S. 396 (2003).

69. Bayzler, *supra* note 63, at 170–71.

70. *See* Iwanova v. Ford Motor Co., 65 F.Supp. 2d 434 (D.N.J. 1999); Burfer-Fischer v. Degussa AG, 65 F.Supp. 2d 248 (D.N.J. 1999).

The law firm of Lieff Cabraser has a Web site that details the Holocaust-era litigation (as well as advertises their role in the litigation): http://www.lieffcabraser.com/holocaust.htm.

71. Bayzler, *supra* note 63, at 77–78; Tom Hayden, *Ex-Slave Laborers Deserve Far Better*, Los Angeles Times B11 (December 30, 1999).

72. *See* Armenian Genocide Victims Insurance Act, Cal. Code Civ. Proc. § 354.4; Marootian v. New York Life Ins. Co., 2001 U.S. Dist. LEXIS 22274 (C.D. Cal. Nov. 30, 2001), discussed in Paul R. Dubinsky, *Justice for the Collective: the Limits of the Human Rights Class Action*, 102 Mich. L. Rev. 1152, 1153 (2004).

73. The act provides in pertinent part:

Notwithstanding any other provision of law, any Armenian Genocide victim, or heir or beneficiary of an Armenian Genocide victim, whether a resident or nonresident of this state, seeking benefits under the insurance policies issued or in effect between 1875 and 1923 . . . may bring a legal action or may continue a pending legal action to recover on that claim in any court of competent jurisdiction in this state, which court shall be deemed the proper forum for that action until its completion or resolution.

Any action, including any pending action brought by an Armenian Genocide victim or the heir or beneficiary of an Armenian Genocide victim, whether a resident or nonresident of this state, seeking benefits under the insurance policies issued or in effect between 1875 and 1923 shall not be dismissed for failure to comply with the applicable statute of limitation, provided the action is filed on or before December 31, 2010. (Armenian Genocide Victims Insurance Act, Cal. Code Civ. Proc. § 354.4)

74. The final order is *available at* http://www.armenianinsurance settlementfund.com/final%20order.pdf.

75. The editorial is quoted in "New York Life Announces $20 Million Agreement Reached on Class Action Suit," *available at* http://www.hairenik .com/armenianweekly/february_2004/history003.html.

76. Mehinovic v. Vuckovic, 198 F.Supp. 2d 1322 (Dist. Ga. 2002). *See also* David Gonzalez, *Torture Victims in El Salvador Are Awarded $54 Million*, N.Y. Times, July 25, 2002. In those race instances, there are identified (though regrettably largely judgment-proof) individuals. And there is still no way of reaching the system of which they were a part. For instance, in the El Salvador case, the two men held liable were leaders of the El Salvador National Guard and Ministry of Defense; yet, the judgment was against them personally, rather than against the government.

77. See also *Suing for Reparations*, Baltimore Sun, January 17, 1999 (discussing importance of recently discovered evidence, which had been hidden by defendants' fraud, on tolling statute of limitations, which led to settlement of Swiss bank litigation). The Swiss Bank litigation was settled before there was a hearing on the statute of limitations. See *Swiss Banks Reach Accord*, N.Y. Times sec. 4 at 2, August 16, 1998. It testifies to the importance of negotiation—and a moral consensus—on claims for reparations. It also testifies to the importance of a credible claim in court.

78. Jackson v. United States, 1994 U.S. Dist. LEXIS 7872 (N.D. Calif.); Lewis v. United States, 1994 U.S. Dist. LEXIS 7868 (N.D. Calif.); Powell v. United States, 1994 U.S. Dist. LEXIS 8628 (N.D. Calif.). *See also* Bell v. United States, 2001 U.S. Dist. Lexis 14,812 (N.D. Tex.) (dismissing suit for reparations for slavery and observing that "without a concrete, personal injury that

is not abstract and that is fairly traceable to the government conduct that plaintiff challenges as unconstitutional, Bell lacks standing").

79. Cato v. United States, 70 F.3d 1103 (9th Cir. 1995). More recently, the U.S. Court of Claims has dismissed a suit seeking reparations for slavery based on an equal protection argument, claiming that victims of slavery are entitled to share in the Civil Liberties Act of 1988, which provided compensation to Japanese Americans interned during World War II. *See* Obadele v. U.S. 52 Fed.Cl. 432 (2002).

80. The cold and businesslike nature of the legal language is captured in the sentence: "As Cato's complaint neither identifies any constitutional or statutory right that was violated, nor asserts any basis for federal subject matter jurisdiction or waiver of sovereign immunity, it was properly dismissed" (70 F.3d at 1106).

81. *Cato*, 70 F.3d 1103, 1106 (9th Cir. 1995).

82. 70 F.3d at 1110. It also followed Supreme Court precedent that refused to recognize a right to sue for constitutional violations to the federal government; individual officers of the government might be liable for constitutional violations, but not the federal government itself. *Id.*

83. *Id.* at 1108 (citing Oneida Indian Nation of New York v. New York, 691 F.2d 1070, 1083–84 (2nd Cir. 1982)).

Sometimes suits by native tribes work out well. For instance, the Seminole Tribe obtained a judgment of $20 million in 1980 for land taken from them in the nineteenth century. The Seneca Nation in upstate New York is pursing a claim to several large tracts of land. Those claims are not barred by the statute of limitations, because they are based on treaties. For a sampling of piecemeal reparations for native Americans, see Eric Yamamoto, *Racial Reparations: Japanese American Redress and African American Claims*, 40 B.C. L. Rev. 477 n. 22 (1998); Lindsay Glauner, *The Need for Accountability and Reparation: 1830–1976 the United States Government's Role in the Promotion, Implementation, and Execution of the Crime of Genocide Against Native Americans*, 51 DePaul L. Rev. 911, 961 (2002). See also Natsu Taylor Saito, *From Slavery and Seminoles to AIDS in South Africa: An Essay on Race and Property in International Law*, 45 Vill. L. Rev. 1135 (2000).

84. *Id.*

85. Sampson v. Federal Republic of Germany, 250 F.3d 1145 (7th Cir. 2001).

86. Second World War Slave or Forced Labor Victims . . ., California Code of Civil Procedure, § 354.6.

87. In re World War II Era Japanese Forced Labor Litigation, 14 F.Supp. 2d 939, 1 942 (N.D. Cal. 2000), affirmed sub nom., Deutsch v. Turner Corp. 317 F.3d 1005 (9th Cir. 2003). *See also* Deutsch v. Turner Corp., 324 F.3d 692 (9th Cir. 2003) (denying rehearing en banc).

88. In re World War II Era Japanese Forced Labor Litigation, 164 F.Supp. 2d 1160 (N.D. Cal. 2001).

89. Hwang v. Japan, 172 F.Supp. 2d 52, 55 (D.C. D.C. 2001).

90. *Id.* at 1110 ("In any case, she does not trace the presence of discrimination and its harm to the United States rather than to other persons or institutions. Accordingly, Cato lacks standing to bring a suit setting forth the claims she suggests").

91. The complaint is *available at* http://news.findlaw.com/cnn/docs/slavery/ fpllmnflt032602cmp.pdf.

For additional commentary, see Anthony J. Sebok, *The Brooklyn Slavery Class Action: More Than Just a Political Gambit, available at* http://writ.news .findlaw.com/sebok/20020409.html.

See also Anthony J. Sebok, *Should Claims Based on African-American Slavery Be Litigated in the Courts? And If So, How?* available at http://writ .news.findlaw.com/sebok/20001204.html.

92. Here, as with many issues in reparations, one could conduct an intriguing thought-experiment about the bases for tort liability.

93. *See generally* Elaine Shoben *et al.*, *Remedies: Cases and Problems* 806 (2002).

94. *See also* In Re African American Slave Descendents Litigation, 304 F.Supp.2d 1027, 1053 ("Plaintiff's Complaint seeks to litigate a generalized grievance over one of the most horrific chapters of our Nation's history rather than a personal dispute, which the federal courts are able to adjudicate").

For more on unjust enrichment claims in the context of reparations, see Hannoch Dagen, *Restitution and Slavery*, 84 Boston University L. Rev. 1139 (2004); Andrew Kull, *Restitution in Favor of Former Slaves*, 84 Boston University L. Rev. 1277 (2004); Emily Sherwin, *Reparations and Unjust Enrichment*, 84 Boston University L. Rev. 1443 (2004).

95. The problems with identification of the class are enormous, though not greater than what courts face in some real property disputes. *See, e.g.,* Brown v. Independent Baptist Church of Woburn, 91 N.E.2d 922 (Mass. 1950) (holding that defeasible fee created in 1849 is violated and requiring distribution of reversion to intestate heirs, who numbered in the dozens and were spread around the world).

96. That avoids the problem that slavery was legal at the time, which plagues tort suits.

97. Please excuse my equation of money with personal property; that's an elision that a court might be willing to overlook.

98. *See, e.g.,* Charles Ogletree, *Litigating the Legacy of Slavery*, N.Y. Times sec. 4 at 9, March 31, 2002 (mentioning endowments funded with money made from slavery at Harvard Law School and Brown and Yale Univer-

sities); Laura Israel, *Anthropology Class Studies Slavery in Medford: Former Medford Slave Leaves Legacy of Freedom and Equality*, Tufts Daily Herald, May 19, 2002 (discussing Royall's twenty-eight slaves); Christopher Greaves, *Reparations Advocate Argues for Redressing America's 'Debt' to Blacks*, Cornell Chronicle, February 15, 2002) (discussing Isaac Royall's endowment at Harvard Law School), *available at* http://www.news.cornell.edu/Chronicle/01/2.15.01/Robinson_cover.html.

99. *See* Joseph Story, A Discourse Pronounced at the Funeral Obsequies of John Hooker Ashmun, Esq., Royall Professor of Law in Harvard University before the President, Fellows, and Faculty in the Chapel of the University, April 5, 1833 (Cambridge: Brown, Shattuck, 1833).

100. *See* Elizabeth Tyler Bates, *Reparations for Slave Art*, 55 Ala. L. Rev. 1109 (2004) (suggesting one way that the statute of limitations may not have run on claims for return of art made by slaves).

101. There are other problems associated with making a claim against descendants of a group of beneficiaries, such as tracing the benefits.

102. *See, e.g.*, Michael J. Bazyler, *Litigating the Holocaust*, 33 U. Rich. L. Rev. 601 (1999).

103. *See* Cal. Ins. § 13812 (2000). The California Commissioner of Insurance is instructed to make that information available to the public, *id* at § 13811, and the descendants of the people whose lives were insured are entitled to full disclosure. *Id.* at § 13813.

104. The legislation poses problems of retroactive legislation. It is subject to close scrutiny, though it is not necessarily unconstitutional. *See, e.g.*, Charles B. Hochman, *The Supreme Court and the Constitutionality of Retroactive Legislation*, 73 Harv. L. Rev. 692, 693 (1960) (discussing ability of Congress to impose retroactive legislation); Debra Lyn Bassett, *In the Wake of Schooner Peggy: Deconstructing Legislative Retroactivity Analysis*, 69 U. Cin. L. Rev. 453 (2001) (discussing confusion in recent retroactive legislation decisions); James L. Huffman, *Retroactivity, the Rule of Law, and the Constitution*, 51 Ala. L. Rev. 1095 (2000) (same). Adopting the analysis of Eastern Enterprises v. Apfel, 524 U.S. 498 (1998), it seems likely that the legislation would be constitutional. Obviously, such legislation would "impose new legal consequences to [an employment relationship] completed before its enactment." *Id.* at 532 (quoting Landgraf v. USI Film Products, 511 U.S. 244 (1994)). Nevertheless, *Eastern Enterprises* emphasized three factors: the economic impact of the statute, its interference with reasonable investment-backed expectations, and the character of the governmental action. 524 U.S. at 523–24. The court focused on proportionality—how distant were the acts for which liability was imposed and what the magnitude of the liability is. *Eastern Enterprises*, 524 U.S. at 534. Applying those factors to a reparations statute that provides a cause of

action against railroad companies, for instance, seems likely to be Constitutional. There is a substantial governmental interest; the liability is small in comparison with the railroad's overall assets, thus limiting its economic impact and its interference with reasonable investment-backed expectations.

105. See *Run of Abuse Claims Seen; Those Who Say They Were Molested by Priests Face a Year-End Deadline for Filing Legal Actions*, Los Angeles Times B1, December 8, 2003.

106. Eastern Enterprises v. Apfel, 118 S.Ct. 2131 (1998).

107. Several articles recently have made the case for reparations in the Jim Crow—rather than slavery—context. *See* Sherrilyn A. Ifill, *Creating a Truth and Reconciliation Commission for Lynching*, 21 Law & Ineq. 263 (2003); Emma Coleman Jordan, *A History Lesson: Reparations for What?* 58 N.Y.U. Annual Survey Am. L. 557 (2003). They both focus on the ugly legacy of lynching, which has captured the attention of historians in recent years. The new lynching studies offer detailed evidence of the community's complicity. As a result, they often offer compact sites for viewing both the evils of Jim Crow and for tracing out the effects on the present.

In a lot of ways, Jim Crow cases are more compelling than reparations for slavery. Often, victims are still alive, the evidence is often stronger than in slavery cases, and they are closer in time than slavery. The common refrain—that all the slaves are dead—does not apply to Jim Crow, where there are people still alive. Reparations for Jim Crow may offer the way to bridge supporters and detractors of reparations for slavery.

108. For a detailed exploration of the riot, see Alfred L. Brophy, *Reconstructing the Dreamland: The Tulsa Riot of 1921—Race, Reparations, Reconciliation* (2002).

109. For more on the Tulsa riot, listen to *Talking History* (December 3, 2002), *available at* http://talkinghistory.oah.org/shows/2002/TulsaRiots.mp3; *Fresh Air* (February 22, 2000), *available at* http://whyy.org/cgi-bin/FAshow retrieve.cgi?2821; and *Tavis Smiley* (February 26, 2003), *available at* http://discover.npr.org/rundowns/segment.jhtml?wfId=1175756.

See also Brophy, *Reconstructing the Dreamland, supra* note 108.

110. Statutes of limitation are undertheorized, although Suzette Malveaux' article is helping to change that. *See* Malveaux, *supra* note 18. We see frequently discussions that remind us that their purpose is repose. *See, e.g.,* Klehr v. A. O. Smith Corp., 521 U.S. 179 (1997) (allowing suits for all acts in a conspiracy based on when the last predicate act occurred extends the statute of limitations to acts dramatically and "thereby conflicts with a basic objective—repose—that underlies limitations periods"). The basis for the repose is an understanding—by legislatures and judges—that memories of witnesses fade and evidence is lost. *See id.* at 187 (citing Wilson v. Garcia, 471 U.S. 261, 271

(1985)). That repose is designed to assure fairness for defendants. *See, e.g.*, Burnett v. New York Central R.R., 380 U.S. 424, 428 (1965). At base is a sense of justice for when someone should be allowed repose. One may, I think, make a very strong argument that certain crimes are so heinous that there should be no repose.

111. 231 F.Supp.2d 1202, 1208 (S.D. Fla. 2002).

112. Bodner v. Banque Paribas, 114 F.Supp.2d 117, 133–34 (E.D.N.Y. 2000) ("the nature of plaintiffs claim is such that the continued denial of their assets, as well as facts and information relating thereto, if proven, constitutes a continuing violation").

113. *See* Jacques deLisle, *Human Rights, Civil Wrongs and Foreign Relations: A 'Sinical' Look at the Use of U.S. Litigation to Address Human Rights Abuses Abroad*, 52 DePaul L. Rev. 473, 539 n. 203 (2003) (citing, among others, Forti v. Suarz-Mason, 672 F.Supp. 1531, 1549 (N.D. Calif. 1987) (impossibility of relief in Argentine courts basis for tolling); Doe v. Unocal Corp, 963 F.Supp. 880, 897 (C.D. Calif. 1997) (fear of retaliation basis for tolling); Barrueto v. Larios, 205 F.Supp. 1325, 1330–31 (S.D. Fla. 2002) (pre-1990 concealment of body and cause of death by Chilean government tolled running until 1990).

114. Hanger v. Abbott, 73 U.S. (6 Wall.) 532 (1867).

115. *See* Osbourne v. United States, 164 F.2d 767 (2nd Cir. 1947).

116. Forti v. Suarez-Mason, 672 F.Supp. 1531, 1550 (N.D. Calif. 1987).

117. *See* Hilao v. Estate of Ferdinand Marcos, 103 F.3d 767, 779 (9th Cir. 1996).

118. *See* Doe v. Unocal Co., 963 F.Supp. 880, 897 (C.D. Calif. 1997).

119. *See* Barrueto v. Larios, 205 F.Supp. 1325, 1330–31 (S.D. Fla. 2002). In the case of Tulsa, the term "equitable estoppel" may not be quite right. Typically, we think of estoppel claims as involving a representation and then reliance on that representation. *See* Cada v. Baxter Healthcare Corp., 920 F.2d 446 (7th Cir. 1990); Douglas Laycock, Modern American Remedies 983 (3rd ed. 2002). In the case of Tulsa, we have affirmative action to stop plaintiffs from using the courts—threats of prosecution to drive out plaintiffs, followed up by violence against those who have the audacity to assert rights.

120. 205 F.Supp.2d at 1331.

121. There are some suggestive cases in which the statute of limitations has been tolled over many years in certain limited and extraordinary circumstances. *See* Bodner v. Banque Paribas, 114 F.Supp.2d 117, 134–35 (E.D. N.Y. 2000). In cases when the plaintiffs could not gain effective relief, particularly when the government made it impossible to pursue the claims, some federal courts have tolled the statute of limitations. In Rosner v. U.S., 231 F.Supp.2d 1202, 1208 (S.D.Fla. 2002), for instance, the plaintiffs alleged that the govern-

ment mistakenly reported that gold taken from French Holocaust victims was unidentifiable and unreturnable. The government's culpability in cases like Tulsa, where the courts were effectively unavailable, goes beyond the government's misleading owners about the identity of property.

122. Equal Credit Opportunity Act, 15 U.S.C. § 1691.

123. Pigford v. Glickman, 185 F.R.D. 82, 85 (D.D.C. 1999), aff'd, 206 F.3d 1212 (D.C. Cir. 2000).

124. See, e.g., Pigford v. Veneman, 143 F.Supp.2d 28 (D.D.C. 2001).

125. See Cal. Civ. Proc. Code secs. 354.4, 354.6 (West 2002), held unconstitutional in In Re World War II Era Japanese Forced Labor Litigation, 317 F.3d 1005 (9th Cir. 2003).

126. U.S. House of Representatives, Report of the Special Committee Authorized by Congress to Investigate the East St. Louis Race Riots, 65th Congress, 2nd Sess., Document 1231 (July 15, 1918). See also Eric Arnesen, *Brotherhoods of Color: Black Railroad Workers and the Struggle for Equality* (2001); Rick Halpern, *Down on the Killing Floor: Black and White Workers in Chicago's Packinghouses, 1904–54* (1997).

127. See Elliott Rudwick, *Race Riot at East St. Louis* (1963). Mr. Rudwick's monograph, so pioneering at the time, brought attention to the tragedy. However, it is outdated in its failure to provide attention to African American culture. The victims of the riot appear in the monograph as little more than pawns in a historical tragedy; we need a study that gives the African American community more attention. How, one wonders, did the great ideas of the renaissance influence the community's arming for self-protection? How did the great migration lead to conflict between African American and white workers? How did the manufacturing and meatpacking companies in East St. Louis manipulate racial dynamics to set the stage for riot?

Moreover, we now have much more sophisticated methods of interpreting the narratives told before the Congressional committee investigating the riot and in the pages of white and black newspapers throughout the country, than were available in Rudwick's time. There are many questions that need answers and, fortunately, hundreds of pages of Congressional testimony, as well as civil and criminal lawsuits, that can help answer those questions. Finally, there is a great need for explorations of the results of riot—essentially, how it was remembered and how that memory affected Chicago, Elaine, Arkansas, and Washington in 1919 and Tulsa in 1921. Much of that work of brining the riot up to date—and again to the attention of a national audience—has been performed recently by Malcolm McLaughlin's *Power, Community, and Racial Killing in East St. Louis* (2005).

128. See City of Chicago v. Sturigs, 222 U.S. 323 (1908) (upholding constitutionality of Illinois statute imposing liability on cities for three quarters value

of mob damage, regardless of fault); *see also* Morton J. Horwitz, *The Transformation of American Law, 1870–1960* 123–26 (1992) (discussing controversy over strict liability).

129. Gregory Mixon, *The Atlanta Riot: Race, Class and Violence in a New South City* (2005); John Fort Godshalk, *Veiled Visions: The 1906 Atlanta Race Riot and the Reshaping of American Race Relations* (2005); Dominic Capeci & Jack C. Knight, *Reckoning with Violence: W. E. B. DuBois and the 1906 Atlanta Race Riot*, 62 J. Southern Hist. 727 (1996).

130. *See generally* Alfred L. Brophy, *The Tulsa Race Riot Commission, Apologies, and Reparations: Understanding the Functions and Limitations of a Historical Truth Commission*, in Taking Wrongs Seriously: Apologies and Reconciliation (Elazar Barkan and Alexander Karn ed. 2006); Ifill, *supra* note 107, at 309–11 (discussing the roles that truth commissions for lynchings might fill).

131. 261 U.S. 86 (1923).

132. *See* Hollins v. Oklahoma, 295 U.S. 394 (1935).

133. *See* James E. Goodman, *Stories of Scottsboro* (1995); Dan T. Carter, *Scottsboro: A Tragedy of the American South* (1972).

134. See Alberto B. Lopez, *$10 and Denim Jacket? Towards a Model Statute for the Wrongfully Convicted*, 36 Ga. L. Rev. 665 (2002).

135. Guinn v. United States, 228 F. 103, 109 (8th Cir. 1915).

136. *Id.* (discussing case of G. I. Curran).

137. *Id.* at 109–10 (discussing cases of Oliver Andrews and Thomas Pettis).

138. Peyton McCreary, *Bringing Equality to Power: How the Federal Courts Transformed the Electoral Structure of Southern Politics, 1960–1990*, 5 U. Pa. J. Const. L. 665 (2003); Michael J. Klarman, *Race and the Court in the Progressive Era*, 51 Vand. L. Rev. 881, 914–15 (1998); Mark V. Tushnet, *Progressive Era Race Relations Cases in Their "Traditional" Context*, 51 Vand. L. Rev. 993, 997 (1998).

139. In some cases, the mere deprivation of a constitutional right—even if there is no harm—may be compensable. *See, e.g.*, Carey v. Piphus, 435 U.S. 247 (1978). Or in some cases, there may be injunctive relief to revote, even if there is little evidence that the vote will come out differently. *See* Bell v. Southwell, 376 F.2d 659 (5th Cir. 1967). The latter remedy is obviously ineffective unless the election misbehavior was recent.

140. Croson, 488 U.S. at 498 (requiring more than "generalized assertion that there has been past discrimination in an entire industry"); Adarand v. Pena, 515 U.S. 200, 220 (1995) ("Societal discrimination, without more, is too amorphous a basis for imposing a racially classified approach").

141. 426 U.S. 229 (1976).

142. Obviously, the discriminatory motive was demonstrated in the legislation struck down in *Guinn*. However, we might learn from the history of vot-

ing right discrimination that we need to be especially vigilant in the protection of voting rights. *See* Kim Forde-Mazrui, *The Constitutional Implications of Race-Neutral Affirmative Action*, 88 Geo. L. J. 2331, 2346–47 (2000) (discussing voting rights). The Voting Rights Act of 1965 ought, in that case, to be considered a key piece of reparations legislation, for it was based so fully on the history of discrimination. 42 U.S.C. § 1973. Indeed, the Supreme Court has recently reacknowledged the role of history in supporting the constitutionality of the act. *See* Garrett v. University of Alabama, 531 U.S. 356, 373 (2001) ("Congress documented a marked pattern of unconstitutional action by the States. State officials, Congress found, routinely applied voting tests in order to exclude African-American citizens from registering to vote. . . . Congress also determined that litigation had proved ineffective and that there persisted an otherwise inexplicable 50-percentage point gap in the registration of white and African-American voters in some States").

143. *See* Arthur LeFrancois, *On Our Chosen Frequency: Norms, Race, and Transcendence in Cadillac Flambé*, 26 Okla. City U. L. Rev. (2001) (discussing Ellison's experience with a segregated library in Oklahoma City); Arthur G. LeFrancois, *A Curious Place for Intolerance: Alabama's Segregated Public Libraries*, 57 Ala. L. Rev. 141 (2005) (reviewing Patterson Toby Graham, *A Right to Read: Segregation and Civil Rights in Alabama's Public Libraries* (2002) (discussing segregation in Alabama's libraries)).

144. Graham, *supra* note 143.

145. Although one might expect that in an area like libraries, whose sole function is to provide education (and therefore educational, social, moral, and economic improvement), the forces supporting uplift for all would suppress tendencies to racial exclusion, libraries were hotly contested sites of integration. *See, e.g.*, Kerr v. Enoch Pratt Free Library of Baltimore City, 149 F.2d 212 (4th Cir. 1945) (discrimination in providing training for library workers); Hainsworth v. Harris County Com'rs' Court, 269 S.W.2d 332 (Tex. 1954) (refusing relief from allegation that County Law Library was segregated). Perhaps because of the symbolic value of libraries, they became an important site for sit-ins during the Civil Rights movement. *See* Brown v. Louisiana, 383 U.S. 131 (1968).

146. There is some experience with court-directed collection development. *See* Taylor v. Perini 421 F.Supp. 740 (D.C.Ohio 1976) (listing more than 100 books on black experience to be added to a prison library).

147. As long as we are thinking about lawsuits for segregated facilities, we might consider segregated parks and swimming pools. Palmer v. Thompson, 403 U.S. 217 (1971) (upholding Jackson, Mississippi's closing of public swimming pools instead of integrating them). The problems with those suits is that the behavior was legal at the time. If the behavior was legal, it becomes diffi-

cult to find a cause of action. How do we go back and impose liability on the city of Jackson—where, because of changing demographics, 70.6% of the city's people were black in 2000? There is the strange phenomenon of the current taxpayers, who are descended from the people who were discriminated against (and are some of the victims themselves) being asked to pay reparations to themselves. And they are asked to pay for decisions that were legal at the time—and presumably still are legal. There are also cemeteries, which were segregated in many places well into the 1960s (and, obviously, those segregation patterns for people buried before the 1960s continue today). *See* Kitty Rogers, *Integrating the City of the Dead: The Integration of Cemeteries and the Evolution of Property Law, 1900–1969*, 56 Ala. L. Rev. 1165 (2004). I am not suggesting any legal remedy, only noting that the system of Jim Crow segregation reached from libraries to the grave and to a lot of places in between, too.

The case works much better when the Jim Crow discrimination was illegal at the time—or at least questionable—and was subsequently prohibited, and then it works particularly well in cases where there is a continuing effect (as in library collections or location) of past illegal conduct.

CHAPTER 6

1. Fullilove v. Klutznick, 448 U.S. 448, 478 (1980). The opinion continued:

Congress had before it, among other data, evidence of a long history of marked disparity in the percentage of public contracts awarded to minority business enterprises. This disparity was considered to result not from any lack of capable and qualified minority businesses, but from the existence and maintenance of barriers to competitive access which had their roots in racial and ethnic discrimination, and which continue today, even absent any intentional discrimination or other unlawful conduct. Although much of this history related to the experience of minority businesses in the area of federal procurement, there was direct evidence before the Congress that this pattern of disadvantage and discrimination existed with respect to state and local construction contracting as well. In relation to the MBE provision, Congress acted within its competence to determine that the problem was national in scope. (*Id.*)

2. The argument I am advancing here is distinct from the more popular—and I think incorrect—assumption that just because someone's ancestors arrived after slavery ended there is no liability. Those ancestors arrived into a so-

ciety in which it was easier for a white person to advance than a black person, and while many immigrants, especially those from southern and eastern Europe and Asia, faced discrimination, it was of a less virulent nature than African Americans faced. Moreover, one who immigrates to the United States takes it with all the liabilities—as well as the opportunities—that the country offers. I would draw an analogy to shareholders' liability for a corporation's actions. Investors are liable (up to the value of their investment) for a corporation's torts, even though the torts may have occurred before the investors purchased their shares.

My point is that in talking about reparations for slavery and Jim Crow, one must be careful in talking about claims of victims against perpetrators, when many of the people against whom claims are being asserted are not perpetrators.

3. On apologies more generally, see Mark Gibney and Erik Roxstrom, *The Status of State Apologies*, 23 Hum. Rts. Q. 911 (2001); Jennifer Robbennolt, *Apologies and Legal Settlement: An Empirical Examination*, 102 Mich. L. Rev. 460 (2004).

4. Lucio Guerrero, *Not Much Known about 'Martha' Besides Name*, Chicago Sun Times, November 25, 2003. For further discussions of the story, see Fran Spielman, *Company Admits Its Ties to Slavery*, Chicago Sun Times, November 24, 2003.

5. See Ralph Ellison, *Going to the Territory*, in The Collected Works of Ralph Ellison 591 (John Callahan ed. 1995).

6. The process might be much like the one that Ralph Ellison described in his speech at Brown, when he received the Inman Page award. Page was Brown's first known black graduate . . . and, many years later, Ellison's teacher in Oklahoma City! As Ellison said of Page, "Dr. Page served as a representative figure. As such he inspired the extremes of ambivalent emotion: love and hate, admiration and envy, fear and respect. . . . Today his influence is such that although he passed away some forty years ago, one has only to bring a group of his old students together and immediately he lives again in apotheosis." *Id.* at 592.

7. See J. P. Morgan Says Two Precursor Banks Held Slaves, Los Angeles Times, January 21, 2005; J. P. Morgan Discloses Past Links to Slavery, Washington Post E02, January 21, 2005; Rebecca Mowbray, Bank Reveals Slavery Links; 2 Louisiana Firms Named, Times-Picayune 1, January 21, 2005.

8. The press release and apology, once available on the bank's Web site, are nowhere to be found. For a BBC story on the apology, *JP Morgan Admits U.S. Slavery Links*, see http://news.bbc.co.uk/2/hi/business/4193797.stm.

9. The data have been taken down from the bank's Web site. There is, one suspects, an interesting tale in why they are not available.

10. Wachovia's Web site details its findings at http://www.wachovia .com/misc/o,,877,00.html.

The apology attracted much attention and opposition. *See, e.g.,* Joseph N. DiStefano, *Wachovia Finds Role in Slavery in Its Past,* Philadelphia Inquirer, June 2, 2005; *Shaking Down Wachovia,* Washington Times, June 15, 2005; Jeff Jacoby, *The Slavery Shakedown,* Boston Globe, June 9, 2005; David Person, *The Real Value of an Apology,* Huntsville Times, June 10, 2005.

11. Makebra M. Anderson, *More Companies Will Share Wachovia's Slavery Woes,* Chicago Defender, June 24, 2005.

12. See BBC, *JP Morgan Admits U.S. Slavery Links, available at* http://news.bbc.co.uk/2/hi/business/4193797.stm.

13. Sharon K. Hom & Eric K. Yamamoto, *Collective Memory, History, and Social Justice,* 47 UCLA L. Rev. 1747, 1764 (2000). See also Eric K. Yamamoto, *Practically Reframing Rights: Cultural Performance and Judging,* 33 U.C. Davis L. Rev. 875 (2000). These themes are explored in more depth in Eric Yamamoto, *Interracial Justice: Conflict and Reconciliation in Post–Civil Rights America* (1998); and Elazar Barkan, *The Guilt of Nations: Restitution and Negotiating Historical Injustices* (2000).

14. *See* American Ins. Co. v. Garamendi, 123 S.Ct. 2374 (2003).

15. Holocaust Victim Insurance Relief Act of 1999, Cal. Ins. Code Ann. secs. 13800–13807.

16. *See, e.g.,* Cal. Ins. Code Ann. 13812 (2000). *See generally L.A. Council Moves toward Slavery Law,* San Diego Union-Tribune A6, June 21, 2003 (discussing city ordinances that require disclosure of corporations' connections with slavery); V. Dion Haynes, *Report Names Slaves, Owners and Insurers,* Chicago Tribune, May 2, 2002.

The California law has resulted in a registry of names of insurance companies that wrote policies, as well as the names of people whose slaves were insured, *see* http://www.insurance.ca.gov/0100-consumers/0300-public-programs/0200-slavery-era-insur/.

For the list of slaves, *see* http://www.insurance.ca.gov/0100-consumers/0300-public-programs/0200-slavery-era-insur/slave-names.cfm.

17. *See* Excerpt of Remarks Delivered by John W. Rowe, M.D., Chairman, President and CEO, Aetna Inc., Annual Shareholders Meeting, April 26, 2002, *available at* http://www.aetna.com/news/2002/slavery_reparations_issue .html. Rowe again apologized and then promised to take positive action:

Today, I wish to reiterate a sincere apology for the actions of our company in its earliest days. Slavery is morally wrong and reprehensible.

Today, there remain significant concerns about race in America. Major disparities continue to exist in education, in economic opportunity and in health care.

The Aetna of today is determined to be a leader in addressing these problems. We are proud of our recent record, but also actively seeking additional ways to be a force for positive change. For example, we have an opportunity to make a difference in eliminating disparities in health care and in health status. I am determined that we will pursue initiatives in this area.

18. *See, e.g.*, Paul Zielbauer, *A Newspaper Apologizes for Slave-Era Ads*, N.Y. Times B1, July 6, 2000 (discussing other newspapers' complicity); James Benson Sellers, Slavery in Alabama 346, 391 (1950) (Harriet E. Amos Doss ed. rev. ed. 1994) (mentioning proslavery arguments in the *Montgomery Advertiser* and *Mobile Register*).

19. Ruth J. Simmons, *Facing Up to Our Ties to Slavery*, Boston Globe A13, April 28, 2004 (op-ed); Joanna Walters, *'Sorry' Seems to Be the Hardest Word: Should Universities Founded Centuries Ago on Money from the Slave Trade Attempt to Make Reparations?* Guardian 22, March 23, 2004; Jennifer D. Jordan, *Brown Begins 2-year Scrutiny of Slavery and Reparations*, Providence Journal, March 15, 2004; DeWayne Wickham, *President of Brown Seeks to Fuel Reparations Debate*, USA Today A13, March 16, 2004; Pam Belluck, *Brown U. to Examine Debt to Slave Trade*, N.Y. Times, March 13, 2004; Frances Fitzgerald, *Peculiar Institutions: Brown University Looks at Slave Traders in Its Past*, New Yorker 68, September 12, 2005.

The best summary of the case for and the controversy surrounding the apology at the University of Alabama appears in Carter Davis, *Race and Reparations*, [Tuscaloosa] City Magazine, April 24, 2004.

20. Brandon Reed, *UNC Highlights Past Ills: Dedication of Memorial, New Exhibit Part of Process*, Daily Tar Heel, November 4, 2005.

21. *See* Peter Schuck, *Slavery Reparations: A Misguided Movement* (listing questions in implementation, which must be answered in order to determine the content of reparations programs), *available at* http://jurist.law.pitt.edu/forum/forumnew78.php.

22. Arthur Serota, *Ending Apartheid in America: The Need for a Black Political Party and Reparations Now!* 147 (1996).

23. Clarence J. Munford, *Race and Reparations: A Black Perspective for the 21st Century* 413 (1996). Munford continues:

Insist on collecting everything owing to us as a people historically, down to the last penny, and not one whit less. Make indemnification item number one on the Black political signboard. We need to calculate the gigantic debt owed the African creators of the wealth luxuriated in by the white industrialized North and once that is done, get right down to negotiating the forms, accrued interests and period of amortization. As Manning Marable observes, public policy toward Afro-Americans has been up in the air ever since desegregation was legally won 30 years ago and more. . . . *Reparations*—and its Siamese twin, Black empowerment—are imperative if the end of formal segregation is ever to amount to anything but a sham leading absolutely nowhere. (*Id.*)

24. *Id.* at 437.

25. *Id.* at 470.

26. *See* Robert Westley, *Many Billions Gone: Is It Time to Reconsider the Case for African American Reparations?* 19 B.C. Third World L. Rev. 464 (1998).

27. *Id.* at 470.

28. *Id.* at 470. He goes on to acknowledge that "determining a method by which all Black people can participate in their own empowerment will require a much more refined instrument than it would be appropriate for me to attempt to describe here."

29. *Id.*

30. Randall Robinson, *The Debt: What America Owes Blacks,* at 244 (2000). L.G. Sherrod, *Forty Acres and a Mule,* Essence 124, April 1993 (suggesting restitution of value blacks contributed to economy during slavery and era of Jim Crow).

31. Robinson, *supra* note 30, at 245.

32. *Id.* at 245–46.

33. *Id.* at 246 ("The ideas I have broached here do not comprise anything near a comprehensive package"). *See also* Kevin Hopkins, *Forgive U.S. Our Debts? Righting the Wrongs of Slavery,* 89 Geo. L.J. 2531 (2001) (reviewing Robinson, *supra* note 30) (discussing Robinson's reparations proposals).

34. Roy Brooks, *Atonement and Forgiveness: A New Model for Black Reparations* 159–63 (2004). Brooks also discusses his atonement model in *Getting Reparations for Slavery Right—A Response to Posner and Vermeule,* 80 Notre Dame L. Rev. 251 (2004).

35. Molefi Kete Asante, *The African American Warrant for Reparations: The Crime of European Enslavement of Africans and Its Consequences,* in Should America Pay? Slavery and the Raging Debate over Reparations 12 (Raymond Winbush ed. 2003). Asante also proposes a commission to study reparations, educate the public about their importance, and make recommendations about further reparations. *Id.*

36. *See* Thomas Bray, *Granholm Tries to Slip Reparations Hook,* Detroit News, October 9, 2002.

37. There has been for a very long time in the African American commu-

nity the idea that life can—and will—be better. That dream has led some, even in the face of long odds, to have a faith in such fundamental documents as the Declaration of Independence and the U.S. Constitution to bring about equality. And they have maintained that faith, in spite of all evidence to the contrary. Indeed, there was an optimism in the black community in the years leading into the Tulsa riot that law might be made fairer. And even though those hopes were dashed in the short term, over many long years of advocacy, the black community worked to remake the law, so that people who lived through the Tulsa race riot—and witnessed its aftermath—saw the triumph of *Brown v. Board of Education* in 1954. There remains much work to be done to explore what Ralph Ellison termed in his 1952 novel *Invisible Man* "The Great Constitutional Dream Book" and how that "book"—those sets of beliefs about the Constitution—were part of remaking American law in the twentieth century. For some initial explorations, see Brophy, *Reconstructing the Dreamland: The Tulsa Riot of 1921*, chapter 1 (2002); "Reading the Great Constitutional Dream Book," paper presented at Vanderbilt University Law School, September 24, 2005. Some of these ideas are explored in a most preliminary way in Alfred Brophy, Book Review, 20 Journal of Law and Religion 567–70 (2004–05) (reviewing James B. Bennett, *Religion and the Rise of Jim Crow in New Orleans* (2005)).

38. Serota, *supra* note 22, at 147.

39. *See, e.g.*, Brooks, *supra* note 34, at 159–63.

40. *See, e.g.*, Eric Posner and Adrian Vermeule, *Reparations for Slavery and Other Historical Injustices*, 103 Columbia L. Rev. 689 (2003); Ronald Dworkin, *Freedom's Law: The Moral Reading of the American Constitution* 25–26, 250–54 (1996). Dworkin explained what he meant by ethical individualism in a discussion over euthanasia in 1997:

> In our society, a society that is marked by the point of view that I recently have been calling ethical individualism, one master idea is accepted: that it is not only the case that human beings each have a life to live, but that each human being has a life to make something of—a responsibility to create a life such that he or she can look back on that life with pride rather than misery and take pride in it rather than account it a waste. That is a fundamental human responsibility. It has been denied over many areas and tracks of human history, but not by us. And it carries with it, I want to suggest, a further responsibility. This is the responsibility that—in our moral tradition—is often referred to as autonomy or self-respect or similar names. I think the nerve of that responsibility is this: so far as decisions are made primarily affecting a person's life, and so far as those decisions are made

with the aim that that person's life go better, be more successful, run less of a risk of waste, then those decisions must be made by the person whose life it is or, when that's not possible, in accordance, so far as this is possible, with the standards that that person chose.

See also Lawrence Solum, Ronald Dworkin, & John Finnis, *Euthanasia, Morality, and the Law,* 30 Loy. L. Rev. 1465, 1490 (1997); Frank I. Michelman, *Relative Constraint and Public Reason: What Is "the Work We Expect of Law"?* 67 Brook. L. Rev. 963, 971 n. 20 (2002); Matthew D. Adler & Eric A. Posner, *Rethinking Cost-Benefit Analysis,* 109 Yale L.J. 165 (1999) (referring to ethical individualism's concern for "the enhancement of community values"). Others have taken up his phrase but seem to have given it somewhat different meanings, which focus more on liberalism's requirement that individual deserts relate closely to an individual's claim against another. *See, e.g.,* Jeremy Waldron, *Does Law Promise Justice?* 17 Ga. St. U. L. Rev. 759, 777 (2001) ("It is a commitment to a particular kind of reason-giving—a kind of reason-giving closely connected to the sort of ethical individualism or individualization of reasons that is identified with justice in the most substantive sense of the word"); James R. Hackney Jr., *Law and Neoclassical Economics: Science, Politics, and the Reconfiguration of American Tort Law Theory,* 15 Law & Hist. Rev. 275, 286 (1997) ("The core of the antistatist stance as articulated in Serfdom grew out of the belief in the uniqueness of individual activity and thought ('ethical individualism'). It was unacceptable, in fact impossible, for anyone other than the individual to make decisions for the individual without imposing an alien set of values. At that point, seemingly benign policy prescriptions dissolved into naked, unjustifiable coercion. Thus, 'individuals should be allowed, within defined limits, to follow their own values and preferences rather than somebody else's'") (quoting Hayek, *Road to Serfdom* 66 (1956 ed.)).

41. For other formulations, see Alfred L. Brophy, *Reparations Talk: The Tort Law Analogy in Reparations for Slavery,* 24 B.C. Third World L.J. 81, 129–30 (2004).

42. Robinson, *supra* note 30, at 207.

43. Robinson, *supra* note 30, at 216. Posner and Vermeuele, *supra* note 40, at 742, provide a more clinical description of the reparationists' case for continuing harm:

Proponents of slavery reparations argue that the wrong done to blacks did not end with slavery, but has continued to this day. This argument could be understood in a number of ways. Slavery disrupted family relationships and social conventions among blacks, and these ruptures continue in the form of various family pathologies—illegitimacy and so forth. Slavery, by depriving blacks of education, placed them at a competitive disadvantage after the Civil War, pushing blacks into economic relationships with peonage-like elements. Slavery promoted negative stereotypes about blacks which have been passed down from generation to generation. If these arguments are correct, calculating reparations is not a matter of determining, say, the difference between the market wage and the actual wage paid to slaves, but must include some assessment of the harm incurred by blacks, and the benefits (if any) obtained by whites, since the Civil War (footnotes omitted).

Posner and Vermeule miss critical elements of the continued harm—the continued limitation of education, of vocational opportunities under Jim Crow, and of other social opportunities. The lack of opportunities—enforced through statutes and norms—continued through the Jim Crow era and, in altered form, to a misdirected welfare policy.

44. The growing literature on the Airline Stabilization Act, Pub. L. 107–42, 115 Stat. 230 (2004), which established the 9/11 Victims' Compensation Fund, has implications for design of reparations programs. *See, e.g.*, Janet Cooper Alexander, *Procedural Design and Terror Victim Compensation*, 53 DePaul L. Rev. 627 (2003); Lawrence M. Friedman & Joseph Thompson, *Total Disaster and Total Justice: Responses to Man-Made Tragedy*, 53 DePaul L. Rev. 251 (2003).

45. *See* Oklahoma City Victim Compensation Act, H.R. 3633 (introduced January 24, 2002).

46. Calvin Massey, *Some Thoughts on the Law and Politics of Reparations for Slavery*, 24 B. C. Third World L.J. 157, 158–66 (2004).

47. *See, e.g.*, Stephen Kershnar, *Reparations for Slavery and Justice*, 33 U. Mem. L. Rev. 277, 292–95 (2003) (discussing setoff of benefits from slavery); Alfred L. Brophy, *Some Conceptual and Legal Problems in Reparations*, 58 N.Y.U. Annual Survey of Am. L. 498, 521–23 (2003) (discussing unjust enrichment factors and offsetting the benefits). Compare *Restatement (Second) Torts* § 920 (1979) (limiting offset of benefits to "the interest of the plaintiff that was harmed") with *Restatement (Second) Contracts*, secs. 347, 349 (1983) (containing no limitation on the interests benefited).

48. Much of reparations writing makes the case for legislative grants, rather than judicial action. *See, e.g.*, Tuneen E. Chisholm, *Sweep around Your Own Front Door: Examining the Argument for Legislative African American Reparations*, 147 U. Pa. L. Rev. 677 (1999); Rhonda V. Magee, *The Master's Tools, from the Bottom Up: Responses to African-American Reparations Theory in Mainstream and Outsider Remedies Discourse*, 79 Va. L. Rev. 863 (1993).

49. George L. Priest, *The Problematic Structure of the September 11th Victim Compensation Fund*, 53 DePaul L. Rev. 527, 538 (2003).

50. *Id.*

51. Roy Brooks and Boris Bittker have argued persuasively that reparations ought to constitutional. *See* Roy Brooks & Boris Bittker, *The Constitutionality of Black Reparations*, in When Sorry Isn't Enough 374 (Roy Brooks ed. 1999).

52. Geduldig v. Aiello, 417 U.S. 484 (1974).

53. *Id.* at 494.

54. *Id.* at 497 n. 20 ("While it is true that only women can become pregnant it does not follow that every legislative classification concerning pregnancy is a sex-based classification . . . . Normal pregnancy is an objectively identifiable physical condition with unique characteristics. . . . The program divides potential recipients into two groups—pregnant women and non-pregnant persons. While the first group is exclusively female, the second included members of both sexes").

55. David B. Cruz, *Disestablishing Sex and Gender*, 90 Cal. L. Rev. 997, 1043 (2002) (citing Sylvia A. Law, *Rethinking Sex and the Constitution*, 132 U. Pa. L. Rev. 955, 983 n. 107 (1984)).

56. Jacobs v. Barr, 959 F.2d 313, 320 (D.C. Cir. 1992).

57. *Id.* at 321. It is significant that the District of Columbia Circuit Court thought it necessary to talk in terms of Congress' racial classification, even though not all Japanese Americans—but only those interned during World War II—were entitled to compensation under the Civil Liberties Act of 1988. That suggests reparations for slavery would also be evaluated as a racial classification.

58. One might consider the grandfather clause cases in this context, which addressed a facially neutral rule (those whose ancestors were eligible to vote before the Fifteenth Amendment) that was in fact discrimination based on race. *See* Guinn v. United States, 238 U.S. 347 (1915).

59. Or that it might be the kind of program that Congress is permitted to pass. *See* Stephen A. Siegel, *The Federal Government's Power to Enact Color-Conscious Laws: An Originalist Inquiry*, 92 Nw. U. L. Rev. 477 (1998) (concluding, based on study of Reconstruction-era legislation, that Congress is permitted to enact race-conscious legislation).

If a *Geduldig*-based argument were upheld, then one might expect that Congress would invoke reparations for slavery in talismanic fashion to uphold its affirmative action programs. Thus, one might see programs like the one struck down in *Adarand* justified as reparations for slavery. (The set-aside scheme would have to be modified to provide preferential treatment for those who are descended from slaves, rather than for all African Americans.) Some commentators have drawn that connection, even before the recent reparations writing. *See* Note, *Forty Megahertz and a Mule: Ensuring Minority Ownership of the Electromagnetic Spectrum*, 108 Harv. L. Rev. 1145 (1995) (invoking imagery of reparations for slavery in discussing Supreme Court's decision in Metro Broadcasting v. Federal Communications Commission, 497 U.S. 547 (1990)).

It is more likely that the Supreme Court will conclude that a program so closely aligned with race would be subject to heightened scrutiny. At the very least, one would expect that there would have to be the same showing of close connection between past harm and remedial purpose that the Supreme Court imposes in affirmative action cases.

60. Adarand v. Pena, 515 U.S. 200, 235 (1995).

61. *Id.* at 226.

62. *Id.* at 237.

63. *See, e.g., id.* at 237 ("The unhappy persistence of both the practice and the lingering effects of racial discrimination against minority groups in this country is an unfortunate reality, and government is not disqualified from acting in response to it"); Richmond v. J. A. Croson, 488 U.S. 469, 509 (1988).

64. *Id.*

65. Justice O'Connor acknowledged the shameful history of racism—and its likely effect on the number of African American contractors. However, that history was insufficiently tied to the quota that Richmond established. *Id.* at 499 ("The 30% quota cannot in any realistic sense be tied to any injury suffered by anyone").

66. *See, e.g.,* Vincene Verdun, *If the Shoe Fits, Wear It: An Analysis of Reparations to African Americans*, 67 Tul. L. Rev. 597, 643 (1993).

67. *See, e.g.,* Melvin L. Oliver & Thomas M. Shapiro, *Black Wealth/ White Wealth: A New Perspective on Racial Equality* (1997) (documenting racial disparities in income and wealth); *id.* at 188–90 (discussing reparations as a partial solution).

68. *See, e.g.,* Wygant, 476 U.S. at 276 (dismissing evidence of disparity in racial composition of students and teachers as evidence of discrimination in employing teachers); Croson, 480 U.S. at 499, 507 (dismissing "outright racial balancing" as appropriate goal of race-based action).

69. Adarand, 515 U.S. at 220 ("societal discrimination, without more, is too amorphous a basis for imposing a racially classified remedy") (quoting Wygant v. Jackson Bd. Ed., 476 U.S. 267, 276 (1986)); Wygant, 476 U.S. at 270; Croson, 488 U.S. at 497 (observing that past cases have distinguished "between 'societal discrimination' which is an inadequate basis for race-conscious classifications, and the type of identified discrimination that can support and define the scope of race-based relief"). Reliance upon evidence of societal discrimination makes figuring an appropriate remedy—and logical stopping point—difficult. *See* Croson, 488 U.S. at 498.

The distinction between "societal discrimination" and more specific evidence of discrimination in a location is—obviously, one supposes—a distinction based on the amount of evidence that one expects before a court will grant relief. This is precisely the issue that critical race scholars criticize the courts for adopting: the requirement of a close nexus between past racial crimes (or discrimination) and current harm. Many of these problems, one supposes, could be solved with further evidence. Thus, the city of Richmond might very well have been able to defend much of its racial set-asides for minority contractors *if* it could have shown evidence of discrimination in the construction trades or in the award of government contracts in the past. *See* Croson, 488 U.S. at 509.

The closeness of this issue—and its contentiousness—is illustrated by the dissenting opinions in Adarand. Four justices have suggested that findings of societal discrimination might support race-conscious action. *See* Adarand, 515 U.S. at 269 (Souter, dissenting, joined by Ginsburg and Breyer); *id.* at 242 (Stevens, dissenting).

70. Croson, 488 U.S. at 507 (implying that private discrimination could meet requirement). But *cf. id.* at 500 ("There is nothing approaching a prima facie case of a constitutional or statutory violation by *anyone* in the Richmond construction industry") (emphasis in original).

71. Adarand, 515 U.S. at 237.

72. Croson, 488 U.S. at 497.

73. *Id.* at 509.

74. Westley, *supra* note 26, at 470–71.

75. Lee A. Harris, *Political Autonomy as a Form of Reparations to African-Americans*, 29 S.U. L. Rev. 25 (2001). Harris locates the reparations debate in concerns about corrective and distributive justice—that is, claims for correcting past injustices and claims for assuring equal (or fairer) distributions of wealth now. His solution, though, is a radical one.

76. Verdun, *supra* note 66, at 638.

77. *Id.* at 642.

78. *Id.* at 642.

79. Croson, 448 U.S. at 507 ("[T]he 30% quote cannot be said to be narrowly tailored to any goal, expect perhaps outright racial balancing. It rests upon 'the completely unrealistic' assumption that minorities will choose a particular trade in lockstep proportion to their representation in the local population") (quoting Sheet Metal Workers v. EEOC, 478 U.S. 421, 494 (1986)).

80. There are some problems in linking the payments to the body doing the discriminating.

81. *See* Westley, *supra* note 26, at 429–30 (lamenting decline of affirmative action).

82. At several places in Croson, for instance, Justice O'Connor suggested there was a need for evidence that there had been discrimination *in* the local construction industry. 488 U.S. at 499 (questioning whether there is "strong basis in evidence" that remedial action is necessary, because "[t]here is nothing approaching a prima facie case of a constitutional or statutory violation by *anyone* in the Richmond construction industry") (quoting Wygant, 476 U.S. at 277) (emphasis in original). By implication, discrimination against African Americans that occurred outside the industry, but had negative effects on the number of African Americans in the industry, is an insufficient basis for race-based action. *See id.* at 501 (rejecting evidence that minorities are underrepresented in employment when there are special qualifications); *id.* at 507 (questioning "'completely unrealistic' assumption that minorities will choose a particular trade in lockstep proportion to their representation in the local population").

83. *See* Croson, 488 U.S. at 507 (observing that Richmond never considered whether there were race-neutral alternatives that would accomplish the same purpose). Croson suggested one race-neutral program—city funding for small businesses—that might increase minority participation in the construction industry. *Id.*

84. The recent Section five cases address Congress's power to prohibit behavior or to otherwise limit states' authority. *See, e.g.,* Kimel v. Florida Bd. of Regents, 528 U.S. 62 (2000) (attempted abrogation of state's immunity from suit under Eleventh Amendment); City of Boerne v. Flores, 521 U.S. 507 (1997) (striking down statute that limited state government's power to burden religious exercise). Congress' power to define violations of the equal protection clause ought to be the same whether Congress is trying to expand its power to prohibit action that it believes would violate the equal protection clause or to take action to promote equal protection. *Cf.* Adarand Constructors v. Pena, 515 U.S. 200, 223 (1995) (Supreme Court applies consistent standard governing equal protection clause, regardless of whether government is burdening or benefiting racial minority). *See generally* Kimberly E. Dean, *In Light of the Evil Presented: What Kind of Prophylactic Antidiscrimination Legislation Can Congress Enact after Garrett?* 43 B.C. L. Rev. 697 (2002) (discussing Congress' power under Section Five).

85. See City of Boerne v. Flores, 521 U.S. 507, 526 (1997).

86. *Id.* at 530.

87. *Id.* at 532.

88. 406 U.S. 205 (1972).

89. 374 U.S. 398 (1963).

90. *See* 42 U.S.C. § 2000bb(a)–(b); Boerne, 521 U.S. at 515 (describing RFRA act).

91. Boerne, 521 U.S. at 530.

92. *Id.* at 532 (RFRA "cannot be understood as responsive to, or designed to prevent, unconstitutional behavior").

93. *See, e.g.*, Garrett v. University of Alabama, 531 U.S. 356, 370 (2001).

94. 383 U.S. 301 (1966).

95. *See* Garrett, 531 U.S. at 373 ("Congress documented a marked pattern of unconstitutional action by the States. State officials, Congress found, routinely applied voting tests in order to exclude African-American citizens from registering to vote. . . . Congress also determined that litigation had proved ineffective and that there persisted an otherwise inexplicable 50-percentage point gap in the registration of white and African-American voters in some States").

96. *See, e.g.*, Emma Coleman Jordan, *A History Lesson: Reparations for What?* 58 N.Y.U. Annual Survey Am. L. 557 (2003). And when Brown University's Steering Committee on Slavery and Justice releases its report in 2006, that will further define the scope of institutions' responses for their relationship to the institution of slavery.

CHAPTER 7

1. Ralph Ellison, *Going to the Territory*, in The Collected Essays of Ralph Ellison 591, 595 (John Callahan ed. 1996). *See also id.* ("Having won its victory, the North could be selective in its memory, as well as in its priorities which developed following the end of Reconstruction. And even the South became selective in its memory of the incidents that led to its rebellion and defeat. Of course a defenseless scapegoat was easily at hand, but my point here is that by pushing significant details of our experience into the underground of unwritten history, we not only overlook much which is positive, but we blur our conceptions of where and who we are.")

2. See *Bridging the Color Line: The Power of African-American Reparations to Redirect America's Future*, 115 Harv. L. Rev. 1689, 1693 (2002) ("Before achieving victory in a court of law, African-Americans must succeed in the court of public opinion").

3. *See, e.g.*, George Schedler, *Responsibility for an Estimation of the Damages of American Slavery*, 33 U. Mem. L. Rev. 307 (2003). *Compare* Stephen Kershnar, *The Inheritance-Based Claim to Reparations*, 8 Legal Theory 243 (2002) (arguing that "the descendants of slaves were not harmed by slavery since they owe their existence to slavery" and that "the inheritance-based claim is defeated by a number of concerns, particularly doubt surrounding the existence and amount of this inheritance-based claim, concern about offsets . . . and problems concerning the identity of any contemporary public or private entity that owes compensation").

4. *See, e.g.*, Indus. Union Dept., AFL-CIO v. Am. Petroleum Inst., 448 U.S. 607 (1980). On the role that considerations of utility have played in U.S. legal history, see Alfred L. Brophy, *Reason and Sentiment: The Moral Worlds and Modes of Reasoning of Antebellum Jurists*, 79 Boston University L. Rev. 1161, 1171–72 (1999).

5. *See generally* Martha Minow, *Between Vengeance and Forgiveness: Facing History after Genocide and Mass Violence* (1998); Mark Gibney & Erik Roxstrom, *The Status of State Apologies*, 23 Hum. Rts. Q. 911–39 (2001). Many ridicule the age of apology. *See, e.g.*, Walter Shapiro, *Mama Mia, That's a Mea Culpa*, Time, June 30, 1997.

6. Report of the Special Committee Authorized by Congress to Investigate the East St. Louis Riots, 65th Cong., 2d Sess., H. Doc. 1231.

7. Chicago Race Relations Commission, *The Negro in Chicago: A Study of Race Relations and a Race Riot* (1922).

8. *See, e.g.*, David W. Blight, *Race and Reunion: The Civil War in American Memory* (2000).

9. *See, e.g.*, James Allen, *Without Sanctuary: Lynching Photography in America* (2000); Nancy MacLean, *Behind the Mask of Chivalry: The Making of the Second Ku Klux Klan* (1994).

10. *See, e.g.*, Roy Brooks, *Rehabilitative Reparations for the Judicial Process*, 58 N.Y.U. Annual Survey Am. L. 475 (2003).

11. See Alfred L. Brophy, *The University and the Slaves: Apology and Its Meaning* (paper presented at University of North Carolina Conference on State Apologies, September 2004) (discussing slavery on the University of Alabama campus and the proslavery ideology of faculty and orators).

12. Among the many sources of proslavery thought in the old South, see *The Ideology of Slavery: Proslavery Thought in the Antebellum South, 1830–1860* (Drew Faust ed. 1981); Shearer Davis Bowman, *Masters and Lords: Mid-19th Century U.S. Planters and Prussian Junkers* (1993); Peter S. Carmichael, *The Last Generation: Young Virginians in Peace, War, and Reunion* (2005); Eugene Genovese and Elizabeth Fox-Genovese, *The Mind of the Master Class: History and Faith in Southern Slaveholders' Worldview* (2005). For a treatment of proslavery thought in the antebellum judiciary, see also Alfred L. Brophy, The Intersection of Slavery and Property in Southern Legal Thought: From Missouri Compromise Through Civil War (Ph.D. dissertation, Harvard University, 2001) and the author's monograph in progress, which is tentatively titled *University, Court, and Slave: Moral Philosophy and Slavery Thought in the Antebellum South*.

13. 42 U.S.C. § 1983.

14. 78 Stat. 255, codified at 42 U.S.C. § 2000.

15. 79 Stat. 439, codified at 42 U.S.C. § 1973c.

16. John McWhorter, *Against Reparations*, The New Republic, June 23, 2001 ("For almost forty years America has been granting blacks what any outside observer would rightly call reparations").

17. *See* Liability of Municipality for Mob or Riot, 13 A.L.R. 751 (1922).

18. *See, e.g.*, James T. Patterson, *Grand Expectations: The United States, 1948–1974* (1996); Irving Bernstein, *Guns or Butter: The Presidency of Lyndon Johnson* (1996); Gareth Davies, *From Opportunity to Entitlement: The Transformation and Decline of Great Society Liberalism* (1996) (tracing changing attitude of Democrats toward Great Society programs).

19. Robert Westley, *Many Billions Gone—Is It Time to Reconsider the Case for Black Reparations?* 40 B.C. Third World L. Rev. 429, 470–71 (1998). For similar suggestions, see Jack E. White, *Sorry Isn't Good Enough: A Simple Apology for Slavery Leaves Unpaid Debts*, Time, June 30, 1997.

20. Charles J. Ogletree, *Reparations for the Children of Slaves: Litigating the Issues*, 33 U. Mem. L. Rev. 245, 261 (2003).

21. David Lyons presents many of the conceptual problems with reparations in *Corrective Justice, Equal Opportunity, and the Legacy of Slavery and Jim Crow*, 84 Boston University Law Review 1375 (2004).

22. *See also* Alfred L. Brophy, *Some Conceptual and Legal Problems in Reparations*, 58 N.Y.U. Annual Survey of Am. L. 498, 523–25 (2003). *See* Swann v. Charlotte-Mecklenburg, 402 U.S. 1, 16 (1971) ("As with any equity case, the nature of the violation determines the scope of the remedy").

23. The issue of unjust enrichment is complex, of course. Although discussion of debt is central to much reparations scholarship (*see, e.g.*, Randall Robinson, *The Debt: What America Owes Blacks* (2000)), unjust enrichment requires consideration of how much one has received, as well as how much one has lost. *See* Brophy, *supra* note 22, at 517, 521–22 (discussing problems with unjust enrichment analysis for slavery reparations).

24. *See, e.g.*, David Kershnar, *Reparations for Slavery and Justice*, 33 U. Mem. L. Rev. 277, 288–89 (2003) (suggesting $500,000 as damages to each person). Or one might propose a settlement in the billions of dollars. Yet, as Jack White has suggested, "the fight for slave reparations is a morally just but totally hopeless cause." *See* Jack E. White, *Don't Waste Your Breath*, Time, April 2, 2001.

25. *See* Dalton Conley, *The Cost of Slavery*, N.Y. Times A25, February 15, 2003.

26. Even among reparations proponents who urge measuring damages according to lost wages or harm to individuals, there is rarely a specific figure. *See, e.g.*, Schedler, *supra* note 6, at 334–35 (proposing methods of estimating damages); Robinson, *supra* note 2, at 370–76 (discussing various methods of calculating damages and suggesting $1.4 trillion as one measure); Alfred L.

Brophy, *Reparations Talk: Reparations and the Tort Law Analogy*, 24 B.C. Third World L.J. 81, 129–30 (2004) (listing damages formulas).

27. *See, e.g.*, Charles Krauthammer, *Reparations for Black Americans*, Time 18, December 31, 1990; David Boyle, *Unexpected Racial Assertions*, 105 W. VA. L. Rev. 711, 713 (2003).

28. As Brent Staples has recently phrased it, how much has there been a collective amnesia about slavery? See Brent Staples, *A Convenient Amnesia about Slavery*, N.Y. Times, December 15, 2005.

29. Ralph Ellison, *Juneteenth* 19 (1999).

FOR FURTHER READING

Reparations scholarship spans a huge spectrum, from general, popular literature to academic articles on very specific topics. Several basic books discuss the case for or against reparations. Much of the recent writing on reparations has been inspired by Randall Robinson's *The Debt: What America Owes to Blacks* (2000). Robinson built in important ways on an intellectual tradition established by James Forman's Black Manifesto. Forman's manifesto received searching attention in the late 1960s and early 1970s, such as Robert S. Lecky and H. Elliott Wright's edited volume, *Black Manifesto: Religion, Racism, and Reparations* (1969), and Boris Bittker's *The Case for Black Reparations* (1973). Bittker's book, which came again to the public's attention after Robinson published *The Debt*, has recently been reissued by Beacon Press. Roy Brooks's 1998 book, *When Sorry Isn't Enough*, is a comprehensive collection of readings on reparations, from the Civil War to the present. Roy Brooks also published the important *Atonement and Forgiveness: A New Model of Black Reparations* (2004). John C. Torpey's *Making Whole What Has Been Smashed: On Reparations Politics* (2005) is an important and sobering look at the politics involved in gaining reparations.

The leading antireparations book is David Horowitz's *Uncivil Wars: The Controversy over Reparations for Slavery* (2001). Much of Horowitz's book is concerned with the conflict swirling around free speech on college campuses and its relationship to the reparations for slavery debate, but the book also makes a strong case against reparations. We are still waiting for a comprehensive, book-length argument against reparations. It builds upon his advertisement, "Ten Reasons Why Reparations for Blacks Is a Bad Idea for Blacks, and Racist Too," available at http://www.frontpagemag.com/Articles/ReadArticle.asp?ID=1153. There are some other popular responses to reparations for slavery, including Peter Flaherty and John Carlisle, *The Case against Slave Reparations*, available at http://www.nlpc.org/pdfs/Final_NLPC_Reparations.pdf.

The responses to David Horowitz include "Ten Reasons: A Response to David Horowitz," by Robert Chrisman and Ernest Allen Jr., available at http://www.umass.edu/afroam/hor.html, and "Ten Reasons for Reparations," by Earl Ofari Hutchinson, available at http://www.alternet.org/story.html?StoryID=10680.

Eric Yamamoto's *Interracial Justice: Conflict and Reconciliation in Post–Civil Rights America* (1999) addresses reparations as one piece of a plan for interracial understanding and justice.

The literature on reparations and apologies in the international context is huge. Probably the best introductions are Elazar Barkan's *The Guilt of Nations* (2000) and Martha Minow's *Between Vengeance and Forgiveness* (1998). Ruti Teitel's *Transitional Justice* (2000) places reparations into an international context, as one of many strategies for countries emerging from dictatorships. Each of those books is accessible to a general audience and worth reading.

Beyond those general works, one searching for reparations scholarship, particularly as it relates to law, must look to shorter essays in the periodical literature. Raymond Winbush's *Should America Pay? Slavery and the Raging Debate over Reparations* (2003) reprints many of the most important recent articles, including Robert Westley's "Many Billions Gone: The Case for Black Reparations," which appeared in the *Boston College Third World Law Journal* in 1998, and John McWhorter's "Against Reparations," which appeared in *The New Republic* in 2001. McWhorter discussed related themes, although he did not mention reparations, in his 2000 book, *Losing the Race: Self-Sabotage in Black America*. I published an essay review of that book: Alfred L. Brophy, "Losing the [Understanding of the Importance of] Race: Evaluating the Significance of Race and the Utility of Reparations," 80 *Texas Law Review* 911 (2002).

There also are five excellent law review symposia on reparations, in the *New York University Annual Survey of American Law* (volume 58 in 2003); in the *University of Memphis Law Review* (volume 33 in 2003); in the *Boston College Third World Law Journal* (volume 19 in 1998 and volume 24 in 2004); and in the *Boston University Law Review* (volume 84 in 200), which includes several important articles by reparations skeptics. Together, their articles present the state-of-the-art legal and moral arguments for and against reparations.

The periodical literature can be divided into several categories: articles primarily about reparations in general; articles on Black Power, nationalism, and reparations; articles about litigation and litigation strategies (or problems with them); philosophical studies of reparations; and critical race scholarship on whiteness and white privilege, which has implications for reparations.

In terms of general articles on reparations, in addition to the Robert Westley and John McWhorter articles mentioned previously, there is Mari Matsuda's "Looking to the Bottom: Critical Legal Studies and Reparations," 22 *Harvard Civil Rights–Civil Liberties Law Review* 323 (1987). Matsuda's article is, in many ways, the fountainhead of academic writing on reparations. Two student notes in the early 1990s were also critical: Rhonda V. Magee, "The Master's Tools, From the Bottom Up: Responses to African-American Reparations Theory in Mainstream and Outsider Remedies Discourse," 79 *Virginia Law Review* 863 (1993) and Tuneen E. Chisholm, "Sweep around Your Own Front Door: Examining the Argument for Legislative African American Reparations," 147 *University of Pennsylvania Law Review* 677 (1999).

There is an important, if small, literature on Black Power, nationalism, and black consciousness and reparations. Perhaps the most important article is by Vincene Verdun, "If the Shoe Fits, Wear It: An Analysis of Reparations to African Americans," 67 *Tulane Law Review* 597 (1993). There are two other important articles by Lee Harris: "Political Autonomy as a Form of Reparations to African-Americans," 29 *Southern University Law Review* 25 (2001), and "'Reparations' as a Dirty Word: The Norm against Slavery Reparations," 33 *University of Memphis Law Review* 409 (2003).

A series of articles, all of them written by or based on work by Charles Ogeltree, assesses the case for lawsuits. The most accessible appeared in *Harper's Magazine* in November 2000, "Making the Case for Reparations" (pp. 37–51). Ogletree's other articles include "The Current Reparations Debate," 36 *U.C. Davis Law Review* 1051 (2003); and "Repairing the Past: New Efforts in the Reparations Debate in America," *Harvard Civil Rights–Civil Liberties Law Review* (2003); see also Eric J. Miller, "Reconceiving Reparations: Multiple Strategies in the Reparations Debate," 24 *Boston College Third World Law Journal* (2004).

A series of articles addresses reparations from the perspective of philosophy. Most are pro-reparations, such as Eric Miller, "Reconceiving Reparations," and Albert Mosely, "Affirmative Action as Reparations," 33 *University of Memphis Law Review* 353 (2003). Several articles are skeptical of reparations, such as Stephen Kershnar, "The Inheritance-Based Claim to Reparations," 8 *Legal Theory* 243–67 (2002); and "Reparations for Slavery and Justice," 33 *University of Memphis Law Review* 277 (2003); and "The Case against Black Reparations," 84 *Boston University Law Review* 1177 (2004).

Reparations for slavery touch on critical issues, like affirmative action, the history of slavery and Jim Crow, and reparations and apologies to other groups. Each of those issues has a huge literature of its own. On affirmative action, one should probably start with Derek Bok, *A Bend in the River*, and Stephan and Abigail Thernstrom, *America in Black and White: One Nation, Indivisible* (1997). On slavery and Jim Crow, one might want to start with Eugene Genovese, *Roll, Jordan, Roll: The World the Slaves Made* (1974), and Leon Litwack, *Trouble in Mind: Black Southerners in the Age of Jim Crow* (1998). There is an important literature on Native American reparations and reparations to Japanese Americans interned during World War II. For Japanese American reparations, the recent casebook by Eric Yamamoto and others, *Race, Rights, and Reparation: Law and the Japanese Internment* (2001) is the key starting point.

Peter Irons's *Justice at War* is about the internment and reveals the government's complicity in the internment. There are many important studies of slavery and Jim Crow. Several that have paid particular attention to the implications for reparations are Alfred L. Brophy, *Reconstructing the Dreamland: The Tulsa Riot of 1921 — Race, Reparations, Reconciliation* (2002) and the Report of the 1898 Wilmington Race Riot Commission, available at http://www.ah.dcr.state.nc.us/1898-wrrc/. The report of the Brown University Steering Committee on Slavery and Justice will, undoubtedly, set the standard for all subsequent discussions of slave history and their implications for the present.

There is also a significant literature on white privilege, which has important implications for how we think about reparations, for it is part of the debate over whether there is any value that has been retained from the system of slavery and Jim Crow. Similarly, there is important literature on the state of black America in education, criminal justice, wealth accumulation, and welfare policy. Those two literatures are joined together in Michael K. Brown et al., *Whitewashing Race: The Myth of a Color-Blind Society* (2003). Two other important works are Douglas S. Massey and Nancy A. Denton, *American Apartheid: Segregation and the Making of the Underclass* (1998), and Melvin L. Oliver and Thomas M. Shapiro, *Black Wealth/White Wealth: A New Perspective on Racial Inequality* (1998). Joe Feagin's *Racist America: Roots, Current Realities, and Future Reparations* (2000) also discusses those issues.

In addition, there are some fine Web sites that have debates available for viewing and listening. Ones that I have found of particular use are the David Horowitz and Dorothy Benton-Lewis debate at MIT (http://Video.C-span.org:8080/ramgen/ndrive/e040701_slavery.rm). Adjoa Aiyetoro and Robert Sedler discuss the "Question of Payback: Reparations for Slavery" at http://www.justicetalking.org/viewprogram.asp?progID=137, and Gerald L. Early's "Multiculturalism, Reparations, and the Politics of Memory" is available at http://ls.wustl.edu/Whatsnew/Confsandevents/vidindexpils.html.

A tag-team debate between Alexander Pires, Christopher Hitchens (at 45 minutes), and a Boston University student, Matt Brown, on the reparations side and Glen Loury, Deroy Murdock, and a Boston University student, Amy Margolius, on the antireparations side appears at http://www.buwi.org/shows/2001/12/20011209.asp. The ninety-minute debate offers substantially more thoughtful discussion than we usually hear.

The pleadings in *In Re African American Slave Descendant Litigation*, which are the fullest exploration yet of the case against reparations for slavery through the legal system, are available on the Aetna Web site: http://www.aetna.com/legal_issues/suits/reparations.html.

Index

Adarand v. Pena, 60
Aetna, 33, 123, 145
affirmative action, as a form of
    reparations, 11
    decline of, 58–62
Africa, conditions in, 8
African American slave descendants' liti-
    gation. See *In re African American
    Slave Descendants Litigation*
against reparations, key arguments, xvi,
    64, 75–94
    compensation already paid, 76, 81–85
    divisive, 76, 86–88, 93
    no legal or moral liability, 76–78
    not best way of overcoming the past, 92
    politically infeasible, 76, 85
    See also opposition to reparations;
    lawsuits
Aiyetoro, Adjoa, 73, 80, 280
Alabama, University of. *See* University of
    Alabama
Alabama Wesleyan College, 172
Alaska Native Claims Settlement Act, xv,
    30, 42
Alexander v. Oklahoma (Tulsa riot
    victims' lawsuit), 4, 128–32
    statute of limitations bars, 128–32
    See also Tulsa riot of 1921
Allen, Ernest, 277
Altmann v. Republic of Austria, 112
America, Richard, 82
American Apartheid, 108, 280
American Baptist Convention, 49
American Dilemma, 108
Anderson, Col. P.H., 21
Anderson, Jourdon, 21–22
Andrews, Rhonda Magee. *See* Magee,
    Rhonda
Anti–Ku Klux Klan Act of 1871, 13,
    28–30, 173

antirent movement, 88
apologetic justice, 170. *See also*
    reparations
apologies. *See* Clinton, William J.;
    Native American reparations;
    Southern Baptist Convention;
    Presbyterian Church in America;
    Presbyterian General Assembly;
    United Church of Christ; United
    States; University of Alabama
apology, as form of reparations, 11–16, 31–32
Arlington National Cemetery, 25
Armenian genocide, 57, 119–20
    Armenian Genocide Insurance Act,
    120
Asante, Molefi Kete, 149
Atkinson, Edward, 24
Atlanta Riot, The, 135
atonement, 73–74, 149. *See also* Brooks,
    Roy L.

"back to Africa" movement, 34
Bakke v. California Regents, 58
Baltimore Sun, 146
Bancroft, George, 89
Barkan, Elazar, 278
    The Guilt of Nations, 278
Barnard, F. A. P., 171
Barnard College, 171
Barrueto v. Larios, 130
Bell, Derrick, 40
Berlin Wall, 46
Birmingham Southern College, 172
Bittker, Boris, 36, 38–40, 277
    The Case for Black Reparations,
    38–40, 277
black codes, xiii, 28
Black Dispatch (Oklahoma City), 84
black farmers, lawsuit, 31, 132. See also
    Pigford v. Glickman

128–33, 280. See also *Alexander v. Oklahoma*
Tuskegee syphilis experiments
  apology, 48
  payments, xiv
Tutu, Nontombi, 3

UDC. *See* United Daughters of the Confederacy
Uganda, 47
United Church of Christ, apology, 31, 49
United Daughters of the Confederacy, 14–16
United Daughters of the Confederacy v. Vanderbilt University, 14–16
United Negro Improvement Association, 34
United States
  Congress and reparations, 141
  deprivation of Hawaiian land, apology for 48
  radiation experiments, apology for, 48
  support for Guatemala's military, apology for 48
  Tuskegee syphilis experiments, apology for 48
University of Alabama, xi
  apology for slavery, 32, 50, 171
University of Arkansas, 172
University of California–Hastings, 137
University of Chicago Law School, 77
University of Georgia, 172
University of Hawaii, 145
University of Mississippi, xi, 172
University of North Alabama, 172
University of North Carolina, xi, 50, 146–47, 172
University of South Carolina, xi, 172
University of the South. *See* Sewanee
University of Virginia, xi, 172
  proposed apology, 50
unjust enrichment, 103–4, 109–11, 123–24
  focus on benefit still retained, 111, 115
  relationship to *The Debt*, 110

Vanderbilt University, xi, 14–16, 87. See also *United Daughters of the Confederacy v. Vanderbilt University*
Verdun, Vincene, 65–66, 162, 279
Vermeule, Adrian, 41, 77, 151
Virginia Law Review, 66
Virginia Military Institute, 172
Voting Rights Act of 1965, xiv, 17, 36, 40, 100, 164, 173

Wachovia Bank, xi, 14, 144
Walker, David, 19
  author of *Appeal to the Colored Citizens of the United States*, 19
Walker, Quock, 20
  lawsuit for freedom, 20
Walker, Timothy, 89
War of 1812 and payments to slaveholders, 23
Washington, Booker T., 75
Washington v. Davis, 138
Washington and Lee University, 172
Washington College, 172
Wayland, Francis, 49
We Won't Pay website, 5
welfare payments as payment of debt, 82
Westley, Robert, 10, 67–69, 73, 148, 278
Whitewashing Race: The Myth of a Color-Blind Society, 280
William and Mary College, 24
Williams, Walter, 82
Wilmington, NC, riot of 1898, 52
  Riot Commission, 147, 280
Winbush, Raymond, 17, 278
Winfrey, Oprah, 18
Wisconsin v. Yoder, 163
World War II. *See* California legislation; Holocaust reparations; lawsuits
Wright, H. Elliott, 38, 277

Yale University, xi,
  connections to slavery, 49
Yamamoto, Eric, 12, 33, 73, 93, 145, 278–79
  Interracial Justice, 73, 278
  Race, Rights, and Reparation, 279

zoning ordinance, Louisville racial, 34